Financial Accounting for the
Hospitality, Tourism and Retail Sectors

About the Authors

Donncha O'Donoghue B.Comm, FCCA

Donncha O'Donoghue is a lecturer in accounting at the Dublin Institute of Technology, based in the Faculty of Tourism and Food. He was educated at University College Galway and Athlone Institute of Technology and has over sixteen years' experience lecturing at undergraduate, postgraduate and professional levels. He also acts as external examiner to a number of tourism programmes in Ireland.

Alice Luby MAAT, ACMA, MSc

Alice Luby is a lecturer in accounting at Dublin Institute of Technology, based in the Faculty of Business. She has thirteen years' lecturing experience at undergraduate and professional levels in addition to twelve years' industrial experience. Educated at Dublin Institute of Technology and Dublin City University she is the author of *Cost and Management Accounting: Learning through Practice* (Gill and MacMillan: 1999) and is also to the forefront in utilising web technology for distance education.

Financial Accounting for the Hospitality, Tourism and Retail Sectors

Donncha O'Donoghue
&
Alice Luby

BLACKHALL
Publishing

This book was typeset by ASHFIELD PRESS for

Blackhall Publishing
33 Carysfort Avenue
Blackrock
Co. Dublin
Ireland

e-mail: info@blackhallpublishing.com
www.blackhallpublishing.com

ISBN: 1 842180 90 8

A catalogue record for this book is available from the British Library.

Printed in Ireland by
ColourBooks Ltd

To my parents, Jack and Margaret.
Donncha

To my family.
Alice

Acknowledgements

We are indebted to many individuals for their ideas and assistance in preparing this book.

- ❑ Ruth Garvey and Gerard O'Connor of Blackhall Publishing whose patience, perseverance and advice was invaluable in producing this text.
- ❑ Our colleagues for their counsel throughout this project especially Marc Mc Donald, Noel O'Connor, Stuart Kent and Frances O'Brien of the Learning Technology Team, DIT.
- ❑ Our colleagues who have made contributions towards the text in particular Gerry Dunne, Eamonn Moane and Daniel King.
- ❑ Our colleagues in the hospitality, tourism and retail sectors especially Karl Reinhardt (IHCI), Failte Ireland, Jury's Doyle Plc, Gresham Hotels Plc, Arnotts Plc and Ryanair Plc for the vast amount of information provided.
- ❑ The academics that reviewed the earlier drafts of this book in particular David Ahern and Eamonn Moane. Your advice and comments were invaluable in developing the final version.
- ❑ The students we have both lectured over the years for their inspiration and feedback.
- ❑ Terri, Jack, Cian and Josh for all your patience.
- ❑ Peter, Emily and Lindsey – thanks for putting up with all the late nights and long phone calls.

Contents

While lecturing on applied management courses it was apparent that the generic accounting texts available did not provide sufficient examples geared towards the relevant sectors. They also focused on many complex issues appropriate only for students of professional accounting. We decided to tackle these limitations with this financial accounting text. In essence, this text is geared for non-accountants and relates specifically to the hospitality, tourism and retail sectors.

Aims and objectives

The aim of this text is to provide a comprehensive guide to accounting for undergraduate students participating in applied management programmes in hospitality, tourism and retail. The text assumes no previous knowledge of financial accounting and seeks to provide a good understanding of the subject area, avoiding complicated technical detail more suited to courses in professional accountancy. A balanced approach to studying accounting is promoted by providing both a conceptual background that is appropriate for managers and a practical application of the subject to the targeted sectors.

Target audience

This text is primarily targeted at undergraduate students studying accounting within applied management programmes relating to the hospitality, tourism and retail sectors. It is also suitable for services management (including transport management), marketing and business studies programmes. The examples and illustrations used throughout provide students with material which they can relate to, either from their studies or from their day-to-day experience as consumers of tourism and retail services. This facilitates student learning by presenting the theory in a practical and easy to understand setting.

Structure

The structure adopted suits both the traditional and modular approach to learning. The text begins with an overview of the structure and characteristics of the hospitality, tourism and retail sectors.

❑ Chapters 1 to 8 focus on the recording and control functions within accounting.
❑ Chapters 9 and 10 focus on accounting for adjustments in accordance with

accounting concepts and how that impacts on the preparation of the final accounts.
❑ Chapter 11 focuses on the preparation of the final accounts for a sole trader.
❑ Chapters 12 and 13 focus on the legal forms of organisation available to a business and the regulatory framework of accounting.
❑ Chapters 14 and 15 focus on the preparation of the final accounts for companies including the format and presentation of accounts for publication and the preparation of cash flow statements.
❑ Chapter 16 provides detailed tools for appraising organisational financial performance.
❑ Finally, Chapter 17 moves towards internal accounting by providing an overview of departmental accounting often used in the targeted sectors.

Pedagogical features

This text adopts a structured approach to learning, with each chapter commencing with clear learning outcomes. There are numerous illustrations and examples explaining each learning outcome clearly. The use of diagrams, tables, charts and accounts provides a visual addition to the text commentary. Real-life examples and accounting news stories provide additional material relevant to the target sectors. A number of additional pedagogical features are employed such as 'Did You Know?' and 'Consider this', which help to relate and illuminate learning points. Chapters conclude with a comprehensive executive summary and review questions. The review questions include conceptual and computational tasks that test the learning outcomes of the chapter. Solutions to the review questions are available to both students and lecturers on the accompanying website (www.blackhallpublishing. com/financialaccounting). References and recommended readings are provided for students who want to explore certain topics in more detail.

Each chapter contains:

❑ Clear learning outcomes.
❑ Illustrations and worked examples relevant to the sectors.
❑ Real-life examples and accounting news stories relevant to the sectors.
❑ A comprehensive executive summary.
❑ End-of-chapter review questions.

Resources

An accompanying website contains resources for both students and lecturers. Student resources include solutions to all review questions. Lecturer resources (password required) include downloadable colour slide presentations for each chapter as well as suggested solutions and additional questions and answers.

NB web address

Sector Overview: Tourism and Hospitality in Ireland

Tourism (incorporating hospitality, travel and leisure) is increasingly being referred to as 'the world's biggest industry', representing 10.7 per cent of the global economy (Youell, 1998). In recent years, many countries have been showing increasing interest in the potential of global travel and tourism as an important contributor to economic development, particularly in terms of investment, revenue, employment and balance of payments. In Ireland, the tourism sector has proved to be a key engine for economic growth. Throughout the 1990s, Irish tourism registered year-on-year growth, consistently outperforming other European countries. The economic benefits accruing from such growth are felt in many areas. Revenue from visitors to Ireland (including receipts paid to Irish carriers by foreign visitors) was estimated to be worth €4.1 billion in 2003. This accounts for almost 4 per cent of national exports (Fáilte Ireland, 2003). Because tourism activity is particularly concentrated in areas which lack an intensive industry base, the sector is credited with having a significant regional distributive effect, i.e. the poorer or less developed regions of the country, such as the western seaboard, tend to benefit particularly well from tourism. Employment is another area where tourism has made a significant impact, with the industry supporting over 230,000 jobs (Fáilte Ireland, 2003). Tourism is commonly regarded as having a high 'people requirement' compared to other industries.

Characteristics of tourism and hospitality businesses

Tourism businesses are commonly regarded as having a number of distinctive characteristics. These include the following:

Sensitivity of demand: Many tourism goods are viewed as being luxury items (for example package holidays) and therefore tend to be quite sensitive to price. This means that economic conditions such as recession, inflation and taxation can play a significant role in the demand for tourism and hospitality products and services. The industry is also sensitive to occurrences and events in the external environment such as terrorism, natural disasters, political instability and other factors. These are usually events which are outside the control of individual businesses but can nonetheless have a dramatic effect on their profits or indeed survival.

Seasonality of demand: many tourism businesses have seasonal demand patterns, for example holiday centres and city sightseeing buses. This results in establishments experiencing uneven cash flow patterns and, in some cases, the reduction or closure of their businesses in off-peak periods.

Fixity of costs: High fixed costs (costs that remain constant and are not affected by volume of business) are a feature commonly associated with the tourism industry. Businesses such as hotels, airlines and tourist attractions employ various yield management systems to try to ensure that they generate sufficient turnover to cover their fixed costs.

Perishability of product: In common with other service industries, tourism consists of products which are perishable by nature, i.e. they have a limited 'shelf life'. If a hotel room or an airplane seat is not sold it cannot be stored or saved and sold at a later date and this results in the loss of potential revenue. Many tourism firms try to counteract this by using tactical pricing techniques to encourage the buying of their products/services.

Scale of operation: Although many large tourism companies exist around the world, the industry is, to a large extent, comprised of quite modest sized enterprises. The majority of tourism businesses in Ireland consists of firms employing less than ten people.

Structure of the tourism and hospitality industry

Tourism is a multi-faceted industry, made up of organisations from the private, public and voluntary sectors. The tourism product itself is made up of an amalgam of businesses which can be loosely divided into three main sectors, each of which is quite distinct but at the same time interdependent.

Transport: This includes air, sea, road and rail carriers. In addition transport providers are often subdivided into those who provide access transport and those who provide internal transport.

Attractions: Tourist attractions can be divided into natural and man-made features and facilities. These include historical sites, museums, theme parks, events, cinemas and a wide range of other attractions and leisure facilities which help to entice visitors to a destination.

Hospitality: This sector usually represents the bulk of businesses that make up the tourism industry. It consists of two main components:

1. *Accommodation*: This consists of hotels, guesthouses, B&Bs, self-catering, hostels and other forms of accommodation.
2. *Restaurants and bars*: This component includes full service and self-service restaurants, fast-food establishments, cafés, bars and pubs.

These businesses represent the main recipients of tourist expenditure at a destination. In Ireland, the accommodation, food and drink sectors receive the majority of overseas tourist spend. The full breakdown can be seen in the table below (note this does not include spend on access transport):

Breakdown of overseas tourists spend in Ireland (%) 2003

Bed and board	27
Other food and drink	36
Sightseeing/entertainment	4
Internal transport	10
Shopping	17
Miscellaneous	6

Source: Failte Ireland Tourism Fact 2003

A number of intermediaries exist in the tourism industry through which the tourism product can be sold. These include travel agents (the traditional retailers of the tourism industry), tour operators (who can be seen as wholesalers) and a variety of specialist intermediaries such as professional conference organisers.

Today, an increasing number of internet websites are being used by customers to purchase travel and tourism products direct from the suppliers. The global tourism industry has been one of the most dynamic sectors in this regard. This trend towards dis-intermediation is having a significant impact on the traditional practices and workings of the industry. The years ahead should prove very interesting in relation to how the industry is structured and how the tourism product is distributed.

Sector Overview: Retail in Ireland

It has been forecast that the services sector will be the largest contributor to Irish employment by 2010. Retail represents the largest element within this sector, generating 11 per cent of the total employment in the Irish economy. According to Forfas, 'retailing is defined as the means by which goods and services are provided to consumers in exchange for payment'. Retailing can be categorised as follows:

RETAILING

Predominantly Food Stores	Predominantly Non-Food Stores	Non-Store Retailing
Hypermarkets	Department stores	Mail order
Supermarkets	Boutiques	Door to door
Symbol groups	Multiples	Vending machines
Convenience stores	Factory outlets	Internet
Independent stores		
Discounters		
Others		

The definition above relates retailing to 'consumers' and therefore wholesaling and business–to–business selling are excluded. There has been a significant change in the make–up of the retailing sector in Ireland over the last 30 years. In the 1970s, it consisted of a large number of small shops offering specialised services such as general stores, bakers, butchers and drapery. Large department stores existed but there were few which matched the size of the stores in existence today. The type and style of products on offer were often dictated by the manufacturers who wielded considerable power.

The retail sector responded to the changes created by the prospering economy in the later half of the 20th century. The make–up of the sector shifted from the small independent stores, to larger retail outlets, particularly in the food sector. This movement has led to the development of a range of retailers who are larger than many of the manufacturers (suppliers). Within the supply chain, the power has shifted from manufacturing to retailing. Diversification (getting involved in different activities) and improved customer services are other trends that have developed in the retail sector today.

In a more consumer–driven society, the retail sector has a significant role to play in the economy. Currently one in five new Irish jobs is in the retail sector.

CHAPTER 1

Introduction to Accounting

Learning Outcomes

By the end of this chapter you will be able to:

- ❑ Describe the nature and purpose of accounting.
- ❑ Identify the main categories of accounting users and their specific accounting information needs.
- ❑ Outline the main financial statements that are produced to satisfy the information needs of the various users of accounting data.
- ❑ Outline and explain the distinctions between financial and management accounting.
- ❑ Give a brief outline of the choice of legal forms of organisation open to a business.
- ❑ Give a brief outline of the regulatory framework of accounting.

Introduction

The purpose of this chapter is to provide a background from which the principles of accounting can be applied. The way in which accounting evolved to a system suitable for modern society is briefly presented. The chapter also introduces the main types of legal organisation that exist and the various stakeholders or users of financial statements. The elements of accounting and its regulatory framework are briefly set out, establishing the context for the coming chapters.

Nature and Purpose of Accounting

'...The process of identifying, measuring and communicating economic information about an organisation or other entity, to permit informed judgements and decisions by the users of the information.'

American Accounting Association

The accounting systems in use today are similar to that developed by Piciolia, an Italian monk, who published a booklet in 1494 outlining a system of accounting. From the beginning of time people have kept records of their belongings or *assets*. They also kept records of their debts to other people or *liabilities*. This was normal practice even when trading took the form of bartering. Accounting developed even further as social structures grew and a division occurred between master/servant and employer/employee. With the ever increasing amount of trade and business transactions a uniform system of accounting was needed.

The above definition from the American Accounting Association indicates that accounting is concerned with:

- ❑ The recording of data or transactions. (This activity is sometimes called book-keeping.)
- ❑ Classifying and summarising the data.
- ❑ Communicating the outcomes of the above.

Accounting has developed from its early years to meet the needs of modern society and now operates in a more regulated environment. Standards have been developed that must be complied with. These standards apply across all business sectors including hospitality, tourism and retail.

Business Organisation Types

Common across all business sectors are legal forms of organisation that can be adopted by a business. This is dealt with in greater detail later on in this book; however, it is useful for students to familiarise themselves with the main characteristics of each type. The three most common types of legal form organisations can take are described below.

The sole proprietor/trader

This is where the business is owned and run by one person or a family. The most important characteristic of this type of business is that there is no difference between the assets of the business and the assets of the owners. Thus should a business fail and have outstanding debts which it cannot pay, then the courts can order the sale of the owner's *private* assets, such as the home or car, to pay back the debts. This is known as *unlimited liability*. Sole traders are generally small businesses and their financial statements are not governed by law and thus they have no need to publish their accounts except to the Revenue Commissioners. Most businesses within the tourism sector would be classed as sole proprietorships made up of B&Bs, small pubs and restaurants. Many small retail outlets would also be sole traders.

Partnerships

 A partnership exists where two or more people own, run and share the profits and losses of the business. The main advantage a partnership has over a sole proprietorship is that, as there are a number of partners involved, the risk is shared and it may be easier to raise finance as more collateral is likely to be available to raise capital/loans. Partnerships also have unlimited liability and are not required to publish their accounts except to the Revenue Commissioners.

Limited liability companies

 A limited company is a legal structure whereby the owners of the business are only legally liable to the value of whatever they have invested in the business. Thus the private assets of the owners are (to some extent) not at risk if the business experiences financial difficulties. The creation of a limited company involves setting up a legal persona. This is normally carried out with the assistance of a solicitor who drafts the necessary documents for registration with the Registrar of Companies. Thus a company is a legal entity created by law that is capable of entering into contracts, incurring liabilities and carrying out business. For the owners, liability is legally limited to whatever they invest in the company. Companies must publish information about their operations, financial transactions and results. This is required under the various Companies Acts that have been enacted since 1963. Should a company choose to float on a stock exchange, the requirements for publication of accounts will increase. The legal forms of organisation will be covered in greater detail in Chapter 12.

Users of Accounting Information and their Needs

Accounting has often been described as the 'language of business'. As it is an information tool for users of economic data, it is essential, as with any information system, to know two things:

1. Who are these users?
2. What are their specific information needs?

The Accounting Standards Board (ASB) was set up in 1990 to improve the standards of financial accounting and reporting. The ASB produced a Statement of Principles in 1999 which sets out fundamental principles for the preparation and presentation of financial statements and which identified the following seven groups of users of financial information (often described as stakeholders in the business).

Stakeholders of a business

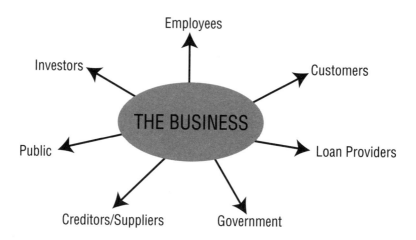

Investors/shareholders: Investors provide capital to the business usually in the form of cash or sometimes in a non-liquid form such as providing an asset (for example, plant and machinery or property). Shareholders are the legal owners of the business and thus are interested in ensuring the business provides a good return (profit) for their investment and that the investment will survive into the future.

Creditors/suppliers: These are made up of other businesses that supply goods and service on credit to 'the business'. Thus there is a period between receiving goods/services and payment. This can help the business' cash flow. Creditors are interested in ensuring the business is a good credit risk and will pay its debts as they fall due. Thus they are primarily interested in the solvency, good name and reputation of 'the business'.

The government: The use and interpretation of accounting information is essential for government departments to implement and monitor state policy. Government policy ranges from taxation of business profits to the regulation of certain activities. Tax assessments are based on financial accounts submitted to the Revenue Commissioners. Income tax, corporation tax, capital gains tax, stamp duty, VAT, PAYE and PRSI returns are all backed up by the accounts of the business.

Loan providers: Banks and financial institutions are concerned primarily with whether the business has the ability to repay loans, plus the interest charged. They will also require security/collateral for any loans given. The nature of the business, the business sector and the quality of the management team are all factors which financial institutions take into account before agreeing to advance any funds.

Employees: Employees and their trade union representatives require information on job security, profitability, wage structures and comparative information about other companies. This information is essential for wage negotiation.

Customers: Customers will be interested in the financial accounts produced by companies from which they intend to purchase goods and services. Their primary interest will be in the ongoing financial stability of the business.

The public: The general public, including communities and pressure groups, would scan the financial statements and reports of local businesses for information that would concern them. For example, the future plans of the businesses (expand or shut down) and environmental issues would be of general public concern.

An eighth group could be added to the above list, namely the management of the business, as they need financial information to support their decision making.

Management: Management run the business and try to ensure that it is profitable and stable/solvent. They are interested in and responsible for every aspect of the business. Management can also be the owners/shareholders of the business. Ultimately, managers require frequent, accurate, relevant information to plan and control business activities. They must ensure that the business is profitable, solvent (likely to remain in business) and run in an efficient and effective manner.

Elements of Accounting

The whole process of accounting can be sub-divided into a number of elements or modules. For example, the definition of accounting put forward by the American Institute of Certified and Public Accounts considers accounting to be:

'...the collection, measurement, recording, classification and communication of economic data relating to an enterprise for the purposes of reporting, decision making and control.'

It follows that accounting can be broken into the following key areas:

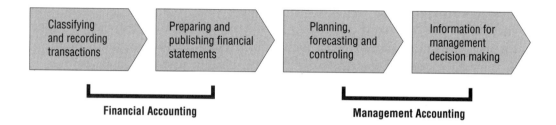

Financial accounting

Financial accounting involves the recording of business transactions, and summarising and communicating that data through uniform financial statements or final accounts. The process of classifying and recording business transactions is often referred to as book-keeping. It is important to remember that businesses are required by law to keep proper records which are available to auditors and the Revenue Commissioners so they can verify the figures given to them in the financial statements.

Businesses produce three main financial statements to satisfy the needs of the various users of accounting information. These financial statements are expensive to produce and thus businesses do not produce a customised set for each user group (although some, like banks and the Revenue Commissioners, could demand them). Thus financial statements are multi-purpose documents and users will have to glean the information they need from these documents. The main statements produced by a business are:

❑ **The balance sheet**: This is a statement showing what the business owns (assets) and what it owes (liabilities) on the very last day of the financial year. It's like a photograph of a business at one point in time and helps to answer the question, Is the business financially stable?
❑ **The profit and loss account**: This shows the amount the business has earned (its income/revenue), less the amounts charged (its expenses) in running the business. The difference between revenues and expenses is the profit or loss earned by the business over a period.

❑ **The cash flow statement**: This statement identifies the main sources of cash and the main uses of cash for a business in a financial period. It shows the flow of cash through the business and summarises the cash performance of a business.

Appendix A contains a sample of the financial statements mentioned above.

Management accounting

In addition to the financial statements outlined above, businesses will produce other statements for their own internal use and these will be tailored to their specific requirements. These internal reports are intended to help management manage more effectively and ultimately to provide timely and relevant management information to improve the decision-making process. To help management in their planning and controlling responsibilities, various statements will be prepared on a weekly/monthly basis. These statements such as cost analyses, budgets (both short and long term) and variance analysis will be produced, examined and acted upon. They are part of the whole management information system known collectively as the management accounts. These statements are not usually available for inspection outside the business on the grounds of confidentiality and also due to the fact that, in management accounting, speed is vital (information must be timely) and more important than absolute accuracy. The process of preparing management accounts is known as management accounting.

Table 1.1: *Financial versus management accounting*

Source	Financial accounting	Management accounting
Primary users	External (shareholders)	Internal (management)
Type of information	Summarised balance sheet, profit and loss account and cash flow statement	A range of very detailed and specifically focused reports
Frequency	Once/twice a year	As required by management – usually weekly/monthly
Time focus	Historic	Both historic and a future focus
Format of accounting governed by	Companies Acts and standards issued by the accounting profession	Not governed by legislation or standards

Adapted from *Accounting Information for Managers* by Peter J. Clarke, 2002

The Regulatory Framework of Accounting

The fact that parties external to an organisation may rely on the financial statements produced from an accounting system generates a need for consistency and regulation in the production of the financial statements.

Abuse in the provision of financial statements in the later end of the last century has brought about the need for more rigorous regulation. The term regulation implies the imposition of rules and requirements. In an accounting context this would relate to the preparation and presentation of reports and statements for external parties.

The objective of an accounting regulatory framework is to ensure adequate relevant disclosure, objectivity and comparability of accounting information for the external users of financial reports. Accounting and the preparation of financial statements and reports is therefore regulated through the following:

1. The government, through relevant legislation. In Ireland, this relates to the Companies Acts 1963 to 2003 and the various Companies (Amendment) Acts.
2. Regulation through the European Union. The EU issues directives to its member states to help ensure greater harmony in the presentation of financial statements. An EU directive requires the government of each member state to incorporate that directive into their laws. The EU's 4th Directive concerned the preparation and presentation of the accounts of companies and this was made law in Ireland through the Companies (Amendment) Act 1986.
3. The stock exchange listing requirements (yellow book) for companies listed on a publicly quoted exchange.
4. The accounting standards issued by the Accounting Standards Board (ASB).

The regulatory framework of accounting and, in particular, the self-regulation by the ASB through the standards they issue will be covered in greater detail in Chapter 13.

Summary

At this stage the nature and purpose of accounting should be clearer to you. It is essential to remember that the main financial statements are multi-purpose documents and are used by all the various categories of users of accounting information. Accounting is divided into a number of different activities of which the two main ones are financial and management accounting. This text specifically focuses on financial accounting.

The main information points covered in this chapter are as follows:

❑ Accounting is concerned with:
   - The recording of data or transactions.
   - Classifying and summarising the data.
   - Communicating what has been learned from the data.
❑ The stakeholders in the business have a reasonable right to information regarding the reporting entity. The ASB identified seven separate categories of users of accounting information.
❑ Businesses produce three main financial statements to satisfy the needs of the various users of accounting information. These are the balance sheet, profit and loss account and cash flow statement.
❑ Financial accounting is involved in recording, summarising and communicating the financial performance of the business through the financial statements or final accounts. Management accounting is another branch of accounting that focuses on the accounting information needs of managers. It satisfies their financial information needs through a wide variety of financial reports.
❑ There are three main legal forms of organisations that a business must choose from. These are sole proprietorships, partnerships and limited liability companies.
❑ The objective of an accounting regulatory framework is to ensure adequate relevant disclosure, objectivity and comparability of accounting information for external users of financial reports.
❑ Accounting, and the preparation of accounting financial statements and reports, is regulated by the following:
   - The government, through the relevant legislation.
   - Regulation through the European Union.
   - The stock exchange listing requirements (yellow book) for listed companies.
   - Accounting standards issued by the ASB and the IASC.

Review Questions

Question 1.1

Briefly describe the main legal forms of organisation a business must choose from.

Question 1.2

List the various users of accounting information and describe their specific information needs.

Question 1.3

Distinguish between financial and management accounting and discuss the role both have in an organisation.

Question 1.4

Briefly describe the elements that make up the regulatory framework that applies to accounting and the presentation of financial statements.

CHAPTER 2

The Balance Sheet and Accounting for Assets, Liabilities and Capital

Learning Outcomes

By the end of this chapter you will be able to:

❑ Explain the importance of the accounting equation.
❑ Understand the structure of a balance sheet, differentiating between assets, liabilities and capital.
❑ Record the effects of transactions on the balance sheet.
❑ Demonstrate a knowledge of the rules of double entry accounting for assets, liabilities and capital, and apply those rules to the commercial transactions that affect the balance sheet.
❑ Outline the role of accounting concepts and the importance of both the separate entity and dual aspect concepts within accounting.

Introduction

Chapter 1 stated that accounting is concerned with recording, summarising and reporting financial information. This chapter's main focus is the balance sheet, which is one of the most important financial statements to understand in accounting. The balance sheet is a financial statement which *reports* on the position of an organisation at a point in time. It is normally drawn up at the end of a period of time, *summarising* what the business owns and owes at that date. The balance sheet is based on or derived from what is known as the accounting equation, which outlines the relationship between the three key components of the balance sheet, namely assets, liabilities and capital.

Before data can be summarised and reported it must be recorded. The system of recording business transactions, called the double entry system of accounting, is explained and illustrated in relation to asset, liability and capital transactions. While every business needs to account for assets, liabilities and capital and produce a balance sheet, the basic examples and transactions presented are in the context of the hospitality, tourism and retail sectors.

The Accounting Equation

The whole of financial accounting is based on a formula called *the accounting equation*. The equation is as follows:

$$\text{Assets} = \text{Capital} + \text{Liabilities}$$

Assets: According to the ASB assets are 'rights or other forms of access to future economic benefits controlled by a business or entity as a result of past transactions or events'. In effect, assets are what the business owns, for example premises, machinery, furniture, motor vehicles and cash. Assets also include debts owed by customers to the business called *debtors* or *amounts receivable*.

Liabilities: According to the ASB, liabilities are 'obligations of an entity to transfer economic benefits as a result of past transactions or events'. Liabilities consist of monies owed by the business. They include loans, monies owed for goods which have been supplied or monies owed for expenses.

Capital: Capital is what the owner invests in the business whether in the form of cash or other assets such as motor vehicles and equipment. According to the ASB, capital or *ownership interest* is the 'residual amount found by deducting all of the entity's liabilities from the entity's assets'.

In simple terms, capital and liabilities are the means by which a business acquires its asset resources. The equation tells us that although the assets, liabilities and capital of a business may change, the total assets of a business will always equal the total of its capital and liabilities.

Business transactions and their effect on the accounting equation

A business transaction occurs when there is a transfer of assets/liabilities between the parties of a transaction. As each transaction is processed it has an effect on the accounting equation; however, the two sides of the accounting equation should always remain equal, irrespective of the transaction that has occurred.

The following simplified example is based on Henry Spud who has started in business selling baked potatoes and other hot foods from a mobile vehicle. He mainly travels to concerts and festivals around Ireland and also caters for private parties. The eight transactions listed below are typical accounting transactions that affect any type of business. The examples show their effect on the accounting equation of this business.

Transaction 1: Introduction of capital

The owner (Henry Spud) commences business investing €50,000, which is lodged in a business bank account.

Here the owner has invested money/capital into the business. An asset (cash at bank) has been created and also capital of €50,000. Thus the accounting equation will look as follows:

The accounting equation: after transaction 1

	Assets	**=**	**Capital + liabilities**	
	€			€
Cash at bank	50,000		Capital	50,000

Transaction 2: Purchase of an asset paying immediately

The business purchases an asset (equipment) costing €10,000, paying for it by cheque.

Here the business creates another asset (equipment) and in the process reduces the original asset (cash at bank) by €10,000 as the equipment was paid for immediately. Capital and liabilities remain unchanged.

The accounting equation: after transaction 2

	Assets	**=**	**Capital + liabilities**	
	€			€
Cash at bank	40,000		Capital	50,000
Equipment	10,000			
	50,000			50,000

Transaction 3: Purchase of an asset on credit

The business purchases another asset (a vehicle) on credit for €15,000.

In this transaction a new asset is created (vehicles) and a liability is created (creditors) as the business has not yet paid for the asset. Creditors are people or other businesses to whom the business owes money.

The accounting equation: after transaction 3

	Assets	=	Capital + liabilities	
	€			€
Cash at bank	40,000		Capital	50,000
Equipment	10,000		Liabilities: creditors	15,000
Vehicles	15,000			
	65,000			65,000

Transaction 4: Purchase of stock on credit

The business purchases the asset of stock on credit for €2,000.

Stock is the term used for the commodities that the business trades in. For example, this business requires potatoes, fillings and other food items. The business makes a profit by selling the stock at a higher price than they paid for it. Stock is an asset for the business as it has bought and now owns the stock. In this transaction a new asset is created (stock) and the liability of creditors is increased.

The accounting equation: after transaction 4

	Assets	=	Capital + liabilities	
	€			€
Cash at bank	40,000		Capital	50,000
Equipment	10,000		Liabilities: creditors	17,000
Vehicles	15,000			
Stock	2,000			
	67,000			67,000

Transaction 5: Payment of a liability

The business decides to pay the full amount owing for the motor vehicle (transaction 3).

This transaction has the effect of reducing a liability (as we no longer owe the money) and reducing the asset of bank (as the bank balance is lower due to this pay-off).

The accounting equation: after transaction 5

	Assets	=	Capital + liabilities	
	€			€
Cash at bank	25,000		Capital	50,000
Equipment	10,000		Liabilities: creditors	2,000
Vehicles	15,000			
Stock	2,000			
	52,000			52,000

Transaction 6: Selling stock and receiving the money immediately

The business sells some stock for €500. Henry has decided that he will sell his produce at cost for the first few weeks thus foregoing a profit in order to get a share of the market.

In this transaction the asset cash at bank increases (more cash), whereas the asset of stock decreases (less stock). Capital and liabilities stay the same.

The accounting equation: after transaction 6

	Assets	=	Capital + liabilities	
	€			€
Cash at bank	25,500		Capital	50,000
Equipment	10,000		Liabilities: creditors	2,000
Vehicles	15,000			
Stock	1,500			
	52,000			52,000

Transaction 7: Selling stock on credit

In this transaction, stock is sold at original cost (no profit) on credit amounting to €300. In this situation Henry catered for a private party and, as it was a friend, he provided the service at cost price and also agreed that the customer could pay him later on in the month.

In this situation the asset of stock decreases while a new asset (debtors) is created. Debtors are people or other businesses who owe the business money. Thus, selling stock on credit will create debtors. Again, capital and liabilities are unchanged.

The accounting equation: after transaction 7

	Assets	=	Capital + liabilities	
	€			€
Cash at bank	25,500		Capital	50,000
Equipment	10,000		Liabilities: creditors	2,000
Vehicles	15,000			
Stock	1,200			
Debtors	300			
	52,000			52,000

Transaction 8: Receiving cash from debtors

Debtors pay the cash owed to Henry by cheque.

In this transaction cash at bank increases by €300 and debtors decreases by €300. Capital and liabilities remain unchanged.

The accounting equation: after transaction 8

	Assets	=	Capital + liabilities	
	€			€
Cash at bank	25,800		Capital	50,000
Equipment	10,000		Liabilities: creditors	2,000
Vehicles	15,000			
Stock	1,200			
	52,000			52,000

Thus one can see from the above examples that the accounting equation still holds after every transaction type has occurred.

The accounting equation can be rearranged and presented as follows:

Assets - Liabilities = Capital

In this approach the left-hand side represents what the business owns, and what is owed to everyone except the owners of the business. The right-hand side represents the owner's resources or what the owner has invested in the business.

The Balance Sheet

The balance sheet is a financial statement showing what the business owns (assets) and what it owes (liabilities + capital) at a specific moment in time. It is like a photograph of a business at a point in time and simply lists the assets and liabilities of the business as well as what the owner has invested (capital). It is effectively governed by the accounting equation and is called the balance sheet as both sides must equate with one another. Just as the accounting equation equates irrespective of the transaction types, the balance sheet must also balance after each transaction type.

The effects of the transactions presented above can be shown in relation to the balance sheet.

After Transaction	1	2	3	4	5	6	7	8
	€	€	€	€	€	€	€	€
Assets								
Cash at bank	50,000	40,000	40,000	40,000	25,000	25,500	25,500	25,800
Equipment		10,000	10,000	10,000	10,000	10,000	10,000	10,000
Vehicles			15,000	15,000	15,000	15,000	15,000	15,000
Stock				2,000	2,000	1,500	1,200	1,200
Debtors							300	
Liabilities								
Creditors			(15,000)	(17,000)	(2,000)	(2,000)	(2,000)	(2,000)
	50,000	50,000	50,000	50,000	50,000	50,000	50,000	50,000
Capital	50,000	50,000	50,000	50,000	50,000	50,000	50,000	50,000

The balance sheet outlined above avoids complex headings and categorisation. Appendix A contains a sample balance sheet with all the headings typically used.

As businesses may have hundreds or even thousands of transactions, it is impractical to restate the balance sheet after every transaction. Thus an accounting system was developed to account for each transaction during a period and a balance sheet is produced at the end of that period to present a summary of what has happened in that time. This system is known as the *double entry accounting system*.

The Double Entry Accounting System

The double entry system was devised to record transactions in such a way that the balance sheet was prepared only after a period of time elapsed, such as a week, one month, three months or twelve months. For this to work, each asset, liability and form of capital has its own account, which changes as transactions occur. For example:

❑ Assets would be made up of a number of accounts for each type such as motor vehicles account, plant and machinery account, fixtures and fittings accounts, furniture account, office equipment account, debtors accounts (which would be the individual accounts of each customer of the business) and bank and cash accounts.

❑ Liability accounts would be made up of individual accounts for the various suppliers/creditors and also individual accounts for the various loans that the business may have received.

❑ The capital account would be the account that deals with the transactions between the owner and the business.

At the end of a period of time these accounts are summarised or balanced and a new balance sheet is prepared based on the new balances in the accounts.

Double entry accounts and rules

Each account would have two sides to it, a debit side and a credit side, as follows:

The name of the account
(for example, **Motor Vehicles Account**)

DEBIT SIDE					**CREDIT SIDE**
Date	Details	Amount €	Date	Details	Amount €

The rules of double entry accounting are as follows:

1. A debit (Dr) represents an asset and a credit (Cr) represents a liability or capital.
2. If a transaction requires you to increase an asset account you debit the asset account with the amount of the increase; to decrease an asset account you credit the asset account.
3. If a transaction requires you to increase a liability or capital account you credit the account with the amount of the increase; to decrease a liability or capital account you debit the capital or liability account.

4. For every transaction, a debit will have a corresponding credit and vice versa.

Double entry accounting ensures that the accounting equation still holds. The summary double entry rules for these three classes of account (asset, liability and capital) are as follows:

Accounts	To record	Entry in the account
Asset	An increase	Debit the asset a/c*
	A decrease	Credit the asset a/c
Liability	An increase	Credit the liability a/c
	A decrease	Debit the liability a/c
Capital	An increase	Credit the capital a/c
	A decrease	Debit the capital a/c

* 'a/c' is shorthand for 'account'.

For some people a simplified approach based on the phrase '*debit the receiver and credit the giver*' is sufficient in applying the double entry rules.

Let us now look at the transaction examples at the beginning of the chapter and apply the double entry rules to them.

Transaction 1: Introduction of capital

The owner put €50,000 into the business bank account on 1 January.
    Here the owner has invested money/capital into the business. An asset (cash at bank) has been created and also capital of €50,000. The two relevant accounts as a result of this transaction are the bank account and the capital account. The transaction increases the asset of bank and also increases capital. Thus we debit the bank account (increasing an asset) and credit the capital account (increasing capital).

The individual accounts and balance sheet would look as follows:

Dr	Bank Account		Cr
	€		€
1 Jan Capital a/c 50,000			

Dr	Capital Account		Cr
	€		€
		1 Jan Bank a/c 50,000	

Balance Sheet	€
Assets:	
Bank	50,000
	50,000
Capital	50,000

Note: The narrative in each account indicates the corresponding account for the transaction.

Alternative approach to understanding entries:
Debit the receiver – the bank account is receiving the cash.
Credit the giver – the capital (owner) account is giving the cash.

Transaction 2: Purchase of an asset paying immediately

The business purchases an asset (equipment) on 2 January, costing €10,000, paying for it by cheque.

Here the business creates another asset (equipment) and in the process reduces the original asset (bank) by €10,000 as the equipment was paid for immediately. The two relevant accounts to this transaction are the equipment account and bank account. We are increasing an asset, equipment thus we debit that account with €10,000 and we are decreasing another asset, bank thus we credit that account.

The individual accounts and balance sheet would look as follows (Note: the bank account now has two transactions recorded in it):

Dr		Bank Account		Cr		Balance Sheet	€
		€		€		**Assets:**	
1 Jan	Capital a/c	50,000	2 Jan Equipment a/c	10,000		Bank	40,000
						Equipment	10,000
Dr		**Capital Account**		**Cr**			50,000
		€		€			
2 Jan	Bank a/c	10,000				**Capital**	50,000

Alternative approach to understanding entries:
Debit the receiver – the equipment account is receiving new equipment.
Credit the giver – the bank account is giving the money.

Transaction 3: Purchase of an asset on credit

The business purchases another asset (motor vehicles) on credit from Bargain City Motors Ltd for €15,000 on the 3 January.

In this transaction a new asset is created (motor vehicles) and a new liability is created (creditors) as the business has not paid for the assets and thus owes Bargain City Motors for them. The two relevant accounts are motor vehicles and creditors – Bargain City Motors Ltd. Thus we debit the asset account, motor vehicles (increasing an asset), and credit the creditor account for Bargain City motors (increasing the liability).

The individual accounts and balance sheet would look as follows:

Dr	Motor Vehicles Account	Cr
	€	€
3 Jan Bargain City a/c 15,000		

Dr	Creditors Account (Bargain City)	Cr
	€	€
	3 Jan Vehicles a/c 15,000	

Balance Sheet   €

Assets:

Bank	40,000
Equipment	10,000
Vehicles	15,000

Liabilities:

Creditors	(15,000)
	50,000

Capital	50,000

Alternative approach to understanding entries:
Debit the receiver – the vehicles account is receiving a vehicle.
Credit the giver – Bargain City is giving the vehicle.

Transaction 4: Purchase of stock on credit

The business purchases the asset of stock on credit for €2,000 from Food Suppliers Ltd on the 4 January.

Stock is an asset for the business as it has purchased and now owns the stock. In this transaction a new asset is created (stock) and a new liability is created (trade creditors/Food Suppliers Ltd). The relevant accounts are stock and trade creditors/Food Suppliers Ltd. The stock account is debited (increasing the asset) and the creditor account is credited (increasing the liability).

The two accounts and balance sheet would look as follows:

Dr	Stock Account	Cr
	€	€
4 Jan Food suppliers a/c 2,000		

Dr	Creditors Account (Food Suppliers)	Cr
	€	€
	4 Jan Stock a/c 2,000	

Balance Sheet   €

Assets:

Bank	40,000
Equipment	10,000
Vehicles	15,000
Stock	2,000

Liabilities:

Creditors	(17,000)
	50,000

Alternative approach to understanding entries:
Debit the receiver – the stock account is receiving food suppliers.
Credit the giver – Food Suppliers Ltd is giving the items.

Capital	50,000

Transaction 5: Payment of a liability

On 5 January the business decides to pay amounts owing for the purchase of motor vehicles of €15,000 (transaction 3).

This transaction has the effect of reducing a liability (as we no longer owe the money) and reducing the asset of bank (as the bank balance is lower due to this pay-off). Thus, the two relevant accounts here are bank which we credit (reducing the asset) and Bargain City Motors, a liability which we are reducing and thus we debit the account.

The two accounts and balance sheet would look as follows:

Dr		Creditors Account (Bargain City)			Cr
		€			€
5 Jan	Bank a/c	15,000	3 Jan	Vehicles a/c	15,000

Dr		Bank Account			Cr
		€			€
1 Jan	Capital a/c	50,000	2 Jan	Equipment a/c	10,000
			5 Jan	Vehicles a/c	15,000

Balance Sheet	€
Assets:	
Bank	25,000
Equipment	10,000
Vehicles	15,000
Stock	2,000
Liabilities:	
Creditors	(2,000)
	50,000
Capital	50,000

Alternative approach to understanding the entries:
Debit the receiver – Bargain City is receiving money.
Credit the giver – the bank account is giving the money.

Transaction 6: Selling stock and receiving the money immediately

On 6 January the business sells some stock for €500 receiving the money by cheque.

The stock was sold at original cost, with the business foregoing a profit just to get a share of the market. In this transaction the asset of bank increases (increasing the cash at bank), whereas the asset of stock decreases (less stock). Thus we debit bank and credit stock with €500.

The accounts and balance sheet would look as follows:

Dr	Bank Account		Cr
	€		€
1 Jan Capital a/c	50,000	2 Jan Equipment a/c	10,000
6 Jan Stock a/c	500	5 Jan Vehicles a/c	15,000

Dr	Stock Account		Cr
	€		€
4 Jan Food supplies a/c	2,000	6 Jan Bank a/c	500

Alternative approach to understanding the entries:
Debit the receiver – the bank account is receiving money from sales.
Credit the giver – the stock account is giving food items.

Balance Sheet	€
Assets:	
Bank	25,500
Equipment	10,000
Vehicles	15,000
Stock	1,500
Liabilities:	
Creditors	(2,000)
	50,000
Capital	50,000

Transaction 7: Selling stock on credit

On 7 January Henry catered for a private party and charged €300 to John Duncan. He performed this service at cost price as John is a friend. He also allowed John to pay him later in the month.

In this situation the asset of stock decreases while a new asset (debtors – J. Duncan) is created. Debtors are people or other businesses who owe the business money. Debtors and stock are the two relevant accounts to this transaction and we credit stock (reducing the asset of stock) and debit debtors (increasing the asset of debtors). Thus selling stock on credit will create debtors.

The accounts and balance sheet will look as follows:

Dr	Debtors Account (John Duncan)		Cr
	€		€
7 Jan Stock a/c	300		

Dr	Stock Account		Cr
	€		€
4 Jan Food supplies a/c	2,000	6 Jan Bank a/c	500
		7 Jan John Duncan a/c	300

Alternative approach to understanding the entries:
Debit the receiver – John Duncan is receiving food supplies and a debt.
Credit the giver – the stock account is giving food items.

Balance Sheet	€
Assets:	
Bank	25,500
Equipment	10,000
Vehicles	15,000
Stock	1,200
Debtors	300
Liabilities:	
Creditors	(2,000)
	50,000
Capital	50,000

Transaction 8: Receiving cheque from debtors

J. Duncan (debtor) pays the cash owed by him to the firm by cheque on 8 January.

In this transaction cash at bank increases by €300 and debtors decreases by €300. The two accounts affected are bank and debtors and thus we debit bank account (increasing the asset of bank) and credit debtors J. Duncan account (reducing debtors) as he no longer owes the business money.

The two accounts and balance sheet would look as follows:

Dr		Bank Account			Cr
		€			€
1 Jan	Capital a/c	50,000	2 Jan	Equipment a/c	10,000
6 Jan	Stock a/c	500	5 Jan	Vehicles a/c	15,000
8 Jan	John Duncan a/c	300			

Dr		Debtors Account (John Duncan)			Cr
		€			€
7 Jan	Stock a/c	300	8 Jan	Bank a/c	300

Alternative approach to understanding the entries:
Debit the receiver − the bank account is receiving the money.
Credit the giver − John Duncan is giving the money.

Balance Sheet	€
Assets:	
Bank	25,800
Equipment	10,000
Vehicles	15,000
Stock	1,200
Liabilities:	
Creditors	(2,000)
	50,000
Capital	50,000

A note on balancing accounts

In order to find the figure for the balance sheet, an account must be totalled or balanced. This is usually done at the end of an accounting period. The bank account would be balanced as follows:

Dr		Bank Account				Cr
		€				€
1 Jan	Capital a/c	50,000	2 Jan		Equipment a/c	10,000
6 Jan	Stock a/c	500	5 Jan		Vehicles a/c	15,000
8 Jan	John Duncan a/c	300			Bal c/d*	25,800
		50,800				50,800
	Bal b/d**	25,800				

*   c/d / 'carried down' represents the closing balance.
** b/d / 'brought down' represents the opening balance.

Accounting Concepts

Accounting concepts are broad basic assumptions which form the basis of the financial accounts of a business. It is essential that all businesses follow these basic assumptions, since they help to ensure that transactions and accounts are recorded and prepared in a uniform manner. At this stage it is timely to introduce two accounting concepts. These are:

1. The business entity concept.
2. The dual aspect concept.

The business entity concept

This concept states that the business is separate from the owner. Thus, the items recorded in a firm's accounting records and books are limited to the transactions that affect the firm and will not concern themselves with the private transactions of the owner. The only transactions between the business and the owner recorded in the business records are:

1. The owner investing resources (usually cash) in the business.
2. The owner taking out resources (usually cash or stock) from the business for their own use (termed *drawings*).

The dual aspect concept

This concept states that there are two aspects to accounting: one represented by the assets of the business and the other by the claims against them (capital and liabilities). This concept states that these two aspects will always be equal.

Assets = Capital + Liabilities

From our eight typical transaction examples above we can see that any transaction will affect a balance sheet in two ways. This is what is meant by the term dual aspect. The name given for recording transactions under the dual aspect concept is double entry accounting.

Summary

The main focus of this chapter has been the balance sheet and the recording of transactions which affect the balance sheet using the double entry approach. The balance sheet is a financial statement listing what the business owns and owes at one point in time. The following are the main information points from the chapter:

❑ The balance sheet is a financial statement based on the accounting equation which states that Assets = Capital + Liabilities.

❑ Assets are the resources used by the business and include premises, furniture, equipment, motor vehicles, bank account balance and stock of goods for resale. Liabilities represent amounts owed by the business including loans. Capital represents the amounts invested in the business by the owner(s).

❑ All business transactions from buying and selling to procuring finance give rise to a dual effect on the balance sheet. Irrespective of the transaction, the accounting equation of Assets = Capital + Liabilities will always hold.

❑ Double entry accounting is a system of accounting used to record business transactions where a debit represents one side of the accounting equation (assets) and a credit represents the other side (capital and liabilities). All business transactions will lead to a debit and credit effect.

❑ Most businesses have computer packages to record business transactions and these packages follow the accounting rules of double entry.

❑ The separate entity concept simply states that business is separate from its owner(s) and hence only the transactions that affect the business are recorded in its accounting records and not the private transactions of its owners.

Review Questions

Question 2.1

Indicate, by circling the correct classification, whether each of the following is an asset or a liability:

Loan from AIF	Asset	Liability
Motor vehicles	Asset	Liability
Office equipment	Asset	Liability
Stock of goods	Asset	Liability
Cash	Asset	Liability
Bank overdraft	Asset	Liability
Debtors	Asset	Liability
Creditors	Asset	Liability

Question 2.2

Indicate, by circling either true or false, whether the following classifications for assets and liabilities are correct:

Machinery = Asset	True	False
Creditors = Asset	True	False
Premises = Asset	True	False
Motor vehicles = Asset	True	False
Stock = Asset	True	False
Bank overdraft = Asset	True	False
Creditors = Liability	True	False
Debtors = Liability	True	False
Cash = Liability	True	False
Loan = Liability	True	False

Question 2.3

Using the accounting equation Assets = Capital + Liabilities complete the gaps in each of the equations below:

Equation 1   If Assets = €100,000 and Liabilities = €62,000 then Capital equals …
Equation 2   If Assets = €85,000 and Capital = €45,000 then Liabilities equals …

Equation 3   If Liabilities = €75,000 and Capital = €75,000 then Assets equals ...
Equation 4   If Assets = €42,000 and Capital = €42,000 then Liabilities equals ...
Equation 5   If Assets = €72,000 and Liabilities = €42,000 then Capital equals ...
Equation 6   If Liabilities = €10,000 and Capital = €15,000 then Assets equals ...

Question 2.4

Indicate in the table below whether Assets/Liabilities/Capital increase, decrease or remain unchanged in each of the transactions described:

	Assets	Liabilities	Capital
1. Owner puts €50,000 into the business by opening a bank account.	*increase*	–	*increase*
2. Bought office equipment on credit from OE Ltd.			
3. The business obtains a loan.			
4. Purchased stock paying by cheque.			
5. Purchased stock on credit from a supplier.			
6. Sold goods on credit.			
7. Paid the amount due to stock suppliers.			
8. Received amount outstanding from a debtor.			

Question 2.5

(a) Gary Dunne operates a successful café bar. You are required to draw up a balance sheet from the following list of balances provided at the 31 December and calculate the capital figure.

	€
Fixtures and fittings	26,000
Loan	78,000
Creditors	22,000
Debtors	15,000
Bank overdraft	5,000
Cash	1,000
Stock of goods	9,800
Equipment	20,000
Premises	298,000

(b) During the first week of January the transactions listed below took place. Prepare a balance sheet as at 7 January taking into account these transactions:

    1. Gary purchased more fixtures for €500 on credit.

    2. Received €9,000 from debtors in cash.

    3. Repaid part of loan €5,000 cash.

    4. Purchased more stock on credit for €1,200.

    5. Gary paid creditors €2,000 by cheque.

Question 2.6

Karen Fox is in the process of opening a new restaurant. Complete the following table with the account and the amount to be debited and credited for each transaction.

Date	Transaction	Account to be debited	Account to be credited
1 May	Karen invested €60,000 in the business opening a business bank account.		
2 May	Bought some kitchen equipment from KE Suppliers on credit for €20,000.		
3 May	Bought restaurant furniture for €15,000 on credit from RF Ltd.		
10 May	Withdrew €1,000 from the bank for a cash float.		
11 May	Paid Interior Designers Ltd €25,000 by cheque for fitting out the restaurant.		
15 May	Bought motor van for €9,000 paying by cheque.		
16 May	Paid KE Suppliers the amount owed by cheque.		
19 May	Paid RF Ltd the amount owing by cheque.		

Question 2.7

Susan Ward has developed a plan where she will provide a bed and breakfast service. The following transactions occurred as Susan established her business venture:

Date	Transaction
1 Sept	Susan invested €40,000 lodging it in a business bank account.
2 Sept	Susan obtained a loan of €300,000 from Irish Business Bank (IBB), lodging the funds into the business bank account.
3 Sept	Property to the value of €330,000 was purchased paying by cheque.
5 Sept	Bought furniture paying by cheque €5,000.
7 Sept	Bought kitchen equipment on credit from QE Ltd for €7,000.
10 Sept	Returned to QE Ltd some of the equipment worth €3,000 for a full allowance.
12 Sept	Paid the amount owing to QE Ltd by cheque.
15 Sept	Withdrew €500 out of the bank for a cash float.
23 Sept	Paid for a computer by cheque costing €1,200.
26 Sept	Bought furniture on credit from Style Interiors Ltd for €1,400.
30 Sept	Paid Style Interiors Ltd €1,200, in part payment, by cheque.

Required

Write up the asset, liability and capital accounts for Susan's business.

CHAPTER 3

The Profit and Loss Account and Accounting for Revenues and Expenses

Learning Outcomes

By the end of this chapter you will be able to:

- ❑ Demonstrate an understanding of the structure of the profit and loss account, differentiating between revenues and expenses.
- ❑ Outline how stock is valued and accounted for.
- ❑ Apply double entry accounting rules to stock, revenues and expenses.
- ❑ Explain the effects of profit or loss on capital.
- ❑ Show an understanding of the money measurement, cost/current value, going concern and realisation concepts, and how they are applied in accounting.

Introduction

The focus in this chapter moves from the balance sheet to another important financial reporting statement, namely the profit and loss account. The measurement of profit is probably the most important function of financial accounting. All users of financial statements are interested in how well the business is performing, and profitability is a key measure of success. This chapter will focus on each element within the profit formula and how these elements are accounted for within the double entry system. It will also explain the effect that profit has on capital. While every business needs to account and report profit, the basic examples and transactions presented are shown in a hospitality, tourism and retail context.

The Profit and Loss Account

The main reason why people set up in business is to make a profit. The profit and loss account shows whether the business is successful in this regard. The calculation of profit follows the following formula:

Revenues - Expenses = Profit or Loss

If revenues exceed expenses, then the business is making a profit. If expenses are higher than revenue, then the business is making a loss. It is essential that a business makes a profit, as no business can sustain continuous losses. Thus making a profit helps to ensure the continuity of the business.

Revenue is the income generated by the business from the sale of its products or services. It is important to note that revenues include both cash and credit sales. Thus a sale is recorded even if the monies are not yet received. This is based on the *realisation concept* (see 49), which states that a transaction is recorded when the purchaser incurs liability for the goods, even though no cash may have changed hands. Revenues do not include any monies received by means of loans or cash received from selling fixed assets; these are transactions that affect the balance sheet, not the profit and loss account. Revenues are income earned (not necessarily received) from the sales of the products or services provided by the business.

Revenue

❏ Revenue is the income generated by the business from the sale (both cash and on credit) of its products or services.
❏ Revenue does not include any monies received by means of loans or cash received from selling fixed assets (balance sheet transactions).

Expenses are the costs incurred in running the business on a day-to-day basis and thus do not include the cost of purchasing fixed assets or the repayment of any loans. Expenses are the cost of using the resources available to the business (people and fixed assets) to produce a product or service and sell it. Examples include purchase of goods for re-sale, wages for personnel, fuel for motor vehicles or machinery, repairs to fixed assets, light and heat in providing the environment in which to produce the product or service, insurance, advertising costs, phone costs, rent, rates, accounting fees and general expenses.

Expenses

- ❑ Expenses are the costs incurred in running the business on a day-to-day basis.
- ❑ Expenses do not include the cost of purchasing fixed assets or the repayment of any loans.

The profit and loss account is normally prepared for a period showing a summary of revenues and expenses over that time. The period could be a month, six months or a full year. This is unlike the balance sheet, which shows what a business owns (assets) and owes (liabilities and capital) at one point in time, usually at the end of the year. The presentation of the profit and loss account will differ for businesses that offer a service (consultants, banks, tour operators) to those that sell a product (retailers and publicans).

Illustration 3.1: *The format and presentation of a profit and loss account*

Profit and loss account for period ended 30 June

SERVICE PROVIDER		
	€	€
Sales		100,000
Less expenses		
Rent	18,000	
Rates	5,000	
Wages and salaries	40,000	
Repairs	3,500	
Advertising	5,000	
Accountants' fees	2,000	
Solicitors' fees	1,000	
Insurance	7,000	
Phone	1,500	83,000
Net profit		**17,000**

Profit and loss account for period ended 30 June

PRODUCT PROVIDER		
	€	€
Sales		130,000
Less the cost of sales		40,000
Gross profit		90,000
Less expenses		
Rent and rates	12,000	
Wages and salaries	25,000	
Repairs	2,100	
Advertising	3,000	
Professional fees	4,000	
Office expenses	14,900	
Insurance	4,500	65,500
Net profit		**24,500**

The difference between the two profit and loss accounts illustrated above is that the provider of services does not purchase stock of goods for resale. Hence there is no stock account, whereas the provider of products purchases stock at one price (cost price) and sells it at another price (selling price). The difference between the two will amount to their gross, or trading, profit (if their selling price is greater than his cost price). For example, if a business buys 10,000 plastic 'Bart Simpsons' at €1 a unit and sells all of them at €10, then the gross profit is €9 per unit multiplied by the number of units sold, i.e. 10,000 x €9 = €90,000. Thus sales, less cost of sales, gives us gross profit and this part of the profit and loss account is known as the trading (buying and selling) account. A provider of services does not get involved in the purchasing and selling of products and therefore does not produce a trading account. If the business manufactured the goods themselves, then they would have to prepare a manufacturing account to calculate the cost of manufacturing the products sold. This text will assume that all businesses are product providers unless specifically stated otherwise.

Did You Know?

The tourism sector has a wide variety of activities, some that supply products and others that provide services. The majority, such as tour operators, travel agents, transport (taxis, bus, rail and air travel) hotels, events (concerts, festivals) leisure activities (including health and fitness, cinema, bowling etc.) provide services. Tourism activities that are product-based include restaurants, pubs and souvenir shops. The retail sector is primarily product based.

Accounting for Expenses and Revenues

Chapter 2 introduced the concept of double entry system accounting for assets, liabilities and capital (the balance sheet entries), where a debit represents assets and a credit represents liabilities and capital. This representation is now extended to include both revenues and expenses (the profit and loss entries).

The following double entry rules apply to revenues and expenses:

❑   A debit represents an expense and a credit represents revenue.
❑   If a transaction creates/increases revenue you credit the revenue account.
❑   If a transaction creates/increases an expense you debit the expense account.
❑   For every debit there is a corresponding credit.

Sales are revenues earned by a business from selling a product or providing a service. In addition to sales, examples of other revenue accounts could include rental income if the business let out part of its premises, and commissions received. A separate account would be kept for sales and each category of other revenue.

Examples of expense accounts could include rent paid to landlord, rates, advertising, insurance, wages and salaries, repairs, general expenses, accounting fees etc. The receipt or payment of a bill will create/increase an expense for a business. These expenses will be presented in the profit and loss account. A separate expense account would be kept for each category of expense.

Example 3.1: *Revenue and expense transactions*

Fred Smith is in the process of starting a new business venture retailing in fruit and vegetables from a stall in a market under the banner of Fred's Veggies. Fred has incurred a number of expense and revenue transactions as he sets up his business.

Transaction 1: Payment of rent

Fred has entered a rental agreement to occupy a stall in a market paying €800 by cheque on 1 July.

Here the owner debits the rent account as the expense of rent is created and credits the bank account as the asset of bank is decreased.

Dr		Rent Payable Account			Cr
		€			€
1 Jul	Bank a/c	800			

Dr		Bank Account			Cr
		€			€
			1 Jul	Rent a/c	800

Alternative approach to understanding entries:
Debit the receiver – the rent account is receiving the expense.
Credit the giver – the bank account is giving the money.

Transaction 2: Payment of insurance

Fred has had to pay an insurance premium of €375 by cheque on 1 July.

Here the owner debits the insurance account as the expense of insurance is created and credits the bank account as the asset of bank is decreased.

Dr		Insurance Account				Cr
		€				€
1 Jul	Bank a/c	375				

Dr		Bank Account				Cr
		€				€
			1 Jul	Rent a/c		800
			1 Jul	Insurance a/c		375

Alternative approach to understanding entries:
Debit the receiver – the insurance account is receiving the expense.
Credit the giver – the bank account is giving the money.

Transaction 3: Advertising expense

On 2 July Fred arranged for promotional leaflets to be produced and distributed to market his new stall and pays €250 by cheque.

Here the owner debits the advertising account as the expense of advertising is created and credits the bank account as the asset of bank is decreased.

Dr		Advertising Account				Cr
		€				€
2 Jul	Bank a/c	250				

Dr		Bank Account				Cr
		€				€
			1 Jul	Rent a/c		800
			1 Jul	Insurance a/c		375
			2 Jul	Advertising a/c		250

Alternative approach to understanding entries:
Debit the receiver – the advertising account is receiving the expense.
Credit the giver – the bank account is giving the money.

Transaction 4: Rent received

On 3 July Fred agreed to sub-let a small portion of his stall and received a cheque for €40.

Here the owner debits the bank account as the asset of bank is increasing and credits a rent received account as it is creating revenue.

Dr			Bank Account		Cr
			€		€
3 Jul	Rent received a/c		40	1 Jul Rent a/c	800
				1 Jul Insurance a/c	375
				2 Jul Advertising a/c	250

Dr		Rent Received Account		Cr
	€			€
		3 Jul	Bank a/c	40

Alternative approach to understanding entries:
Debit the receiver – the bank account is receiving the money.
Credit the giver – the rent received account (representing the tenant) is giving the money.

In the scenario above, Fred is in the initial stage of setting up the business. One of his most significant expenses will be the purchase of stock for resale. This brings us to the accounting procedures for stock.

Accounting for Stock

For businesses buying and selling products the selling price is normally set at a price above the cost price – otherwise the business would not make a profit. Stock is bought at one price, the purchase price, and sold at another price (normally higher), the selling price. It makes no sense to have one account for stock, as goods are purchased and sold at different prices. Thus the actual stock account is divided into four separate accounts as follows:

1. Sales account – detailing all stock sold at selling price.
2. Sales returns account – detailing all stock returned at selling price.
3. Purchases account – detailing all stock purchased at cost price.
4. Purchases returns account – detailing all purchases returned at cost price.

} Stock A/C

These four accounts record all stock going into the business (either through purchases or sales returns) and stock going out of the business (either through sales or purchases returns).

Three points need to be made here:

1. The terms sales and purchases have very specific meaning in business. The term *purchases* means the buying of goods which the business intends to sell. Sometimes the goods are altered or added to but the intention when buying is re-sale. Similarly the term *sales* means the sale of goods in which the business normally trades and which were bought with the prime intention of selling. The specific definition is to ensure purchases or sales of fixed assets are not confused as purchases and sales of stock. The distinction is that fixed assets are not purchased with the intention to be sold but are purchased to be used in the business.
2. Stock is an asset that the business needs to sell to make a profit. Thus the sales account is a revenue account and the purchases account is an expense account in the trading, profit and loss account. Should there be any stock left over (unsold) at the end of a period, or accounting year, this stock is the amount that appears in the balance sheet. *The stock figure left over at the end of a period is normally ascertained by counting the amount of stock unsold at that date.*
3. Any unsold stock at the period end is valued at cost or its recoverable amount — whichever is the lowest (see cost/current value concept below).

Double entry for stock

As stock is an asset:

1. When purchasing stock we are increasing the asset of stock, therefore we debit the purchases account.
2. When purchases are returned for whatever reason (damaged goods etc.), then the asset of stock is reduced and hence we credit the purchases returns account. You should never need to debit the purchases returns account.
3. When selling stock we are reducing the asset of stock and thus we credit the sales account with the amount of the sale. You should never need to debit the sales account.
4. When goods sold are returned then the asset of stock is increasing and thus we debit the sales returns account. You should never need to credit the sales returns account.

Thus the rules could be summarised as follows:

Dr	Purchases and sales returns, as these transactions result in an increase in the asset of stock
Cr	Sales and purchases returns, as these transactions result in a decrease in the asset of stock

Or alternatively:

Dr	Purchases account	*Debit the receiver* (receive stock)
Cr	Purchases returns account	*Credit the giver* (give back stock)
Dr	Sales returns account	*Debit the receiver* (receive back stock)
Cr	Sales account	*Credit the giver* (give out stock)

Example 3.2: *Stock transactions*

Returning to the scenario relating to Fred Smith of Fred's Veggies we can see how stock is accounted for. The transactions below are a sample from Fred's first week of trading relating to stock.

Transaction 1: Cash purchases

Fred bought stock of fresh fruit and vegetables from a supplier paying €500 by cheque on 1 July.

Here the owner debits the purchases account as it is increasing stock of goods for resale and credits the bank account as it is decreasing the asset of bank.

Dr		Purchases Account		Cr
		€		€
1 Jul	Bank a/c	500		

Dr		Bank Account		Cr
		€		€
			1 Jul Purchases a/c	500

Alternative approach to understanding entries:
Debit the receiver – the purchases account is receiving the stock.
Credit the giver – the bank account is giving the money.

Transaction 2: Credit purchases

On 2 July Fred bought stock of vegetables amounting to €750 from Market Suppliers, a wholesale business, who agreed to grant Fred credit.

Here the owner debits the purchases account again as it is increasing stock of goods for re-sale and credits a creditor/supplier showing the amount owed to the supplier.

Dr		Purchases Account			Cr
		€			€
1 Jul	Bank a/c	500			
2 Jul	Market Suppliers a/c	750			

Dr		Creditor (Market Suppliers) Account			Cr
		€			€
			2 Jul	Purchases a/c	750

Alternative approach to understanding entries:
Debit the receiver – the purchases account is receiving the stock.
Credit the giver – Market Suppliers is giving the stock.

Transaction 3: Purchases returns

On 3 July Fred returned €100 of sub-standard vegetables to Market Suppliers and received an allowance for the full amount.

Here the owner debits the creditor/supplier account with the value of goods returned and credits a purchases returns account as it is reducing its stock of goods for re-sale.

Dr		Creditor (Market Suppliers) Account			Cr
		€			€
3 Jul	Purchases Returns	100	2 Jul	Purchases a/c	750

Dr		Purchases Returns Account			Cr
		€			€
			3 Jul	Market Suppliers a/c	100

Alternative approach to understanding entries:
Debit the receiver – Market Suppliers is receiving back the stock.
Credit the giver – purchases returns account is giving the stock back.

Transaction 4: Cash sales

Fred sold stock of fresh fruit and vegetables for cash totalling €880 on 4 July.

Here the owner debits the cash account with €880 cash received and credits the sales account with the amount of the sale. In this example the asset of stock is reduced due to the sale.

Dr		Cash Account		Cr
		€		€
4 Jul	Sales a/c	880		

Dr		Sales Account		Cr
		€		€
			4 Jul Cash a/c	880

Alternative approach to understanding entries:
Debit the receiver – the cash account is receiving the money.
Credit the giver – the sales account is giving the stock.

Transaction 5: Credit sales

On 5 July Fred sold stock of vegetables amounting to €260 to the Dame Café on credit.

Here the owner credits the sales account with the amount of the sale and debits a debtor account with the amount owed by the debtor Dame Café.

Dr		Debtor (Dame Café) Account		Cr
		€		€
5 Jul	Sales a/c	260		

Dr		Sales Account		Cr
		€		€
			4 Jul Cash a/c	880
			5 Jul Dame Cafe a/c	260

Alternative approach to understanding entries:
Debit the receiver – the Dame Café is receiving the stock.
Credit the giver – the sales account is giving the stock.

Transaction 6: Sales returns

On 6 July a customer returned vegetables amounting to €15 to Fred and received a cash refund.

Here the owner debits the sales returns account as the asset of stock for re-sale has increased due to this transaction and credits the cash account with €15 as the asset of cash is reduced.

Dr		Sales Returns Account			Cr
		€			€
6 Jul	Cash a/c	15			

Dr		Cash Account			Cr
		€			€
4 Jul	Sales a/c	880	6 Jul	Sales returns a/c	15

Alternative approach to understanding entries:
Debit the receiver – the sales returns account is receiving back the stock.
Credit the giver – the cash account is giving the cash refund.

The Effect of Profit or Loss on Capital

Profit is the excess of revenues earned (not necessarily received) over expenses charged (not necessarily paid) within a time-frame or period. Revenues consist of the monetary value of goods and services supplied to customers whereas expenses consist of the monetary value of the costs created in producing and selling the product/service. If a business makes a profit then this profit belongs to the owner and, should the owner decide to keep the profit in the business rather than take it out for personal use, then profit increases capital (the amount the owner puts into the business). Conversely, losses decrease capital. In general, most businesses will retain a significant proportion of profits, as this is an important form of finance to enable the business to expand.

Example 3.3 shows the effect profits or losses have on the capital figure in the balance sheet.

Example 3.3: *The effect profit/loss has on capital*

This example examines two scenarios, firstly a profitable first week in March and subsequently revised figures indicating a loss in the first week.

When a profit is made

During the first week of March the total stock which cost €5,000 was sold for €8,000 making a profit of €3,000. The monies were received and banked immediately.

The effect of the transaction is that the business is out of stock but the bank balance has increased by €8,000 and hence total assets increasing by €3,000 to €177,000.

With creditors and loans unchanged then the balancing figure of capital (Assets = Capital + Liabilities) increases by €3,000 to €79,000. Thus profit increases capital.

Balance sheet as at	1 March	7 March
Assets	€	€
Premises	100,000	100,000
Equipment	56,000	56,000
Stock	5,000 ➡	0
Debtors	10,000	10,000
Bank	3,000 ➡	11,000
	174,000	177,000
Liabilities		
Creditors	11,000	11,000
Loans	87,000	87,000
	98,000	98,000
	76,000	79,000
Capital	76,000	76,000
Profit	0 ➡	3,000
	76,000	79,000

When a loss is incurred

During the first week of March the total stock which cost €5,000 was sold for €3,000. The monies were received and banked immediately. In this situation a loss of €2,000 is made.

The effect of the transaction is that the business is out of stock but the bank figure increases to €6,000 and total assets amount to €172,000.

With creditors and loans remaining unchanged then capital would fall to €74,000 showing that a loss reduces capital.

Balance sheet as at	1 March	7 March
Assets	€	€
Premises	100,000	100,000
Equipment	56,000	56,000
Stock	5,000 ➡	0
Debtors	10,000	10,000
Bank	3,000 ➡	6,000
	174,000	172,000
Liabilities		
Creditors	11,000	11,000
Loans	87,000	87,000
	98,000	98,000
	76,000	74,000
Capital	76,000	76,000
Loss	0 ➡	-2,000
	76,000	74,000

In summary the effects of profits or losses on capital are as follows:

Old capital + profit = new capital
Old capital - losses = new capital

Drawings

Capital represents the monies invested by the owner of the business. If the owner of a business decides to invest €5,000, the bank account is debited with €5,000 and the capital account is credited with €5,000. Should the owner decide to take money or any other assets out of the business for their own use, this is known as *drawings*. For example, if the owner of the business withdrew €200 from the business bank account for their own use then we would account for it by debiting the drawings account and crediting the bank account. If the business was an off-licence and the owner took some beverage for their own use then we would debit drawings and credit the purchases account. Drawings is the opposite to capital and, in the balance sheet, drawings is deducted from capital to show the net capital invested by the owner.

Summary of Double Entry Accounting

At this stage all the key transactions likely to occur in a business have been explained. The transactions for assets, liabilities, those involving stock, transactions for revenue and expenses all combine to provide a complete set of accounts. Some of the transactions will affect the balance sheet while others affect the profit and loss statement. Example 3.4 revises some of the key transactions covered.

Example 3.4: *Summary of double entry transactions*

	Account to be Debited	Account to be Credited
Owner invests new capital in the business *Here we increase the asset of bank, which we debit (Dr), and increase the capital, which we credit (Cr).*	Bank a/c	Capital a/c
Owner withdraws cash for his own personal use *Here we increase the owner's drawings,*		

which we debit (Dr), and reduce the asset of cash, which we credit (Cr).	Drawings a/c	Cash a/c
Purchase stock of goods paying by cheque *Here we increase the expense of purchases, which we debit (Dr), and decrease the asset of bank, which we (Cr).*	Purchases a/c	Bank a/c
Sold goods for cash *Here we increase the asset of cash, which we debit (Dr), and increase the revenue of sales, which we credit (Cr).*	Cash a/c	Sales a/c
Paid rent by cheque *Here we decrease the asset of bank, which we credit (Cr), and increase or create the expense of rent, which we debit (Dr).*	Rent a/c	Bank a/c
Purchase stock of goods on credit from A. Dunne *Here we increase the expense of purchases, which we debit (Dr), and increase the liability of creditors, which we credit (Cr).*	Purchase a/c	A. Dunne Creditor a/c
Paid rates by cheque *Here we increase the expense of rates, which we debit (Dr), and reduce the asset of bank, which we credit (Cr).*	Rates a/c	Bank a/c
Paid advertising bill by cheque *Here we increase the expense of advertising, which we debit (Dr), and reduce the asset of bank, which we credit (Cr).*	Advertising a/c	Bank a/c
Purchased motor vehicles paying by cheque *Here we increase the asset of motor vehicles, which we debit (Dr), and decrease the asset of bank, which we credit (Cr).*	Motor vehicles a/c	Bank a/c
Paid for petrol and insurance for motor vehicle by cheque *Here we increase/create motor expenses, which we debit (Dr), and decrease the asset of bank, which we credit (Cr).*	Motor expenses a/c	Bank a/c
Purchased office equipment on credit from OE Ltd *Here we create/increase the asset*		

of office equipment, which we debit (Dr), and increase creditors OE Ltd, which we credit (Cr).	Office equipment a/c Creditor a/c	OE Ltd
Repairs to office equipment paid by cheque *Here we create/increase the expense of repairs, which we debit (Dr), and decrease the asset of bank, which we credit (Cr).*	Repairs a/c	Bank a/c
Paid light and heat bill by cheque *Here we increase the expense of light and heat, which we debit (Dr), and decrease the asset of bank, which we credit (Cr).*	Light and heat a/c	Bank a/c
Paid wages and salaries by cheque *Here we increase the expense of wages and salaries, which we debit (Dr), and decrease the asset of bank, which we credit (Cr).*	Wages and salaries a/c	Bank a/c

Note: You will note that included above are a few transactions that create or increase assets and liabilities. For example, the purchase of a car creates a fixed asset which goes to the balance sheet and thus we debit the car account. The receipt or payment of a bill for car repairs or for petrol creates an expense which goes to the profit and loss account and thus the account is debited.

A summary of the rules of double entry for assets, liabilities, revenues, expenses and capital is as follows:

1. A debit (Dr) represents assets and expenses and a credit (Cr) represents liabilities, capital and revenues.
2. If a transaction requires you to increase an asset or expense, you debit the asset or expense account with the amount of the increase. To decrease an asset/expense, you credit the account.
3. If a transaction requires you to increase a liability, capital or revenue account, you credit the account with the amount of the increase. To decrease a liability, capital or revenue account, you debit the account.
4. For every debit there is a corresponding credit and vice versa.

Consider this

1. Why does a debit represent an asset as well as an expense?
2. Why does a credit represent a revenue and a liability?

It may at first seem strange that a debit would represent assets and expenses. However, in reality assets are like expenses as to acquire them involves the outlay of some resource, usually money. Assets, expenses and losses are a cost to an organisation. Also expenses have the effect of reducing profit and this has the effect of reducing capital. To reduce capital one must debit the account. Thus expenses and assets are represented by debits in double entry accounting.

It also may seem strange that a credit would represent capital, liabilities and revenues. In fact, capital, liabilities, revenue and profit fund a business. An increase in sales has the effect of increasing profit and thus increasing capital so it makes sense that a credit would represent both capital and sales/revenues.

Accounting Concepts

As mentioned in Chapter 2, accounting concepts are broad basic assumptions which form the basis of the financial accounts of a business. They help to ensure that the attributes of comparability, accountability and transparency are upheld in the recording process. We have already covered two accounting concepts, namely the dual aspect concept and the separate entity concept. At this stage we can now introduce you to four more accounting concepts. These are:

1.   The money measurement concept.
2.   The cost/current value concept.
3.   The going concern concept.
4.   The realisation concept.

The money measurement concept

The assets of the business must be measured in some uniform way. Obviously this has to be in some monetary form. It follows that some assets of the business cannot appear on the balance sheet of a company because to put a monetary value on them would be too subjective. The most obvious example is the human asset of a good work force or excellent management team. These assets cannot appear on the balance sheet as it is very difficult, if not impossible, to put an objective monetary value on them. The exception to this rule is football clubs.

Did You Know?

Robbie Keane would be valued at £7 million on the balance sheet of Spurs F.C. if the valuation basis is historic cost. The reason why he (a human asset) is on their balance sheet is because he cost that amount (according to newspaper reports) and thus his value can be objectively ascertained.

The cost/current value concept

In presenting financial statements a measurement basis must be chosen for each category of asset and liability. The choice is:

❑ **Historical cost**: This is where the asset or liability is valued at its initial transaction cost. This may be subsequently re-measured if the recoverable amount of the asset is lower than cost.

❑ **Current value**: This is where the asset is valued based on its current value at the time it was acquired. Assets and liabilities measured on the current value basis are carried at up-to-date current values and thus will be re-measured frequently. Re-measurement, however, will only be recognised if there is sufficient evidence that the monetary values of the asset/liability have changed and the new amount can be measured with sufficient reliability. For example, once a business has decided to apply current values to its property assets then they will be re-measured constantly on the basis of an independent valuer's assessment.

Did You Know?

For many hotels and retail businesses the main asset is property. Such businesses are often located in prime, city centre locations and the value of these properties would increase significantly as time goes by. Hence for these businesses it is essential that property assets are shown at realistic values and if the company policy is to show asset at current values, then their property assets are re-measured frequently.

The going concern concept

The going concern concept states that in preparing the accounts we assume the business will continue into the foreseeable future. This ensures the basis of measuring and valuing assets and liabilities will remain at either cost or current value. If the accounts were to be prepared on the basis that the business was to be sold or about to go into liquidation, then an alternative basis for valuing the assets would have to be considered such as the break-up value. Thus unless the business entity is in liquidation or the directors have no alternative but to cease trading or liquidate, then the going concern basis will apply and all assets and liabilities will be valued at historic cost or current value, whichever is appropriate.

The realisation concept

The realisation concept clarifies when a business accounts for a transaction and thus the related profits or losses on the transaction. For example: When is a sale a sale? When is a purchase a purchase? When do we account for expenses? There are three clear stages in the life of a transaction:

1.   The order stage.
2.   The transfer of goods and acceptance of liability by the purchaser.
3.   The payment or cash stage.

Obviously if some businesses account for sales based on orders received (and some still try to do this to boost sales) and other businesses account for sales based only on cash received, then there is no point in comparing the businesses performances as they recognise sales and profits at different periods. The realisation concept holds the view that a transaction should be accounted for at the transfer of goods and acceptance of liability stage, *not* at the order stage. Effectively the realisation concept tells us when to recognise the profits or loss on a transaction. It states that profits or losses on transactions can only be accounted for when realisation has occurred. A number of criteria have to be observed before realisation can occur. The most critical of these is that goods or services have been provided to a buyer who accepts liability for them and the monetary value of the goods or services has been established. Ultimately it is essential that all businesses account for transactions on the same basis. The realisation concept is very much a part of the prudence concept, which will be considered in Chapter 10.

Summary

In this chapter you have been introduced to the profit and loss account and the variables that calculate profit or loss, namely revenues and expenses. Profit is the ultimate measure of the success of a business and most users of accounting information will be interested in the profit levels achieved by a business. The following are the main information points covered in this chapter:

❑ The profit and loss account is a statement showing the revenues earned and expenses charged for a business. Where revenues exceed expenses a profit is earned by the business. Where expenses exceed revenues the business records a loss.

❑ Revenues are the income generated by the business from the sale of its products or services. It is important to note that revenues include cash and credit sales.

❑ Expenses are the costs incurred in running the business on a day-to-day basis and do not include the cost of purchasing fixed assets or the repayment of any loans.

❑ There are differences in the presentation of a profit and loss account for businesses that sell products and those that provide a service.

❑ The double entry accounting rules also apply to revenues and expenses where a debit represents an expense and a credit represents revenue.

❑ In accounting for stock of goods for re-sale, the stock account is divided into four revenue and expense accounts, namely sales, sales returns, purchases and purchases returns. As stock is bought and sold, a business may have amounts of unsold stock at the end of an accounting period. This is called the closing stock and appears in the balance sheet of the business. Closing stock is normally ascertained through a stock count at the year-end. Stock is valued at the lower of cost, or its recoverable amount.

❑ The effect of profit is to increase the wealth and capital of the owners of the business. A net loss reduces the capital of the business.

❑ The money measurement, historic cost/current value, going concern and realisation concepts all underpin the values we apply to assets, liabilities, expenses and revenues. They help ensure businesses account for transactions in a uniform manner and that the attributes of comparability, accountability and transparency are upheld in the recording process.

Question 3.1

What is the difference between a profit and loss statement for a service provider compared to one produced by a product provider?

Question 3.2

Distinguish between revenues and expenses using examples to illustrate your answer.

Question 3.3

The following transactions relate to Le Med, a cheap and cheerful Spanish restaurant located in downtown Athlone. Complete the following table containing transactions relating to their expense and revenue items.

Transaction	Account to be Debited	Account to be Credited
	€	€
1. Paid electricity by cheque.		
2. Paid for stationery by cash.		
3. Paid insurance by cheque.		
4. Returned some stationery for a cash refund.		
5. Paid wages by cheque.		
6. Received rent in cash from a tenant.		
7. Paid motor expenses in cash.		

Required

(a) Complete the table indicating the accounts to be debited and credited for each transaction.

(b) Record the transactions above in the appropriate ledger accounts.

Question 3.4

What four accounts make up the asset of stock and why?

Question 3.5

Explain how a debit can represent both an asset and an expense.

Question 3.6

Complete the table below which contains transactions relating to Sure Build, a DIY retail outlet.

Transaction	Account to be Debited	Account to be Credited
1. Purchased stock of goods €5,000 on credit from Irish Wholesalers Ltd.	€	€
2. Purchased stock of goods paying €3,500 by cheque.		
3. Sold goods for cash of €2,800.		
4. Sold goods on credit to D&D Ltd for €1,750.		
5. Returned some of the goods purchased from Irish Wholesalers Ltd for a €500 allowance.		
6. Some goods worth €200 were returned to us as damaged from D&D Ltd.		
7. Paid €4,500 to Irish Wholesalers Ltd by cheque.		
8. Received a cheque for €1,000 from D&D Ltd.		

Question 3.7

The transactions listed 1 to 15 below relate to Alpha Retail Ltd. Complete the table indicating the accounts to be debited and credited in each case.

Transaction	Account to be Debited	Account to be Credited
	€	€
1. Purchased stock of goods on credit from AA Ltd.		
2. Paid rent by cheque.		
3. Paid for stationery by cash.		
4. Purchased stock of goods paying by cheque.		
5. Sold goods for cash.		
6. Sold goods on credit to BB Ltd.		
7. Returned some of the goods purchased from AA Ltd.		
8. Some goods were returned to us as damaged from BB Ltd.		
9. Paid rates by cheque.		
10. Paid wages by cheque.		
11. Paid cleaning expenses in cash.		
12. Purchased new equipment paying by cheque.		
13. Repairs to equipment paying by cash.		
14. Owner took some cash for his own use.		
15. Owner took some stock for his own use.		

Question 3.8

Write up the following transactions in the books of O'Donoghue Souvenirs for the month of May.

Date	Transaction
1 May	Owner put €25,000 into a business bank account.
2 May	The business purchased office equipment for €5,000 paying by cheque.
4 May	The business purchased motor vehicles on credit from AA motors Ltd €8,000.
5 May	Purchased stock of goods on credit from Jackod Ltd for €2,000.
6 May	Purchased stock of goods paying by cheque for €3,000.
10 May	Sold goods for €4,000 receiving the money by cheque.
15 May	Paid rent by cheque €1,000.
16 May	Paid stationery bill by cheque €400.
16 May	Paid advertising by cheque €250.
18 May	Returned some of the goods purchased on credit from Jackod Ltd for €500.
20 May	Owner took €300 out of bank for his own use.
22 May	Paid the balance owed to Jackod Ltd by cheque.
23 May	Paid wages by cheque €800.
25 May	Let part of the premises receiving rent by cheque €280.
26 May	Paid for travel and motor expenses €200 by cheque.
27 May	Owner took stock to the value of €100 for his own use.
29 May	Sold goods on credit to G. Dunne €350.
30 May	Paid AA motors Ltd the amount outstanding by cheque.

Question 3.9

(a) Explain in your own words the relationship between 'net profit' and 'capital'.
(b) What do you understand by the term 'drawings'?

CHAPTER 4

Balancing Accounts and the Trial Balance

Learning Outcomes

By the end of this chapter you will be able to:

- ☐ Balance off ledger accounts.
- ☐ Prepare a trial balance.
- ☐ Outline the errors a trial balance will identify.
- ☐ Describe the six errors a trial balance will fail to identify.
- ☐ List the advantages of preparing a trial balance.

Introduction

Up to this we point we have been concerned with recording transactions through the double entry accounting system. The next step in the recording process is to summarise, at the end of an accounting period, the various asset, liability, expense and revenue accounts and list the balance in each of these accounts in what is called a trial balance. It is from this trial balance or list of account balances that we prepare the trading, profit and loss account (focusing on expense and revenue accounts) and balance sheet (focusing on asset, liability and capital accounts) for a business. Thus summarising or balancing accounts and preparing a trial balance is an integral part of the recording process.

Balancing Asset and Liability Accounts

So far, the emphasis has been on the recording of transactions in the asset, liability, expenses and revenue accounts. We now move on to the balancing process. The balancing process works as follows:

The balancing process

1. Add up both sides (debit and credit) to find out the total for each side.
2. Calculate the difference between each side (by taking the lower amount from the higher).
3. Enter this difference on the side that has the smallest total so that the totals on each side are equal and thus the account is balanced. The narrative for this entry is 'balance'.
4. You should enter the total figures for each side with a double line under each total.
5. Enter the balance underneath the totals on the opposite side of the original balance, as this balance represents either an asset or a liability for the new period and is a part of the new period's accounts.

Illustration 4.1: *Balancing an account*

Step 1: Total both sides					
Dr			**Furniture Account**		**Cr**
		€			€
1 May	Bank a/c	1,500	17 May	ABC Ltd a/c	250
15 May	ABC Ltd a/c	2,250			
		3,750			**250**

Step 2: Find the difference between the two totals
The difference is €3,750 - €250, giving €3,500. This is the balance.

Step 3: Enter the balance on the lower side					
Dr			**Furniture Account**		**Cr**
		€			€
1 May	Bank a/c	1,500	17 May	ABC Ltd a/c	250
15 May	ABC Ltd a/c	2,250	**30 May**	**Bal c/d**	**3,500**

Step 4: Enter the total figure for each side				

Dr		Furniture Account			Cr
		€			€
1 May	Bank a/c	1,500	17 May	ABC Ltd a/c	250
15 May	ABC Ltd a/c	2,250	30 May	Bal c/d	3,500
		3,750			3,750

Step 5: Enter the balance below the total on the opposite side				

Dr		Furniture Account			Cr
		€			€
1 May	Bank a/c	1,500	17 May	ABC Ltd a/c	250
15 May	ABC Ltd a/c	2,250	30 May	Bal c/d*	3,500
		3,750			3,750
1 June	*Bal b/d***	*3,500*			

★ c/d / 'carried down' represents the closing balance.
★★ b/d / 'brought down' represents the opening balance.

All asset, liability and capital accounts must be balanced, as it informs the business how much has been invested in assets and how those assets have been financed. The balance in the above example tells us that we have invested €3,500 in furniture at 1 June. In the same way, by balancing all loan accounts and the capital accounts we can see how the company has financed its investment in assets. This information is essential in preparing the balance sheet.

Balancing accounts is even more crucial in terms of debtors and creditors. It is important that each individual debtor account is summarised, with the balance in the account telling us how much the debtor owes us or, conversely, if the customer has overpaid his account and is in credit. This summary is sent to the debtor as a reminder every month for payment.

The same applies to creditors. A business should keep account of the credit it receives and this is done through the balancing of accounts, which can tell us what we owe to individual creditors. It is also important because creditors will obviously send us reminders of the outstanding balance on our account and we should be able to check their records with ours which can help to highlight errors.

Example 4.1: *Balancing a debtor account*

The following transactions took place between our firm and a debtor, A. Mullins, over the period January and February of 2001. You are required to write up the debtor account of A. Mullins only, for each month balancing off the account at the end of January and February.

Date	Transaction
2 Jan	Sold goods on credit to A. Mullins for €500.
10 Jan	Sold goods on credit to A. Mullins for €1,000.
20 Jan	A. Mullins returned goods to the value of €200.
31 Jan	Received €400 from A. Mullins.
10 Feb	Received €900 from A. Mullins.
20 Feb	Sold goods on credit to A. Mullins €300.
28 Feb	A. Mullins returned goods valued at €150.

Solution

Mullins' account for both months will look as follows:

Dr			A. Mullins	(Debtor)		Cr
		€				€
2 Jan	Sales	500	20 Jan	Sales returns		200
10 Jan	Sales	1,000	31 Jan	Bank		400
			31 Jan	Bal c/d		900
		1,500				1,500
1 Feb	Bal b/d	900	10 Feb	Bank		900
20 Feb	Sales	300	28 Feb	Sales returns		150
			28 Feb	Bal c/d		150
		1,200				1,200
1 Mar	Bal b/d	150				

Explanation

❏ At the end of January Mullins owes us €900. This €900 will be part of the overall debtors figure in the balance sheet (end of January). At the end of February he owes us €150.

❏ A debit balance is where the debit side is greater than the credit side, which is the case in Mullins' account for both months. Hence, we place the balance on the credit side and bring it down on the debit side for the next period as Mullins is a debtor who owes us money and is represented by a debit. On 1 February Mullins owes us €900 and on 10 February pays us that amount. However, we sold more goods to him on credit on 20 February and he returned half those goods to us on the 28 February with the balance of €150 representing the amount he owes us.

❑   For all asset accounts it is rare that there would be a credit balance unless a debtor overpaid his account and thus was in credit or if a bank account went into overdraft.

Example 4.2: *Balancing a creditor account*

The following transaction took place between our firm and A. Cooke, a supplier:

Date	Transaction
2 Jan	Purchased goods on credit from A. Cooke for €500.
10 Jan	Purchased goods on credit from A. Cooke for €1,000.
20 Jan	Returned goods to the value of €100 to A. Cooke.
31 Jan	Paid A. Cooke €500 by cheque.
10 Feb	Paid A. Cooke €900 by cheque.
20 Feb	Purchased goods on credit from A. Cooke for €300.
28 Feb	Returned goods to A. Cooke valued at €150.

You are required to balance the account of A. Cooke for both January and February.

Solution

The account of A. Cooke (creditor) would be as follows:

Dr			A. Cooke (creditor)			Cr
		€				€
20 Jan	Purchases returns	100	2 Jan	Purchases		500
31 Jan	Bank	500	10 Jan	Purchases		1,000
31 Jan	Bal c/d	900				
		1,500				1,500
10 Feb	Bank	900	1 Feb	Bal b/d		900
28 Feb	Purchases returns	150	20 Feb	Purchases		300
28 Feb	Bal c/d	150				
		1,200				1,200
			1 Mar	Bal b/d		150

Explanation

❑   At the end of January, we owe Cooke €900. This €900 is part of the overall creditors figure in the balance sheet at the end of January. At the end of February we owe €150.

❑   A credit balance would occur where the credit side is greater than the debit side and thus the balance in the account will be on the debit side but is brought down on the credit side as it represents a liability for the business. On 1 February we owe Cooke €900 and on 10 February we pay that amount by cheque. However, we purchased more goods from him on credit on 20 February, returning half those goods to him on 28 February with the balance representing the amount we owe.

❑   It is very rare that any liability accounts would have a debit balance except where a creditor was overpaid.

Computers and Accounts

We have focused on the traditional (manual) means of presenting the ledger accounts of a business. Within computerised systems, double entry accounting is also used. However, it is presented in columnar form with a debit, credit and balance column, similar to a monthly bank statement.

Below is the account of A. Mullins (debtor) in columnar format:

Date	Transaction	Debit	Credit	Balance
		€	€	€
1 Jan	Balance fwd			0
2 Jan	Sales	500		500 Dr
10 Jan	Sales	1,000		1,500 Dr
20 Jan	Sales returns		200	1,300 Dr
31 Jan	Bank		400	900 Dr
10 Feb	Bank		900	0
20 Feb	Sales	300		300 Dr
28 Feb	Sales returns		150	150 Dr

Balancing Expense and Revenue Accounts

In balancing expense and revenue accounts the process is the same. However, one should be mindful that expenses and revenues are allocated to specific years and do not carry forward into the next year. For example, sales for 2004 are exactly that and do not appear again in 2005, unlike assets and liabilities that carry on for as long as they are owned and used in the business. For example, equipment used in 2004 will also be used in 2005 and will appear as part of the opening balance in the equipment account for 2005.

Example 4.3: *Balancing an expense account*

The following is a rent payable account for a business for January 2003:

Dr		Rent Payable Account		Cr
		€		€
7 Jan	Bank	250		
14 Jan	Bank	250		
21 Jan	Bank	250		
28 Jan	Bank	250		

You are required to balance the rent payable account for January 2003.

This expense account is balanced as follows:

Dr		Rent Payable Account		Cr
		€		€
7 Jan	Bank	250		
14 Jan	Bank	250		
21 Jan	Bank	250		
28 Jan	Bank	250	31 Jan Bal c/d	1,000
		1,000		1,000
1 Feb	Bal b/d	1,000		

Note:The balance on the rent payable account is brought down to the next monthly period. This is only to accumulate the total rent expense for the annual accounting period and to satisfy double entry. However, at the end of the year the total rent payable for the year is transferred to the profit and loss account for 2003. The rent account in 2004 will have no opening balance brought down from 2003. This will be dealt with in greater detail in Chapter 10.

The Trial Balance

The trial balance is a means of checking that double entry has been adhered to, effectively checking that every debit has a corresponding credit and vice versa. If this is the case when balancing the accounts at the end of a period, the total debit balances should correspond to the total credit balances.

    The trial balance is thus a list of balances, both debit and credit, which is drawn up at the end of a period from the accounts to check if the total of all debit balances equals the total of all credit balances.

> ## The trial balance checks that all debit balances = all credit balances

A trial balance would look as follows:

	Dr €	Cr €
Sales		100,000
Sales returns	10,000	
Purchases	50,000	
Purchases returns		5,000
Expenses		
Rent	7,000	
Rates	2,000	
Advertising	3,000	
Light and heat	4,000	
Insurance	10,000	
Wages and salaries	15,000	
Motor vehicles	25,000	
Premises	250,000	
Furniture and equipment	40,000	
Debtors		
A. Dunne	2,500	
J. O'Donoghue	1,500	
P. O'Meara	3,000	
M. McDonald	4,000	
B. Gibson	3,000	
Bank overdraft		23,000
Creditors		
B. Winne		10,000
L. Lamb		5,000
C. Gardge		3,000
Loans		150,000
Capital		134,000
	430,000	430,000

The debit column will contain all debit balances representing assets and expenses whereas the credit column will contain all credit balances representing revenues, liabilities and capital.

Example 4.4: *Balancing accounts and preparing a trial balance*

Joseph Brennan is in the process of setting up a retail outlet. The following accounts have been written up but need to be balanced for the end of January and a trial balance is required.

Capital Account

	€		€
		25 Jan Bank a/c	50,000

Rent Account

	€		€
25 Jan Bank a/c	3,000		

Bank Account

	€		€
25 Jan Capital a/c	50,000	25 Jan Rent a/c	3,000
		26 Jan Equipment a/c	4,500
		30 Jan Ace Motors a/c	5,000

Creditors Account (Ace Interiors)

	€		€
30 Jan Bank	5,000	25 Jan Shop fittings a/c	12,000

Creditors Account (ABC Limited)

	€		€
		29 Jan Equipment a/c	3,500

Equipment Account

	€		€
26 Jan Bank a/c	4,500		
29 Jan ABC Ltd a/c	3,500		

Shop Fittings Account

	€		€
25 Jan Ace Interiors a/c	12,000		

Approach

This is a very basic example with only asset and liability accounts, as Joseph has not yet commenced retailing. Each account should be balanced using the steps outlined in Illustration 4.1.

Capital Account

	€		€
31 Jan Bal c/d	50,000	25 Jan Bank a/c	50,000
		1 Feb Bal b/d	50,000

Rent Payable Account

	€		€
25 Jan Bank a/c	3,000	31 Jan Bal c/d	3,000
1 Feb Bal b/d	3,000		

Bank Account

	€		€
25 Jan Capital a/c	50,000	25 Jan Rent a/c	3,000
		26 Jan Equipment a/c	4,500
		30 Jan Ace Motors a/c	5,000
		31 Jan Bal c/d	37,500
	50,000		50,000
1 Feb Bal b/d	37,500		

Creditors Account (Ace Interiors)

	€		€
30 Jan Bank	5,000	25 Jan Shop fittings a/c	12,000
31 Jan Bal c/d	7,000		
	12,000		12,000
		1 Feb Bal b/d	7,000

Equipment Account			
	€		€
26 Jan Bank a/c	4,500		
29 Jan ABC Ltd a/c	3,500	31 Jan Bal c/d	8,000
	8,000		8,000
1 Feb Bal b/d	8,000		

Creditors Account (ABC Ltd)			
	€		€
31 Jan Bal c/d	3,500	29 Jan Equipment a/c	3,500
		1 Feb Bal b/d	3,500

Shop Fittings Account			
	€		€
25 Jan Ace Interiors a/c	12,000	31 Jan Bal c/d	12,000
Feb Bal b/d	12,000		

When the balancing is complete, a trial balance should be prepared to check the arithmetic accuracy of the double entry transactions.

Trial Balance at 31 January

	Dr	Cr
	€	€
Capital		50,000
Bank	37,500	
Equipment	8,000	
Shop fittings accounts	12,000	
Rent account	3,000	
Creditors – Ace Interiors		7,000
Creditors – ABC Ltd		3,500
	60,500	60,500

It is important to remember that while the trial balance is a test to assess if the double entry process has been maintained accurately in the recording of all transactions, it does not detect all types of errors. It is merely a check on the arithmetic accuracy of the double entry system.

If a trial balance does not balance, the following errors could have occurred:

❑   There was an adding error when balancing the accounts.
❑   Only one side of a transaction was entered.
❑   Different amounts have been posted on the debit side and the credit side.

All the transactions need to be scrutinised until the errors are found and a balanced trial balance is prepared.

Errors the trial balance fails to detect

The trial balance detects whether proper double entry has occurred but it cannot be relied upon to check the proper recording of all transactions. For example, if a book-keeper improperly recorded a sales invoice for €100 as €1,000 then the trial balance would still balance but sales would be overstated. The following are the type of errors that a trial balance does not detect.

❑ **Errors of commission**: This occurs where the correct amount is recorded but in the wrong accounts. For example, a credit sale to G. Dunne for €1,000 is credited to sales but debited to B. Dunne's account instead. Thus while total sales and debtors are correct and the trial balance balances, the individual debtor balances are incorrect.

❑ **Errors of principle**: This is where a transaction is entered into the wrong type of account. For example, a business pays €400 on repairs to motor vehicles. The book-keeper credits the bank account and debits motor vehicles account (asset account) instead of motor expenses account (expense account). Thus the trial balance balances, but assets are overstated and expenses are understated.

❑ **Errors of original entry**: This occurs where a book-keeper records the wrong figure in the right accounts. For example, a sales invoice for €100 is debited and credited as €1,000 to the debtor and sales accounts respectively. The trial balance will still balance but sales and debtors are overstated and thus incorrect.

❑ **Compensating errors**: This is where two errors have occurred and they cancel each other out. For example, an expense account is over-added by €1,000 and a revenue account is over-added by €1,000. The trial balance still balances, but expenses and revenues are overstated.

❑ **Complete reversal of entries**: This is where the correct accounts are used but each item is shown on the wrong side of the account. For example, we made a credit sale to M. Mitchel for €500. The correct entry is to credit sales and debit Mitchel with €500. However, the book-keeper debits the sales account and credits debtors with €500. In this case the trial balance still balances, but sales and debtors are both understated.

❑ **Error of omission**: This occurs where a book-keeper fails to record a transaction in the books. Thus as long as all other transactions are recorded properly then the trial balance will balance but a transaction is omitted.

The advantages of the trial balance

The big advantage of using a trial balance is that although it does not highlight all errors it does highlight a significant proportion of errors and thus should be used as one of many checks to ensure proper control over the recording of transactions. When the trial balance does not balance then accounting personnel are alerted to the possibility of errors and should begin investigations.

Summary

In this section we have focused on balancing off accounts and preparing a trial balance to check and ensure transactions are properly recorded. In preparing and reviewing a trial balance it is essential to be aware that it does not highlight all possible recording errors.

The following are the main information points from the chapter:

- ❑ All accounts must be balanced and transferred to a trial balance.
- ❑ A debit balance occurs when the debit side is greater than the credit side. In this case the balance is inserted on the credit side but is brought down on the debit side for the next accounting period.
- ❑ A debit balance represents either an asset or an expense.
- ❑ A credit balance occurs when the credit side is greater than the debit side. In this case the balance is inserted on the debit side but is brought down on the credit side for the next accounting period.
- ❑ A credit balance represents revenue, liabilities or capital.
- ❑ The trial balance is a control mechanism for checking that all debit balances equal all credit balances.
- ❑ While a trial balance does highlight certain types of errors it is no guarantee that all transactions have been properly recorded.

Review Questions

Question 4.1

What are the main advantages and disadvantages of preparing a trial balance?

Question 4.2

Jack O'Donoghue has just set up a small specialist retail outlet selling model transport kits for children. Write up the following transactions in the books of Jack O'Donoghue for the month of May balancing off all accounts and preparing a trial balance

Date	Transaction
1 May	Jack O'Donoghue put €25,000 into a business bank account.
2 May	The business purchased office equipment for €7,000 paying by cheque.
4 May	The business purchased furniture on credit from Bargain Pieces Ltd. €5,000.
5 May	Purchased stock of goods on credit from Cianod Ltd for €2,000.
6 May	Purchased stock of goods paying by cheque for €3,000.
10 May	Sold goods for €5,000 receiving the money by cheque.
15 May	Paid rent by cheque €1,800.
16 May	Paid stationery bill by cheque €500.
16 May	Paid advertising by cheque €650.
18 May	Returned some of the goods to the value of €800 purchased on credit from Cianod Ltd.
20 May	Jack took €900 out of bank for his own use.
22 May	Paid the balance owed to Cianod Ltd by cheque.
23 May	Paid wages by cheque €1,800.
25 May	Let part of the premises receiving rent by cheque €1,000.
26 May	Paid for travel and motor expenses €75 by cheque.
27 May	Jack took stock to the value of €200 for his own use.
28 May	Sold goods on credit to G. Dunne €950.
30 May	Paid Bargain Pieces Ltd the amount outstanding.

Question 4.3

Write up the accounts to record the following transactions in the books of Alan Gibson, a retailer of health and fitness products, for the month of May, balancing off all accounts and preparing a trial balance.

Date	Transaction
1 May	Started the business with €7,000 in the bank.
2 May	Paid rent €1,200 by cheque.
3 May	Purchased some office equipment on credit from Equip Suppliers Ltd for €5,000.
4 May	Purchased stationery paying by cheque €200.
6 May	Purchased stock of goods paying by cheque €950.
7 May	Paid wages by cheque €550.
8 May	Sold goods for €900 receiving the money by cheque.
9 May	Sold goods on credit to MM Ltd for €1,000.
10 May	Bought office furniture on credit from OF Ltd for €3,000.
12 May	Purchased more stock paying by cheque €1,300.
14 May	Paid wages by cheque €1,500.
15 May	Returned office equipment worth 600 to Equip Suppliers Ltd.
16 May	Sold goods for €800 receiving the money by cheque.
17 May	Paid rates bill €600 by cheque.
18 May	Paid insurance €500 by cheque.
19 May	Purchased some stock on credit from SS Ltd for €750.
21 May	Paid Equip Suppliers Ltd €3,000 by cheque.
22 May	Sold goods on credit to BB Ltd for €1,400.
23 May	Paid OF Ltd €2,200 by cheque.
24 May	Purchased goods on credit from ZZ Ltd €1,450.
25 May	Received a loan from A. Dunne for €1,500.
26 May	Returned some of the goods purchased from ZZ Ltd for €200.
28 May	BB Ltd returned some goods to the value of €300.
29 May	BB Ltd made a part payment of €500 on their account by cheque.

Question 4.4

'My trial balance is balanced so I know my whole book-keeping system has been recorded accurately and no errors have occurred.'

Discuss the validity of the above statement.

CHAPTER 5

The Organisation of Accounts

Learning Outcomes

By the end of this chapter you will be able to:

❑ Outline and explain the separate components and stages within an accounting system.
❑ Appreciate the legal and tax requirements for businesses to keep proper accounting records.
❑ Write up the books of prime entry.
❑ Organise the ledger accounts.
❑ Be aware of computerised accounting packages available.
❑ Document the benefits of computerising an accounting system.

Introduction

Every business requires an accounting system. Its purpose is to ensure proper accounting records are kept, that the systems of recording and summarising accounting transactions will minimise errors and fraud, and that the financial statements produced at the end of an accounting period are accurate. Ultimately this is the responsibility of the owners or directors of a business and is legally enshrined under the Companies Acts. Businesses are also required to keep proper records for tax purposes. Thus businesses are required to organise their accounts and this is achieved through the development of a proper accounting system.

This chapter deals primarily with the component parts of any accounting system (whether manual or computerised) and shows how they integrate through a worked example.

The Accounting System – Overview

An accounting system is about how the recording of commercial transactions is organised within a business. While a business is very small all transactions can be recorded under double entry accounting in one book called a ledger. However, as a business grows and the volume of transactions grows, then the accounting records and books of account need to be organised. The accounting system can be broken down into a number of stages/components, as illustrated in Diagram 5.1.

Diagram 5.1: *Overview of an accounting system*

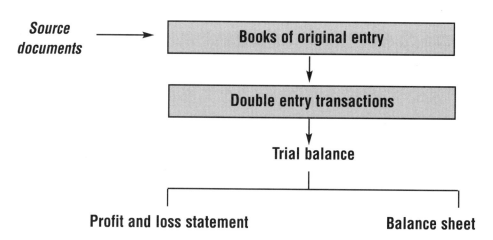

At this stage we have concentrated on double entry transactions, the trial balance and briefly introduced you to the profit and loss account, and balance sheet. We have not, however, looked at the books of original entry and before we do this we must focus on the various documents that give evidence of commercial transactions.

The accounting system – documentation

For transactions to occur there must be proper documentation to prove the existence of such transactions. The following are the commercial documents that give proof to the existence of such transactions:

1. A sales invoice gives rise to the recording of a sale.

2. A purchase invoice gives rise to the recording of a purchase.
3. A credit note which is issued to a customer gives evidence of a sales return.
4. A debit note which is issued to suppliers gives evidence of a purchases return.
5. Copy receipts issued to customers, cheques received and till rolls give evidence of monies and cheques received. Copies of cheques written, receipts, bank statements and supplier statements give evidence of monies paid out.
6. Purchase and sales invoices give evidence for the purchase and sale of fixed assets.

These commercial documents give rise to transactions, which are all recorded in what is known as the books of original entry.

The accounting system – books of original entry

The books of original entry are the books in which transactions are first recorded. The books are referred to as 'day books' or 'journals'. There is a separate book for each type of transaction. Diagram 5.2 shows the books that an organisation may keep.

Diagram 5.2: *Books of original entry*

Sales journal	Sales returns journal	Purchases journal	Purchases returns journal	Cash book	General journal
Recording all credit sales	Recording all sales returns	Recording all credit purchases of stock for resale	Recording all stock purchases returns	Recording all payments and receipts	Recording all other transactions

For example, a transaction involving the sale of goods on credit to J. James would be recorded in the sales journal. There is no double entry system for the books of original entry. All that is recorded is:

1. The date of the transaction.
2. Details of the transaction, for example the customer we sold to and the invoice number.
3. The amount of money involved in the transaction.

The books of original entry are essentially a list or record, in date order, of the transactions that occurred over a period of time.

The accounting system – the ledger accounts

Ultimately the transactions recorded in the books of original entry must be recorded in double entry format to show the effects on the assets, liabilities, capital, revenue and expenses of a business and to prepare the trading, profit and loss, and balance sheet. Chapters 2 and 3 showed in detail how this double entry stage operates. At the end of a period of time the transactions recorded in the books of original entry are recorded in the ledger accounts. Again as a business develops, the ledger accounts must be organised. Thus the ledger accounts are sub-divided into three ledgers:

1. The sales ledger, which contains the accounts of all customers/debtors.
2. The purchases ledger, which contains all trade creditors/suppliers accounts.
3. The general ledger containing all the other double entry accounts including all revenue and expense accounts, and assets (except trade debtors), liabilities (except trade creditors) and capital accounts.

Diagram 5.3: *Accounting system ledgers*

Sales ledger	Purchases ledger	General ledger
Contains all the individual debtor/customer accounts	Contains all the individual creditor/suppliers accounts	Contains all other accounts

Some accounting systems categorise all ledger accounts as either personal accounts or impersonal:

❑   Personal accounts are the individual debtor and creditor accounts in the sales and purchases ledgers.
❑   Impersonal accounts can be classified into two categories:
   — Real accounts, which focus on tangible assets such as property, machinery, fixtures, motor vehicles and equipment.
   — Nominal accounts, which focus on the expense and revenue accounts including the capital and drawings accounts.

Diagram 5.4: *Accounting system ledgers (alternative approach)*

General ledger	Sales ledger	Purchases ledger	Cash books
Real and nominal accounts	Debtors accounts	Creditors accounts	Cash and bank accounts

From these accounts at the end of a period a trial balance is extracted and the final accounts (profit and loss, and balance sheet) are produced.

Example 5.1: *Stages in an accounting system*

Jack O'Donoghue manages and owns a souvenir shop in a popular tourist location in County Kerry. His accounting transactions are generally made up of buying and selling souvenirs, paying wages and general expense items for running the business including rent, light and heating, insurance etc. He needs to record all of these transactions in his accounting records system.

Outline the stages within his financial record keeping cycle.

Approach

Stage 1

Depending on the nature of the transactions that occur, the details will be entered in the following books of original entry for Jack O'Donoghue:

❏   Cash book.
❏   Purchases journal.
❏   Purchases returns journal.
❏   General journal.

Note: There is no mention of the sales journal or sales returns journal, as a souvenir shop would be categorised as a cash-type business that has zero credit sales and returns.

Stage 2

The details are transferred from the book of original entry into the ledger accounts. The ledger accounts for Jack are divided into the following categories:

❏   Purchases ledger.
❏   General ledger.

For this business, as there are no credit sales there will be no debtors and hence no sales ledger accounts.

Stage 3

The ledger accounts are totalled at the end of the accounts period and balances are transferred to a trial balance.

Stage 4

From the trial balance the final accounts are prepared.

A worked example

The following worked example is quite comprehensive and covers most of the types of transactions that occur in a business. It shows how the various transactions are recorded in the books of prime entry and then transferred to the ledger accounts, and finally the accounts are balanced and a trial balance is produced.

Example 5.2: *A worked example*

The following transactions occurred in the books of Sandy's Restaurant for the month of May:

Date	Transaction
1 May	The owner put €5,000 into the business bank account.
1 May	The restaurant credit sales were to S. Small for €500 and N. Mills for €600.
2 May	The business purchases stock of food and beverages from R. Raymond for €500 and S. Sneem for €700 on credit.
4 May	The business purchases motor vehicles on credit from AA Motors Ltd €13,000.
5 May	Purchases stock of food and beverages on credit from Jackod Ltd for €2,000 and F. Franks for €600.
6 May	Purchased stock of food paying by cheque for €3,000.
10 May	Cash takings from the restaurant amounted to €1,000.
15 May	Paid rent by cheque €1,000.
16 May	Paid stationery bill by cheque €500.
16 May	Paid advertising by cash €250.
18 May	Returned some of the beverages purchased on credit from Jackod Ltd for €500.
20 May	Paid the balance owed to Jackod Ltd by cheque €1,500.
22 May	Paid wages by cheque €800.
23 May	Paid travel expenses by cash €200.
25 May	The restaurant's credit sales were to G. Dunne for €300 and W. Disney for €200.
29 May	Received the amount outstanding from S. Small, €500, and N. Mills, €600, by cheque.

Required

(a) Write up the books of original entry.
(b) Write up the ledger accounts from the books of original entry.
(c) Extract a trial balance from the ledger accounts.

Approach

(a) The books of prime entry *(Note: we have included document reference numbers in the solutions to give a more realistic view.)*

Sales Journal

Date	Details	Invoice No.	Amount
			€
1 May	S. Small	8622	500
	N. Mills	8623	600
25 May	G. Dunne	8625	300
	W. Disney	8626	200
30 May			1,600

Purchases Journal

Date	Details	Invoice No.	Amount
			€
2 May	R. Raymond	5555	500
	S. Sneem	5556	700
5 May	Jackod	5557	2,000
	F. Franks	5558	600
30 May			3,800

Purchases Returns Journal

Date	Details	Debit note no.	Amount
			€
18 May	Jackod	601	500
30 May			500

General Journal

Date	Details	Dr	Cr
		€	€
4 May	Motor vehicles	13,000	
	AA Motors		13,000
	The business purchased motor		
	vehicles from AA Ltd on credit		

Cash Book

Dr Date	Details	Cash	Bank	Date	Details	Cash	Bank Cr
		€	€			€	€
1 May	Capital		5,000	6 May	Purchases		3,000
10 May	Sales	1,000		15 May	Rent		1,000
29 May	S. Small		500	16 May	Stationery		500
	N. Mills		600	16 May	Advertising	250	
				20 May	Jackod		1,500
				22 May	Wages		800
				23 May	Travel	200	
30 May	Bal c/d		700	30 May	Bal c/d	550	
		1,000	6,800			1,000	6,800

Notes

❏ You will note the journals are all recorded in date order and do not involve any double entry accounting except for the general journal, which is in effect a memorandum of various transactions that are not recorded in the other journals. After each transaction there is a narrative describing the transaction that took place.

❏ The cash book has both cash and bank columns and involves double entry accounting. The cash book is effectively the cash and bank accounts that would appear in the general ledger. Thus the cash account is both a book of original entry and a ledger account. There is no need to show this account in the general ledger. The balances will be transferred straight to the trial balance.

(b)   The ledger accounts

GENERAL LEDGER ACCOUNTS

Capital Account

		€			€
30 May	Bal c/d	5,000	01 May	Bank	5,000
			01 Jun	Bal b/d	5,000

Motor Vehicles Account

		€			€
02 May	AA Motors	13,000	30 May	Bal c/d	13,000
01 Jun	Bal b/d	13,000			

Purchases Account

		€			€
06 May	Bank	3,000			
30 May	Purchases journal	3,800	30 May	Bal c/d	6,800
		6,800			6,800
01 Jun	Bal b/d	6,800			

Sales Account

		€			€
			10 May	Cash	1,000
30 May	Bal c/d	2,600	30 May	Sales journal	1,600
		2,600			2,600
			01 Jun	Bal b/d	2,600

Purchases Returns Account

		€			€
30 May	Bal c/d	500	30 May	Purch ret journal	500
			01 Jun	Bal b/d	500

Rent Account

		€			€
15 May	Bank	1,000	30 May	Bal c/d	1,000
01 Jun	Bal b/d	1,000			

Stationery Account

		€			€
16 May	Bank	500	30 May	Bal c/d	500
01 Jun	Bal b/d	500			

Advertising Account

		€			€
16 May	Bank	250	30 May	Bal c/d	250
01 Jun	Bal b/d	250			

Wages Account

		€			€
22 May	Bank	800	30 May	Bal c/d	800
01 Jun	Bal b/d	800			

Travel Expense Account

		€			€
23 May	Cash	200	30 May	Bal c/d	200
01 Jun	Bal b/d	200			

SALES LEDGER ACCOUNTS

G. Dunne Account

		€			€
25 May	Sales journal	300	30 May	Bal c/d	300
01 Jun	Bal b/d	300			

S. Small Account

		€			€
1 May	Sales journal	500	29 May	Bank	500

N. Mills Account

		€			€
01 May	Sales journal	600	29 May	Bank	600

W. Disney Account

		€			€
01 May	Sales journal	200	30 May	Bal c/d	200
01 Jun	Bal b/d	200			

PURCHASES LEDGER ACCOUNTS

Jackod Account

		€			€
18 May	Purchases returns	500	05 May	Purchases	2,000
20 May	Bank	1,500			
		2,000			2,000

R. Raymond Account

		€			€
30 May	Bal c/d	500	02 May	Purchases journal	500
			01 Jun	Bal b/d	500

S. Sneem Account

		€			€
30 May	Bal c/d	700	02 May	Purchases journal	700
			01 Jun	Bal b/d	700

F. Franks Account

		€			€
30 May	Bal c/d	600	05 May	Purchases journal	600
			01 Jun	Bal b/d	600

AA Motors Account

		€			€
30 May	Bal c/d	13,000	02 May	Motor vhe	13,000
			01 Jun	Bal b/d	13,000

(c)   Trial balance as at 30 May

	Dr	Cr
	€	€
Trade Debtors		
G. Dunne	300	
W. Disney	200	
Trade creditors		
R. Raymond		500
S. Sneem		700
F. Franks		600
Creditors		
AA Motors		13,000
Travel expenses	200	
Wages	800	
Purchases returns		500
Advertising	250	
Stationery	500	
Rent	1,000	
Sales		2,600
Purchases	6,800	
Motor vehicles	13,000	
Bank		700
Capital		5,000
Cash	550	
	23,600	23,600

Notes

❑   As shown in the worked example above, one of the benefits of the books of original entry is that the sales, purchases, sales returns and purchases returns accounts in the general ledger are not packed with multiple transactions. The totals of the journals in the books of original entry are transferred to the sales, purchases, sales returns and purchases returns accounts to avoid cramming too much detail in the general ledger accounts.

❑   Note also the way the ledger accounts are organised into three separate ledgers. The sales ledger dealing with all debtor accounts, the purchases ledger dealing with all creditor accounts and the general ledger dealing with all other asset, liability and capital accounts as well as revenue and expense accounts. One of the main advantages of this, apart from general organisation, is that errors can be identified and corrected more quickly.

The following detailed diagram summarises the process and shows the link to the final accounts.

Diagram 5.5: *The accounting system for recording transactions*

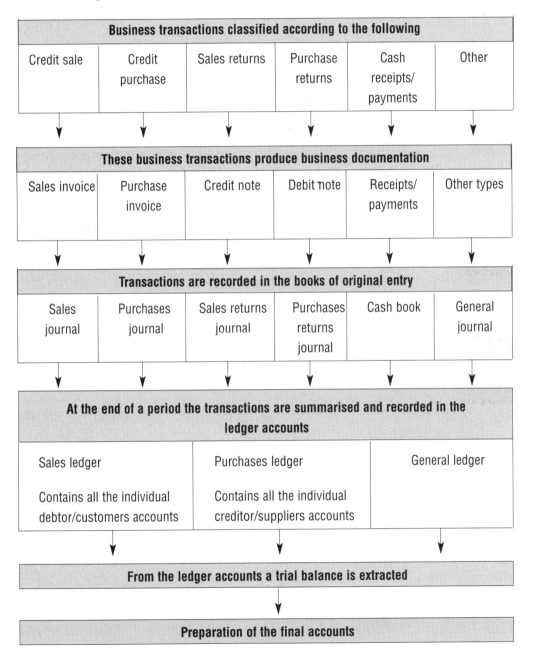

Business transactions classified according to the following					
Credit sale	Credit purchase	Sales returns	Purchase returns	Cash receipts/ payments	Other

These business transactions produce business documentation					
Sales invoice	Purchase invoice	Credit note	Debit note	Receipts/ payments	Other types

Transactions are recorded in the books of original entry					
Sales journal	Purchases journal	Sales returns journal	Purchases returns journal	Cash book	General journal

At the end of a period the transactions are summarised and recorded in the ledger accounts		
Sales ledger Contains all the individual debtor/customers accounts	Purchases ledger Contains all the individual creditor/suppliers accounts	General ledger

From the ledger accounts a trial balance is extracted

Preparation of the final accounts

The Use of Information Technology in Accounting

The accounting system forms a major part of the information system for management and thus it can provide much more information than a set of final accounts for a period. The accounting system should be flexible enough to provide a wide variety of reports and analyses to help managers in their decision-making role.

Obviously larger businesses will require greater outputs from their accounting system than smaller organisations. As would be expected, businesses often opt for the use of computers for most, if not all, their recording and accounting needs. Some businesses develop their own computerised accounting system to satisfy their particular information needs whereas other business can choose a standard computer system which is significantly cheaper but provides them with sufficient information to run their business efficiently. Many small businesses still use a manual accounting system but this is rapidly changing as 'off the shelf' accounting packages get cheaper and are more user friendly. Ultimately, as with any buying decision, the benefits of the purchase must exceed the costs.

Computerised software organises the accounts of a business in a similar format to the manual system described above. They do, however, give the following added advantages:

- ❑ Greater accuracy of calculation.
- ❑ Speed in the preparation of financial reports to provide more timely information for managers.
- ❑ A greater variety of financial reports for management. Thus management can tailor their financial reporting more closely.
- ❑ Ultimately they reduce the cost of providing the required financial information for the organisation.
- ❑ Greater information at the fingertips of management. For example, a comprehensive credit history of customers, analyses of purchases and stock requirements, bank reconciliations, access to statistics on order and stock levels, payroll etc.
- ❑ The saving of time, as the owners/managers can devote themselves to the proper running of their businesses.

The following websites have been set up by the main accounting software specialists:

Sage:	www.sage.com
Pegasus:	www.pegasus.co.uk
Tas books:	www.tassoftware.com
Dosh:	www.dosh.co.uk

The above accounting and business management software companies provide a range of accounting software systems to suit small, medium and large companies. Some of the companies are willing to tailor their software to suit the needs of a particular organisation or sector. Obviously the bigger an organisation, the greater the accounting system, and thus the requirements for that system increase. Some of the websites above provide a number of customer case studies of businesses both large and small from the tourism, hospitality and retail sectors that use the accounting packages on offer.

In Ireland at present Tas software is one of the more popular accounting software systems in use in the tourism, hospitality and leisure sectors. Its basic features include the following:

❑   Customers/sales ledger database.
❑   Suppliers and purchases ledger database.
❑   General ledger database.
❑   Cash and bank account database.
❑   Purchases and sales journals.
❑   Returns journals.
❑   VAT accounting forms and reports.

From these accounting databases management can access information at the tips of their fingers and can ensure periodic, timely reporting of accounting data to inform their decision making.

Hotel Accounting Systems

One of the main reasons a hotel will differ from other businesses within the tourism and hospitality industry is that its systems are required to record a wide variety of sales transactions, many of a low value such as bar sales, in addition to sales transactions that may be quite large and less frequent in nature (albeit they may be made up of many smaller elements). Charging for conference and banqueting revenue, for example, may require a single invoice to be raised but within this invoice there will likely be a number of smaller elements such as room hire, food and beverage, equipment hire etc.

In general, most bar, restaurant and accommodation sales would be cash or credit card based, with a small number of regular business clients receiving credit for accommodation, bar and restaurant services used. From an accounting and profit point of view it is important that all sales or services used are recorded and ultimately billed for. In large hotels this can consist of several point of sales (POS) terminals situated throughout the hotel, for example in the bar, restaurant, accommodation floors, all connected via an interface to a central billing database (often the front office system). This interface will be required also to deal with automated charges as a result of guest usage of items such as telephone or pay TV etc. In addition a user interface (such as a front office package) will be required for manual billing of other charges such as newspapers, laundry services etc. The benefit of an integrated system such as that outlined above is that guest accounts are immediately updated

In many cases this front of house system will in turn be linked to a back of house accounting package facilitating automatic updating of company accounts.

Summary

This chapter focused on the organisation of accounts through the use of accounting systems, both manual and computerised. All transactions give rise to documents which form proof of the transaction and which must be recorded. The accounting system organises all the transactions to ensure the outputs (trial balances, final accounts, management reports, cost analysis) from the accounting system are what the business needs and requires. Also, businesses are required by law (whether tax law or company law) to keep proper records and this requires a proper accounting system. It is also important to note that a good accounting system can help protect against internal and external fraud.

The following are the main information points covered in this chapter:

❏ The directors/owners of businesses are required through the Companies Acts and tax law to keep proper accounting records.

❏ The installation of a proper accounting system can also help protect against internal and external fraud.

❏ An accounting system organises all the transactions to ensure the outputs (trial balances, final accounts, management reports, cost analysis) from the accounting system are what the business needs and requires.

❏ For transactions to occur there must be proper documentation to prove the existence of such transactions. For example, a sales invoice gives evidence of a sales transaction whereas a credit note gives evidence of sales returns.

❏ The books of original entry are the books in which transactions are first recorded. The books are referred to as 'day books' or 'journals'. There is a separate book for each type of transaction. The books of original entry are essentially a list or record, in date order, of the transactions that have occurred over a period of time.

❑   The ledger accounts are sub-divided into three ledgers:

1.   The sales ledger, which is a list of the accounts of all customers/debtors.

2.   The purchases ledger, which is a list of all creditors/suppliers accounts.

3.   The general ledger, containing all the other double entry accounts, including all revenue and expense accounts, and assets (except trade debtors), liabilities (except trade creditors) and capital accounts.

❑   Computerised software organises the accounts of a business in a similar format to the manual system as described with added advantages such as speed and accuracy of information, savings in time and costs, more information and a greater variety of reports for management.

❑   Accounting computer systems can be geared to the characteristics and needs of any business in any sector.

Review Questions

Question 5.1

Distinguish between the following:

(a) Books of original entry and the ledger accounts.
(b) The sales ledger and the purchases ledger.
(c) The general ledger and the general journal.
(d) The cash book and sales journal.

Question 5.2

Describe the commercial documents that give evidence of the following transactions and identify the books of original entry the transaction should be recorded in:

(a) Purchased stock of goods on credit.
(b) Purchased stock of goods paying by cheque.
(c) Purchased new computer system on credit.
(d) Paid rent by cheque.
(f) Received cash from a debtor.
(g) Returned some of the goods bought on credit.
(h) Paid rates by cheque.
(i) A customer returned goods as damaged.

Question 5.3

Mr Senator is a publican who rents his premises from Lessors Ltd, paying rates and repairs. He has renovated the premises and owns the furniture and fittings as well as a motor vehicle. He has a current account with his bank. The current account has an overdraft facility of €15,000. He makes all payments by cheque and received credit of two weeks from his suppliers. All bar sales are for cash. He uses the double entry system of accounts for his business.

You are required to advise Mr Senator on the various books of accounts he should keep.

Question 5.4

Michael Robbins started trading as a restaurateur on 1 January 2004. He spent November and December 2003 preparing and fitting the restaurant with furniture and equipment. He also sourced six employees for his restaurant and was ready to open on 1 January 2004. His transactions were as follows for the first week of January:

Date	Transaction
1 Jan	Purchases of food and drink on credit from GGS Ltd for €6,000.
2 Jan	Banked sales amounting to €2,000.
3 Jan	Bought food on credit from XYZ Ltd for €1,000.
	Banked sales amounting to €1,000.
	Paid rent by cheque.
4 Jan	Bought cutlery from Catering suppliers Ltd for €500 paying by cheque.
	Banked sales amounting to €1,500.
5 Jan	Paid wages by cheque €3,000.
	Banked sales amounting to €2,500.
6 Jan	Purchased food on credit from XYZ Ltd for €2,000.
	Returned some purchases from XYZ Ltd for €200.
	Banked sales amounting to €3,000.
7 Jan	Paid GGS Ltd €2,000 by cheque.
	Banked sales amounting to €3,250.
	Returned some drink purchased from GGS for €500.

Required

(a)   Enter the above transactions in the books of prime entry.
(b)   Show the accounts in the appropriate ledgers.
(c)   Extract a trial balance as at 7 January 2004.

CHAPTER 6

Preparing Financial Statements – An Introduction

Introduction

'Annual income twenty pounds, annual expenditure nineteen ninety six, result happiness Annual income twenty pounds, annual expenditure twenty pounds ought and six, result misery.'

Mr Micawber's famous formula for the good life in Charles Dickens' *David Copperfield*

For most businesses the main objective is to make a profit. Profit occurs where revenues exceed the expenses of a business over a defined period. If a business makes a profit then it is considered a success. Profits help ensure the long-term survival of a business because if the profits are reinvested in the business then it has the finance to buy new stocks and to expand its services. If the business is making a loss (expenses exceed revenues) then the owner will need this information as soon as possible to take timely corrective action and guide the business into profit. Profitability is also an important criteria when providers of finance are considering investing either in the form of capital or loans. The Revenue Commissioners also require information on profitability as business taxation is based on the level of profit achieved by the business. Thus on a number of levels, profitability and the calculation of profit is extremely important. However, this is only one element of the financial statements. Management, potential investors, providers of finance and credit also require information on the existing assets, liabilities and capital of a business and this information is provided in the balance sheet.

The double entry accounting system merely records day-to-day transactions. It cannot provide a profit figure without further work. The trial balance (the end product of the double entry system) provides the summary totals from all the accounts, from which the financial statements for a period can be prepared. The profit and loss account and balance sheet make up the so-called final accounts or financial statements of a business. They are called the final accounts as they provide a summary of all the information provided through the recording process and are thus in reality the final summarised accounts.

This chapter focuses on understanding and preparing the financial statements of a business from the trial balance stage of the recording process. Before we do this, relevant material covered in Chapters 2 and 3 is summarised to recap on key explanations.

Revision of relevant material

The **profit and loss statement** tells whether the business has made a profit or loss for the period under review. Profit is calculated by deducting expenses from revenue.

Revenue is the income generated by the business from the sale of its products or services. It is important to note that revenues include cash and credit sales. Revenues do not include any monies received by means of loans or from selling fixed assets.

Expenses are incurred in running the business on a day-to-day basis and thus do not include the cost of purchasing fixed assets or repayment of any loans. Expenses represent the day-to-day running costs of a business.

The **profit and loss account** is normally prepared for a period of time showing the summary revenues and expenses for that period. This is unlike the **balance sheet**, which shows what the business owns (assets) and owes (liabilities and capital) at one point in time, usually the end of the year.

The **balance sheet** is based on a formula called the accounting equation which states that Assets – Liabilities = Capital.

Assets are the resources used by a business. In effect, assets are what the business owns.

Liabilities consist of monies owed by the business. This can include loans, monies owed for goods supplied or monies owed for expenses.

Capital is what the owner invests in the business whether in the form of cash or other assets such as motor vehicles, premises, expertise.

A sample of a balance sheet and a profit and loss account can be found in Appendix A.

Trading, Profit and Loss Account and the Balance Sheet

The financial statements are prepared from the trial balance. The trial balance provides a useful starting point, as it contains the balances of all the ledger accounts. Every item in the trial balance will appear in either the profit statement or the balance sheet. The profit statement starts with the trading account, which is simply sales less cost of sales. The trading account shows the profit made on the main trading activity before any expenses are deducted. This profit is known as the gross profit. The profit and loss account commences with gross profit and other income is added and expenses are deducted to arrive at the net profit.

It is essential to be familiar with the layout of the accounts. Illustration 6.1 shows a sample of what the financial statements should look like. It includes new headings and categories which are explained in the notes following the accounts.

Illustration 6.1: *Sample of Financial Statements*

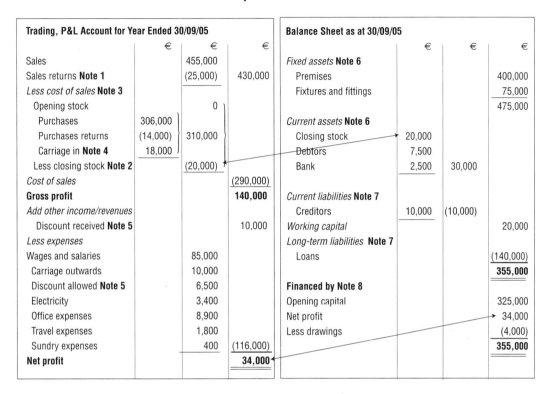

Note 1: Sales and purchases returns

Obviously in any business there will be goods purchased and sold that, for whatever reason, are unsatisfactory and need to be returned. The double entry accounting for these type of transactions was outlined in Chapter 3. Sales returns and purchases returns will appear in the trial balance with all the other accounts. In preparing the trading, profit and loss account, sales returns are simply deducted from sales to get the net sales figure, and purchases returns are deducted from purchases to get the net purchases figure.

Note 2: Stocks

It is important to understand the difference between opening and closing stock. Opening stock is the unsold stock from the previous period. There are only three possible situations in which a business will have no opening stock:

1. If the business is service based.
2. If the business is in a start-up situation, as they will not have traded in the previous period.

3. If the business sold all its stock in the previous period.

Closing stock is the stock from the current period that remains unsold when the accounts are prepared. Closing stock from this period will be the opening stock for the next period.

Closing stock appears in the trading account as a deduction from purchases, as it is unsold and cannot be matched against sales (see below). Closing stock also appears in the balance sheet under current assets, as it is something the business owns at the end of the year. It is important to note that a business calculates its closing stock simply by counting whatever stock is left over and then putting a cost value on it. Thus closing stock is not part of the double entry system and although some computerised accounting systems will be able to calculate what should be in stock at the end of a period, this should also be verified by a physical stock-take.

Note 3: Cost of goods sold

In calculating profit, it must be ensured that only related expenses are deducted from sales. The actual cost of the goods sold is deducted from sales to calculate gross profit.

Example 6.1: *Correct cost of sales figures*

Joseph trades in one product only which is sold at €5 per unit. It can be purchased at a cost of €3 per unit. How much should be charged as *cost of sales* in a period when 11,000 units were bought and only 10,000 units sold?

If a sales figure of €50,000 was based on selling 10,000 units/products at €5, then only the cost of buying 10,000 units should be deducted in calculating gross profit. If we purchased 11,000 units at €3 each, then we would have a stock of units left amounting to 1,000 at a cost value (cost concept) of €3 each. Thus our closing stock is valued at €3,000 and this is deducted from purchases to arrive at a cost of sales figure of €30,000.

Trading Account

		€	€
Sales	10,000 units x €5		50,000
Less cost of sales			
Opening stock		0	
Purchases	11,000 units x €3	33,000	
Less closing stock	1,000 units x €3	(3,000)	
Cost of sales	10,000 units x €3		30,000
Gross profit			20,000

Thus in calculating gross profit, the actual cost of the goods sold is deducted from sales. In the above example the cost of 10,000 units is deducted from the sale of 10,000 units. Costs are matched with related revenues. (See matching or accruals concept on page 97.) The trading account usually states monetary values only; units amounts are not shown.

Note 4: Carriage inwards

Carriage is the expense associated with the transport of goods. Carriage outwards is the cost of transferring goods sold to a customer. Carriage inwards is the cost of transferring the goods purchased from a supplier into the firm. Both are expenses of the firm but a distinction is made due to the fact that carriage inwards is an expense associated with the purchasing of goods and thus should be presented in the trading account section, added to purchases, rather than the profit and loss account section. *The definition of purchases is not just the purchase price of the goods but also any costs in bringing the goods to their present location and condition.*

Carriage inwards would be considered a trading expense, as it involves transferring the goods to their present location. Should there be any additional work on the goods or in packaging the goods, then this would also be considered a trading expense. Carriage outwards is not part of the expense of buying and bringing goods to their present location and condition and thus is presented as an expense in the profit and loss account. It is important to note that some suppliers do not charge for carriage, selling the goods on a 'free delivery' basis, and others will have a policy of charging for delivery.

Example 6.2: *Trading account with returns and carriage*

C. Maguire operates a small retail business in a Dublin suburb. Draw up a trading account from the following extracts in the books of C. Maguire for the year ended 31 December.

	Dr	Cr
	€	€
Purchases	55,000	
Carriage inwards	8,000	
Sales returns	10,000	
Purchases returns		6,000
Sales		167,000
Opening stock	11,000	

Note: C. Maguire's closing stock amounted to €12,000 at the year-end.

Solution

Trading Account for Year Ended 31 December

	€	€	€
Sales			167,500
Less sales returns			(10,000)
			157,500
Less cost of sales			
Opening stock		11,000	
Purchases	55,000		
Less purchases returns	(6,000)		
Add carriage inwards	8,000	57,000	
Less closing stock		(12,000)	
Cost of sales			(56,000)
Gross profit			**101,000**

The closing stock figure of €12,000 will also be shown in the balance sheet and will appear as the opening stock for next year.

Note 5: Cash discounts

A cash discount is the reduction in an amount due to encourage early payment of an account. A business, for example, could offer a discount for payment made within say ten days rather than the standard thirty-day credit period. Businesses may offer or receive discounts for early payment; hence they may have two types of cash discounts to account for:

1. **Discounts allowed:** This is where a business offers their customers a discount for early payment. Should customers avail of this discount it is treated as an expense for the business and thus charged to their profit and loss account. The accounting process is achieved by debiting a discount allowed account and crediting the debtors account with the amount of discount allowed.
2. **Discount received:** Businesses are also offered discounts from their suppliers for early payment. Should they avail of these discounts they are treated as a gain and added to gross profit in their profit and loss account. The accounting process is achieved by debiting the creditors account and crediting the discount received account with the amount of discount received.

Note 6: Assets (resources owned by the business or debts owed to the business)

1. **Fixed assets**: These are assets which are purchased by the business to generate sales and profits over a long period of time. For example, the investment in property, equipment and furniture as well as computer systems requires a large financial outlay and will expect to produce sales and profits over a long period. Fixed assets are bought by a business to be used by the business, not to be sold.
2. **Current assets**: These are assets that are constantly flowing through a business. Current assets can be cash or items held by the business with the intention of turning them into cash (stock and debtors). For example, a business can sell stock, which if sold on credit will turn into debtors and if sold for cash will turn into cash or bank. Stock, debtors and cash/bank are the main categories of current assets.

Did You Know?

Companies involved in providing accommodation, transport, leisure activities, travel agents and tour operators are mainly fixed-asset based and would have very little current assets in their balance sheet. For example, in hotel companies, current assets would generally amount to only 5 per cent of total assets. This is because their main stock is their stock of bedrooms and seats, which are classified as fixed assets.

Within the retail sector current asset levels are significantly higher than tourism and hospitality due to the fact that it is mainly a product-based sector, which by its nature requires high stock levels.

Note 7: Liabilities (generally debts owed by the business)

1. **Current liabilities**: These are liabilities that are owed and expected to be paid within one year. Current liabilities are legally termed 'creditors due in less than twelve months'. These include trade creditors (suppliers of goods for re-sale), expenses owing, bank overdraft and portions of loans that are due for repayment within twelve months.
2. **Long-term liabilities**: These are simply liabilities that are due for payment in more than twelve months. The legal term is 'creditors due for payment in greater than twelve months'. These generally include long-term loans.

Did You Know?

The current liabilities for companies involved in hospitality, transport, leisure activities, travel agents and tour operators tend to be greater than the current assets. This is due to the low levels of current assets in such companies. For example, the norm for the hotel and leisure sector is that current assets would amount to 40 per cent of current liabilities. This is in marked contrast to the manufacturing sector, whose high investment in current assets ensures the norm is that they exceed current liabilities by as much as two or three times.

In retail, high levels of stock can be funded through credit, therefore high levels of trade creditors may exist. The high levels of stock in retail companies, ensures that the expected norm for current assets levels is 80 per cent of current liabilities.

Note 8: Capital

Capital represents the amount invested in the business by the owner. If a business makes a profit, this profit belongs to the owner and thus capital is increased by any profit made by the business. Should the owner take drawings (money or stock) out of the business for their own use then this reduces the amount of capital invested in the business. The capital section of the balance sheet would look as follows:

	€
Opening capital	100,000
Add net profit	20,000
Less drawings	(10,000)
Closing capital	110,000

The best approach to understanding the process of preparing a trading, profit and loss account from a trial balance is through a worked example.

Example 6.3: *Preparing the trading, profit and loss account and balance sheet*

The following trial balance has been extracted from the accounts of Mr T. Raftery for the year ended 31 December 2004. Mr Raftery operates a retail business with a tourism focus, selling souvenir china and glass crafted items. You are required to prepare a trading, profit and loss account for the period.

Trial Balance as at 31 December 2004

	Dr	Cr
	€	€
Sales		110,000
Purchases	55,000	
Expenses		
Rent	7,000	
Rates	2,000	
Advertising	3,000	
Light and heat	4,000	
Insurance	10,000	
Wages and salaries	15,000	
Motor vehicles	25,000	
Premises	250,000	
Furniture and equipment	40,000	
Debtors		
A. Dunne	2,500	
D. O'Donoghue	1,500	
P. O'Meara	3,000	
M. McDonald	4,000	
B. Gibson	3,000	
Bank overdraft		23,000
Creditors		
B. Winne		10,000
L. Lamp		5,000
C. Gardge		3,000
Drawings	9,000	
Loans		140,000
Capital		143,000
	434,000	**434,000**

Note: At the 31 December 2004 the business had stock of unsold goods worth €5,000.

Solution

Trading, Profit and Loss Account for the Year Ended 31 December 2004

	€	€
Sales		110,000
Less cost of sales		
Opening stock	0	
Add purchases	55,000	
Less closing stock	(5,000)	
Cost of sales		(50,000)
Gross profit		60,000
Add other income/revenues		0
Less expenses		
Rent	7,000	
Rates	2,000	
Advertising	3,000	
Light and heat	4,000	
Insurance	10,000	
Wages and salaries	15,000	(41,000)
Net profit		19,000

Balance Sheet as at 31 December 2004

	€	€	€
Fixed assets			
Premises			250,000
Furniture and equipment			40,000
Motor vehicles			25,000
			315,000
Current assets			
Closing stock	5,000		
Debtors	14,000		
Bank	0	19,000	
Current liabilities			
Creditors	18,000		
Bank overdraft	23,000	(41,000)	
Working capital			(22,000)

Long-term liabilities			
Loans			(140,000)
			153,000
Financed by			
Capital			143,000
Net profit			19,000
Less drawings			9,000
			153,000

Explanation

❑   Working capital is current assets less current liabilities.

❑   Total assets less liabilities is (fixed assets + current assets) less (current liabilities + long-term liabilities).

❑   The capital section heading is 'financed by', as it tells us that the net assets (total assets – total liabilities) are financed or bought through the owner's contribution to the business.

❑   The business made a profit of €19,000 and this must be added to opening capital.

❑   The opening capital figure represents the capital invested by the owner before it is adjusted for any profit/loss and drawings. If the owner does not contribute new capital into the business next year his opening capital will be €153,000.

The Accruals Concept

The calculation of profit is based on the accruals concept which requires that the effects of transactions should be accounted for when they occur and are included in the statements for the periods they relate to. Knowledge of this concept is essential in understanding the net profit figure and the differences between cash and profit.

The accruals concept requires two things:

1.   When calculating net profit, expenses should be matched against related revenues. Thus in the trading account, if 100 units are sold in January then only

the cost of 100 units is deducted in calculating gross (trading) profit. In the profit and loss section only the expenses of January are deducted when calculating net profit for January. In the trading account of a product-based company, purchases are matched to sales on a unit basis. In the profit and loss account expenses are matched on a time basis. For a service company all expenses are matched on a time basis.

2. Net profit is the difference between revenues earned (not necessarily received) and expenses charged (not necessarily paid). Thus net profit is worked on a transactions basis. That is, if a transaction occurs it should be accounted for irrespective of whether cash has passed hands. Thus revenues and expenses are accounted for as soon as an invoice has been issued and liability has been accepted. For businesses that buy and sell on credit, sales and purchases in the trading account will be a mixture of cash and credit transactions. Also, expenses that relate to a period will be deducted from sales in the calculation of net profit for that period, whether or not those expenses have actually been paid. Any unpaid expenses will also be shown in the balance sheet under liabilities.

Table 6.1: *Accruals concept key points*

- ❏ The calculation of net profit involves the matching of expenses to related revenues. In the trading account, purchases are matched against sales on a unit basis and in the profit and loss account expenses are matched against sales on a time basis.
- ❏ Sales in the trading account are made up of cash sales and credit sales.
- ❏ Debtors in the balance sheet will be made up of credit sales for which monies have not been received by the end of the period.
- ❏ Purchases in the trading account are made up of cash and credit purchases.
- ❏ Trade creditors in the balance sheet will be made up of credit purchases for which no payment has been made by the period end.
- ❏ Expenses in the profit and loss account are made up of expenses paid and expenses owed.
- ❏ Expenses owed at the year-end will be shown in the balance sheet under current liabilities.

Summary

This chapter provides the first real introduction to preparing the financial statements (trading, profit and loss and balance sheet) of a business. It is very important as it introduces for the first time the accruals concept. Understanding the accruals concept is essential to understanding what profit means and how to calculate profit. The accruals concept is one of the main reasons why there is a difference between the net profit of a business and its end of period bank balance.

The following are the main information points covered in this chapter:

❏ For most businesses the main objective is to make a profit.

❏ For a business that sells products, a trading account is prepared calculating a gross or trading profit. Other income is added and expenses are deducted from gross profit in the calculation of net profit.

❏ For businesses that provide services a trading account is not prepared and thus the profit and loss account is simply sales less expenses.

❏ The calculation of profit is based on the accruals concept which states that in calculating profit, expenses are matched against related revenues and that profit is the difference between revenues earned (not necessarily received) and expenses charged (not necessarily paid).

❏ The balance sheet is presented in the format Assets - Liabilities = Capital. Assets are categorised into fixed and current assets, and liabilities are categorised into current and long-term liabilities.

❏ Capital of the business represents what the owner has invested in the business and this increases when a business makes a profit and decreases when the business makes a loss. If the owner withdraws any assets (cash, stock) for their own use this reduces capital.

Review Questions

Question 6.1

Briefly describe the purpose of:

(a) The profit and loss account.
(b) The balance sheet.

Question 6.2

Describe the accruals concept and state its purpose.

Question 6.3

(a) What is the difference between the trading account and the profit and loss account?
(b) Prepare a trading account from the following information relating to the business of Anthony Rice, who sells motorbikes, for the period ending 31 December 2004.

	Dr	Cr
	€	€
Purchases	300,000	
Carriage inwards	20,000	
Sales		500,000
Returns inwards	30,000	
Returns outwards		50,000
Stock as at 1 January 2004	42,000	

Note: Stock counted at 31 December 2004 was valued at €36,000.

Question 6.4

From the following trial balance of Niall Daly, who operates a number of fast-food outlets you are required to prepare a trading, profit and loss account for the year ended 31 January 2005 and a balance sheet at that date.

	Dr	Cr
	€	€
Purchases	102,763	
Sales		282,233
Carriage inwards	10,152	
Purchases returns		7,894
Wages and salaries	78,456	
Motor expenses	12,356	
Rent	59,400	
Rates	12,456	
Insurance	15,000	
Sundry expenses	4,520	
Light and heat	12,564	
Stock as at 1/2/04	10,900	
Creditors		56,120
Bank		21,300
Office furniture	56,000	
Office equipment	40,000	
Plant and equipment	70,120	
Capital		90,000
Loan		40,000
Cash	560	
Drawings	12,300	
	497,547	497,547

Note: Stock counted at 31 January 2005 was valued at €12,000.

Question 6.5

The following is the trial balance of Mike McDonald, who operates a pub, restaurant and adventure centre in Achill Island. You are required to prepare a trading, profit and loss account for the year ended 31 December 2005 and a balance sheet at that date.

	Dr	Cr
	€	€
Wages and salaries	102,763	
Motor expenses	20,000	
Rent	40,152	
Rates	15,689	
Purchases	150,456	
Sales		452,728
Carriage inwards	8,900	
Purchases returns		12,300
Insurance	15,000	
Marketing and sales	4,520	
Office expenses	5,200	
Sundry expenses	2,900	
Furniture	85,300	
Equipment	80,309	
Adventure equipment	167,079	
Stock as at 1/1/05	15,600	
Drawings	35,000	
Debtors	40,000	
Capital		200,000
Loan		100,000
Cash	1,160	
Creditors		70,000
Bank	45,000	
	835,028	**835,028**

Note: Stock counted at 31 December 2005 was valued at €10,250.

Question 6.6

Tony Smith has been operating a business retailing and delivering electrical goods for the past few years. Using the trial balance extracted on 31 October 2005 (shown below), prepare a trading, profit and loss account and a balance sheet for the year ended October 2005.

Trial Balance as at 31 October 2005

	Dr	Cr
	€	€
Advertising	87,562	
Bank balance		24,650
Buildings	1,188,000	
Capital		1,744,570
Carriage in	25,000	
Carriage out	12,600	
Communication expenses	9,354	
Creditors		126,900
Debtors	164,400	
Discount allowed	7,200	
Discount received		15,000
Drawings	71,110	
Fixtures and fittings	237,600	
General expenses	7,310	
Insurance	12,704	
Light and heat	24,000	
Loan (to be repaid 20/12/2005)		50,000
Motor expenses	36,000	
Motor vehicles	100,000	
Purchases	1,517,700	
Rent payable	80,000	
Rent received		20,000
Returns in	39,460	
Returns out		45,880
Sales		1,973,000
Stock (at 1/11/04)	90,000	
Wages	290,000	
	4,000,000	4,000,000

Note: Stock remaining on the 31 October 2005 was valued by Tony at €120,000.

CHAPTER 7

Accounting for VAT

Learning Outcomes

By the end of this chapter you will be able to:

❑ Describe the nature of value added tax (VAT) and how it affects businesses.
❑ Distinguish between zero rated, exempt and taxable activities for VAT purposes.
❑ Calculate VAT.
❑ Account for VAT.
❑ Be aware of the regulations surrounding the payment and returning of VAT.

Introduction

This chapter focuses on value added tax (VAT). VAT is a tax on the supply of goods and services within the state and affects all businesses within the hospitality, tourism and retail sectors. Thus it is important that one understands VAT, how it works and the role of businesses within the whole VAT system.

Value Added Tax

VAT is a tax on consumer spending. Businesses (whether sole traders, partnerships or companies) charge VAT on the supply of goods and services and they act as a collector of these monies for the Revenue Commissioners. The following short examples explain how VAT works.

Example 7.1: *A Single VAT transaction*

The VAT system can be illustrated by examining a transaction where an item of furniture is sold by a furniture retailer for €1,000. VAT will be charged on that sale at 21 per cent. Thus the customer pays €1,210 for the furniture.

The furniture retailer records the sale at €1,000 and owes the Revenue Commissioners €210 in VAT. The furniture retailer bought the item from a manufacturer for €600 and was charged VAT at the rate of 21 per cent. The retailer owes the manufacturer €726 (€600 + VAT of €126). As the VAT on purchases can be offset against the VAT on sales, the furniture retailer now owes €84 (€210 less €126) to the Revenue Commissioner. The manufacturer owes €126 to the Revenue Commissioners. Ultimately the Revenue Commissioners get the full €210 VAT on the final sale of which the manufacturer remits €126 and the furniture business remits €84. It is important to note that VAT is not an expense for either the retailer or the manufacturer as both are only remitting to the revenue commissioners the monies given to them from the final consumer.

Example 7.2: *Calculation of VAT liability*

The following is a summary of the transactions for a stationery retailer for one week:

Purchases	Sales
€3,000 + VAT €630	€10,000 + VAT €2,100

Calculate the VAT liability of the stationery retailer.

The stationery retailer will charge VAT on the supply of stationery at the rate of 21 per cent. The VAT on sales owed to the Revenue Commissioner is €2,100 (€10,000 by 21 per cent). However, as the stationery retailer paid €3,000 in purchasing the stationery and was charged VAT at the rate of 21 per cent on those purchases, then the amount of VAT paid through his purchases is €630 (€3,000 by 21 per cent). The VAT on purchases of €630 can be offset against the VAT on sales of €2,100 resulting in the retailer owing the Revenue Commissioners €1,470. The Revenue Commissioners will receive €630 from the manufacturer and the balance of €1,470 from the retailer.

VAT is charged on the supply of goods or services (taxable activities) within the state carried out by individuals, partnerships or companies who are taxable (taxable persons). Let's take a closer look at what is meant by both taxable persons and taxable activities.

Taxable persons

According to the Revenue Commissioners a taxable person 'is an individual, partnership or company which is, or is required to be, registered for VAT'. Businesses (whether sole traders, partnerships or companies) charge VAT on the supply of goods and services and they act as a collector of these monies for the Revenue Commissioners. For a business to be required to register for VAT it must be involved in the supply of goods or services that constitute a taxable business activity and whose turnover in any financial year exceeds the following limits:

Supply of goods   €51,000
Supply of services   €25,500

Taxable activities

For VAT purposes business activities are classified into three types:

1. **Taxable activities**: If the activities of an individual, partnership or company are taxable then the business must charge VAT on its sales at the appropriate rate. However, the VAT incurred on purchases, expenses and assets can be offset against the VAT liability on sales.
2. **Exempt activities**: Businesses that carry on exempt activities are not required to charge VAT on the sale of goods and services and do not get a refund of VAT paid on their expenses and outgoings. Also it must be remembered that should annual turnover be less than the limits above you can be treated as exempt for VAT purposes.
3. **Zero rated activities**: Businesses that carry on zero rated activities charge VAT on the sale of their products or services at the rate of 0 per cent. However, they still can get a refund for any VAT paid on the normal outgoings of the business. In this case, businesses that carry on zero rated activities will never have a VAT liability. The Revenue Commissioners will always owe monies to these businesses.

Rates of VAT

For taxable activities the main rates of VAT are 13.5 per cent (lower rate) and 21 per cent. The Revenue Commissioners set out what activities are subject to the 13.5 per cent and 21 per cent rates. These are outlined in Table 7.1. There is also a special rate of 4.3 per cent but this is exclusively for the sale of livestock including cattle, horses, sheep, goats, pigs, deer as well as greyhounds and hire of horses. Rates of VAT can be changed by the government at budget time so check www.revenue.ie for current rates.

Table 7.1: *Examples of VAT activities*

Taxable – higher rate	Taxable – lower rate	Exempt	Zero rated
Alcoholic drinks Consultancy Accounting services Computers Furniture Flowers Telephone Stationery Most electrical goods	Food/drink provision (hotels, pubs) Sporting activities Supply of videos Supply of property Electricity	Dentists Insurance Funeral/undertaking Transport of persons Postal services Educational services Hospital/medical services	Export services Animal feeds Fertiliser Medicines Printed books Children's clothes Certain food/drink

Calculation of VAT

VAT is chargeable on the total sum 'paid or payable to the persons supplying the goods or services including all taxes, commissions, costs and charges whatsoever but not including the VAT chargeable in respect of the transaction'.

The Revenue Commissioners

In calculating the VAT on a transaction it is simply the price paid multiplied by the relevant VAT rate. However, should the figure be quoted gross (including VAT) then to calculate the VAT element one must multiply the gross figure by the following formula:

$$\text{VAT element} = \text{Gross sales} \times \frac{\text{rate of VAT}}{100\% + \text{rate of VAT}}$$

For example, should sales including VAT amount to €2,210 using a VAT rate of 21 per cent, then the VAT element could be calculated as follows:

$$€2,210 \times \frac{21}{100 + 21} = €210$$

The sales figure excluding VAT could be calculated as follows:

$$€2,210 \times \frac{100}{100 + 21} = €2,000$$

Accounting for VAT

It is only taxable and zero rated businesses that must account for VAT. They must comply with the following rules regarding accounting for VAT:

1. VAT charged on sales is not part of the revenues of the business and should not appear as part of sales in the trading, profit and loss account. Thus sales and VAT must be separated. This is done as follows:

    ❑   For all credit sales the sales journal shows the gross and net sales and the VAT separately for each sales invoice. Two extra columns are inserted in the journal for this.

    ❑   For cash sales an extra column is inserted in the cash book to show the VAT element of each cash sale. The actual amount received (including VAT) will be shown in the cash or bank column

    ❑   In the ledger accounts all sales (excluding VAT) are credited to a sales account and the VAT element credited to a VAT account. Thus VAT and sales are separated. All debtor accounts are shown inclusive of VAT. The double entry for a credit sale would be as follows:

	Dr	Cr
	€	€
Debtor account (inclusive of VAT)	121	
Sales account		100
VAT account		21

2. For any expenses for which the business has been charged VAT they will receive an allowance for this VAT. Therefore it is not a true cost to the business and should not appear in the trading profit and loss account as part of the expenses. Thus expenses and VAT must be shown separately. This is recorded as follows:

    ❑   For all credit stock purchases the purchases journal shows the gross and net purchases and the VAT separately for each purchase invoice. Two extra columns are inserted in the journal for this.

    ❑   For all cash purchases and other expenses an extra column is inserted in the cash book to show the VAT element of all cash purchases and expenses separately and the actual amount paid (including VAT) will be shown in either the cash or bank column.

    ❑   In the general ledger all expenses are debited to the expense account net of VAT and the VAT element debited to the VAT account. All creditor accounts are shown inclusive of VAT. The double entry for credit purchases is as follows:

	Dr €	Cr €
Creditor account (inclusive of VAT)		121
Purchases account	100	
VAT account	21	

3. If the business purchased any fixed assets and were charged VAT on their purchases, this VAT is not part of the cost of fixed assets as the business can get an allowance for it. Thus the VAT and the purchase cost of fixed assets must be shown separately. Hence in accounting for the purchase of a new computer, the bank account is credited with the monies paid for the asset (including VAT) and the asset account and VAT account are debited with their respective amounts. Thus the asset is recorded in the asset account net of VAT.

	Dr €	Cr €
Bank account (inclusive of VAT)		121
Asset account	100	
VAT account	21	

Example 7.3: *Accounting for VAT*

The following transactions occurred in May for Catering Equipment Suppliers Ltd:

		Net €	VAT €	Gross €
1 May	Sold goods on credit to JD Ltd.	2,000	420	2,420
4 May	Sold goods on credit to SS Ltd.	1,000	210	1,210
10 May	Purchased goods on credit from XY Ltd.	1,500	315	1,815
12 May	Cash sales.	1,200	252	1,452
15 May	Cash purchases.	500	105	605
20 May	Purchased goods on credit from RR Ltd.	3,000	630	3,630
23 May	Sold goods lodging the cheque received.	2,500	525	3,025
27 May	Paid advertising by cheque.	800	168	968

You are required to:

1. Prepare the books of original entry for the above transactions.
2. Show entries to the ledger accounts.

1. The books of prime entry would appear as follows:

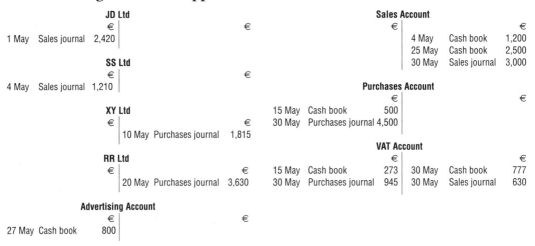

		Sales Journal		
		Net	**VAT**	**Gross**
		€	€	€
1 May	JD Ltd	2,000	420	2,420
4 May	SS Ltd	1,000	210	1,210
30 May		3,000	630	3,630

		Purchases Journal		
		Net	**VAT**	**Gross**
		€	€	€
10 May	XY Ltd	1,500	315	1,815
20 May	RR Ltd	3,000	630	3,630
30 May		4,500	945	5,445

Cash Book

		VAT	**Cash**	**Bank**				**VAT**	**Cash**	**Bank**
		€	€	€				€	€	€
12 May	Sales	252	1,452		15 May	Purchases		105	605	
23 May	Sales	525		3,025	27 May	Advertising		168		968
30 May		777	1,452	3,025				273	605	968

2. The ledger accounts appear as follows:

JD Ltd

€				€
1 May	Sales journal	2,420		

Sales Account

€				€
		4 May	Cash book	1,200
		25 May	Cash book	2,500
		30 May	Sales journal	3,000

SS Ltd

€			€
4 May	Sales journal	1,210	

XY Ltd

€				€
		10 May	Purchases journal	1,815

Purchases Account

		€		€
15 May	Cash book	500		
30 May	Purchases journal	4,500		

RR Ltd

€				€
		20 May	Purchases journal	3,630

VAT Account

		€			€
15 May	Cash book	273	30 May	Cash book	777
30 May	Purchases journal	945	30 May	Sales journal	630

Advertising Account

€			€
27 May	Cash book	800	

Notes

❑ From the example, all sales and expense accounts are recorded net of VAT and will be shown in the profit and loss account net of VAT. All debtor and creditor accounts are shown inclusive of VAT as this is the amount they owe or are owed.

❑ The VAT account shows the VAT on sales less the VAT on any purchases, expenses and fixed assets. In the above case, the company owes the Revenue Commissioners €210. This will be shown as a current liability in the balance sheet.

❑ For companies that carry on zero rated activities there would be no entries in the credit side of the VAT account (as there is no VAT on sales) and thus the account would have a debit balance representing amounts owed by the Revenue Commissioners to the business.

Example 7.4: *Accounting for VAT*

The following transactions occurred in March for Extra-fit Ltd, a company with a chain of fitness centres:

1. Sales takings were €11,350 which was banked.
2. Purchased some leisure equipment paying by cheque €2,420.
3. Paid telephone bill amounting to €121 by cheque.
4. Paid electricity bill amounting to €113.50 by cheque.
5. Paid rent by cheque €500.

Note: The rates of VAT applicable are as follows:

❑ Leisure centre sales 13.5 per cent.
❑ Leisure equipment 21 per cent.
❑ Telephone 21 per cent.
❑ Electricity 13.5 per cent.
❑ VAT does not affect the payment of rent.

You are required to show the relevant ledger account.

Approach

It is helpful to first calculate and study the VAT amounts involved.

Transaction	Net Amount	VAT	Total incl. VAT
Sales	10,000 i.e. 11,350 x 100/113.5	@ 13.5% = 1,350	11,350
Equipment	2,000 i.e. 2,420 x 100/121	@ 21% = 420	2,420
Telephone	100 i.e. 121 x 100/121	@ 21% = 21	121
Electricity	100 i.e. 100 x 100/113.5	@ 13.5% = 13.50	113.50
Rent			500

1. Books of prime entry

As there are no credit transactions, the only book of prime entry required would be the cash book, which would look as follows:

Cash Book

VAT	Cash	Bank		VAT	Cash	Bank	
	€	€	€		€	€	€
Sales	1,350.00		11,350.00	Equipment	420.00		2,420.00
				Telephone	21.00		121.00
				Electricity	13.50		113.50
				Rent			500.00
				Bal c/d			8195.50
	1,350.00		11,350.00		454.50		11,350.00

2. The ledger accounts

Sales Account

	€			€
Bal c/d	10,000	Bank		10,000
	10,000			10,000
		Bal b/d		10,000

VAT Account

	€			€
Bank	454.50	Bank		1,350.00
Bal c/d	895.50			
	1,350.00			1,350.00
		Bal b/d		895.50

Equipment Account

	€			€
Bank	2,000	Bal c/d		2,000
	2,000			2,000
Bal b/d	2,000			

Telephone Account

	€			€
Bank	100	Bal c/d		100
	100			100
Bal b/d	100			

Electricity Account

	€			€
Bank	100	Bal c/d		100
	100			100
Bal b/d	100			

Rent Account

	€			€
Bank	500	Bal c/d		500
	500			500
Bal b/d	500			

Summary Trial Balance

	Dr	Cr
	€	€
Sales		10,000.00
Equipment	2,000.00	
Bank	8,195.50	
Telephone	100.00	
Electricity	100.00	
VAT		895.50
Rent	500.00	
	10,895.50	10,895.50

Notes

❑ You will note that for all expense and asset accounts we are crediting the bank account with the gross amount and debiting each expense and asset account with the net amounts and debiting the VAT account with the VAT element. Thus, we are adhering to double entry principles.

❑ The credit balance on the VAT account represents a liability to the business and will be shown under current liabilities in the balance sheet.

Example 7.5: *How VAT impacts on the final accounts*

The following are the summary transactions for Bagels Forever, a catering company, for the month of January:

	€
Sales including VAT @ 13.5%	113,500
Purchases of foods VAT @ 0%	40,000

Purchase of furniture including VAT @ 21%	12,100
Rent and rates	10,000
Phone including VAT @21%	605
Advertising including VAT @ 21%	968
Accounting fees including VAT 21%	1,210
Repairs including VAT @ 21%	363
Stock as at 1 January	1,000
Stock as at 31 January	1,200

You are required to show relevant extracts from the trading, profit and loss account and balance sheet for January.

Trading, Profit and Loss Account

	€	€
Sales **Note 1**		100,000
Less cost of goods sold		
Opening stock	1,000	
Purchases **Note 2**	40,000	
Closing stock	(1,200)	(39,800)
Gross profit		60,200
Less expenses		
Rent and rates **Note 3**	10,000	
Phone	500	
Advertising	800	
Accounting	1,000	
Repairs	300	12,600
Net profit		47,600

Balance Sheet (extracts)

	€	€
Fixed assets		
Furniture **Note 4**		10,000
Current assets		
Stock		1,200
Current liabilities		
VAT **Note 5**		10,854

Notes
1. The figures in the example show the sales and expense figures including VAT. To calculate the sales element excluding VAT we simply divide the sales figure by 113.5 (100 per cent + 13.5 per cent) and multiply by 100. For any expense items including VAT at 21 per cent we divide by 121 (100 per cent + 21 per cent) and multiply by 100.
2. Some foods (unprocessed foods) are chargeable to VAT at the rate of 0 per cent. For simplicity we have assumed this to be the case for all food purchases in this example.
3. VAT is not chargeable on expenses such as rent, rates, insurance, wages and salaries.
4. As stated already, for taxable and zero rated activities, the VAT paid on any assets purchased are allowed against any VAT due on sales. Thus the assets must be shown in the balance sheet at cost, excluding VAT. This amounts to €10,000 (€12,100 x 100/121).
5. The VAT account would look as follows:

VAT Account

	€		€
VAT on furniture	2,100	VAT on sales	13,500
VAT on phone	105		
VAT on accounting	210		
VAT on advertising	168		
VAT on repairs	63		
Bal c/d	10,854		
	13,500		13,500
		Bal b/d	10,854

The balance of €10,854 in the VAT account represents a VAT liability which is owed and must be paid to the Revenue Commissioners.

Payment of VAT

VAT is due and payable by the nineteenth day of the month following the end of a two-month taxable period. For example, any VAT liability for January/February must be returned and paid by 19 March. All taxable persons must fill in a prescribed return form (VAT 3) giving details of the VAT on sales and all VAT deductibles/allowances. If the deductible VAT exceeds the VAT on sales the excess will be repaid to the taxable person by the Collector General. In addition taxable persons are required to provide an annual return on form RTD EUR, which is a return showing annual trading details of purchases and sales broken down by VAT rate.

If VAT is not paid within the proper period, interest is chargeable for each day at the rate of 0.0322 per cent per day. For further details on VAT see the following website www.revenue.ie.

Summary

Value added tax is a consumer tax and affects all businesses whether they are involved in taxable, exempt or zero rated activities. VAT affects most accounting transactions and thus it is important to understand VAT, the role of businesses within the VAT system and how to account for VAT.

The following are the main information points from this chapter:

❑   VAT is a tax on the supply of goods and services within the state and affects all companies within the hospitality, tourism and retail sectors.

❑   Businesses (whether sole traders, partnerships or companies) charge VAT on the supply of goods and services and they act as a collector of these monies for the Revenue Commissioners.

❑   For a business to be required to register for VAT it must be involved in the supply of goods or services that constitute a taxable activity and whose turnover in any financial year exceeds the following limits:

Supply of goods	€51,000
Supply of services	€25,500

❑   For VAT purposes activities are classified into three categories: exempt, zero rated and taxable.

❑   Exempt activities do not charge VAT on the supply of goods and services and do not get a refund for any VAT charged on purchases, expenses and fixed assets.

❑   Zero rated activities charge VAT at the rate of 0 per cent and get an allowance for any VAT charged on purchases, expenses and fixed assets.

❑   Taxable activities normally charge VAT on the supply of their products or services at either 13.5 per cent or 21 per cent and get an allowance for any VAT charged on purchases, expenses and fixed assets.

❑   For taxable persons, VAT is neither a revenue nor an expense and thus will not appear in the trading, profit and loss account of the business. The fixed assets in the balance sheet will also be recorded net of VAT.

❑   VAT is due and payable by the nineteenth day of the month following the end of a two-month taxable period.

Review Questions

Question 7.1

Describe the operation of VAT and explain why in most cases it is not considered a business expense.

Question 7.2

Distinguish between exempt and zero rated activities for VAT purposes.

Question 7.3

The following transactions occurred in June for Leisure Solutions Ltd:

		Net €	VAT €
1 Jun	Sold goods on credit to Fitness Clubs Ltd.	3,000	630
5 Jun	Sold goods on credit to Slender Hips Ltd.	1,500	315
9 Jun	Purchased goods on credit from JJ Ltd.	1,000	210
12 Jun	Cash sales.	1,500	315
16 Jun	Cash purchases.	600	126
19 Jun	Purchased goods on credit from TR Ltd.	2,500	525
24 Jun	Sold goods on credit to Fitness Clubs Ltd.	2,000	420
29 Jun	Paid accounting fees by cheque.	2,000	420

Required

(a) Prepare the books of original entry for the above transactions.
(b) Show entries to the ledger accounts.
(c) Explain the balance in the VAT account.

Question 7.4

The following details relate to the books of Jordan's Restaurant and B&B for the first week of February:

	Purchase invoices received	Net	VAT
		€	€
1 Feb	Good Food Company	270	0
2 Feb	SGS Drinks	700	147
3 Feb	C&B Drinks Suppliers	800	168
4 Feb	Quality Meat Producers	300	0
5 Feb	O'Reilly Growers	500	0
7 Feb	SGS Drinks	700	147

Required

(a) Write up the purchases journal.
(b) Post transactions to the general and purchases ledger.
(c) If sales for the first week in February amounted to

Accommodation	€1,000 including VAT
Restaurant	€2,700 including VAT

calculate the VAT liability for the first week in February.

Question 7.5

The following summary transactions occurred in the January/February period for Beauty Treatments Ltd:

1. Sales takings were €6,050 which was banked.
2. Purchased three sun-beds paying by cheque €2,420.
3. Purchased a range of cosmetics paying by cheque €605.
4. Paid telephone bill amounting to €363 by cheque.
5. Paid electricity bill amounting to €227 by cheque.
6. Paid advertising by cheque €363.
7. Paid insurance for the year amounting to €5,000.

Note: All the figures above are shown inclusive of VAT of which the rates of VAT applicable are as follows:

- Beauty treatment manicures including sun-bed sessions 13.5%.
- Purchasing sun bed equipment 21%.
- Purchase of cosmetics 21%.
- Telephone 21%.
- Electricity 13.5%.
- VAT does not apply to the payment of insurance.
- Advertising 21%.

Required

(a) Show the entries to the cash book in the books of prime entry.
(b) Show the relevant ledger account.
(c) Prepare a trial balance from the ledger accounts.

CHAPTER 8

Bank Reconciliation Statements

Learning Outcomes

By the end of this chapter you will be able to:

❑ Explain and understand the terminology used in banking.
❑ Update and correct the cash book for items in the bank statement not in the cash book and for errors.
❑ Prepare a bank reconciliation statement.
❑ Outline the purpose and advantages of preparing bank reconciliation statements.
❑ Appreciate the various procedures required to ensure control over cash and bank transactions.

Introduction

Control is an important element within any accounting system. It can help protect the business against error and fraud. Chapter 4 provided an outline of the trial balance as a means of checking the arithmetic accuracy of the recording process. Bank reconciliation statements are a control mechanism that check the accuracy of a business' own records, relating to banking transactions, as well as checking the accuracy of the bank's records of the same. A bank will issue a statement of their record of the bank account of the business regularly. This statement lays out all the transactions that have gone through the business' bank account according to their records. The balance in the bank statement should be checked against the business' own bank account records normally recorded in a *cash book*. This check is called a *bank reconciliation* and a statement is prepared regularly reconciling the bank statement to the business' own cash book.

Cash book

In Chapter 5 we saw that the cash book was part of the books of prime entry and replaced the need for keeping two separate accounts for bank and cash transactions. The cash book contains two money columns on each side: one representing cash transactions, the other representing bank transactions. It avoids the need to maintain two separate accounts for bank and cash. Only the bank columns can be reconciled to a bank statement.

Cash Book

Date	Details	€	€	Date	Details	€	€
		Cash transactions	*Bank transactions*			*Cash transactions*	*Bank transactions*

The term 'cash book' is used in the remainder of this chapter to refer to the banking transactions recorded by the business.

The nature of many businesses operating within the hospitality, tourism and retail sectors results in a very high volume of cash transactions. Therefore the control and handling of cash is of particular importance and requires extra stringent control procedures. These are also covered in this chapter.

Before we focus on these control mechanisms, let us familiarise ourselves with banking terminology.

Banking Terminology

The following are common banking terms that one should understand when dealing with financial institutions:

❏   **Current account**: This is an account maintained with a bank or building society with a view to operating it regularly by making deposits into it and making payments out of it by writing cheques. To facilitate making deposits, the bank provides its customers with a pad of lodgement slips (paying-in slips) and a cheque book for making payments out of it. Both of these are usually sequentially pre-numbered. At agreed intervals (usually monthly) the bank reports to the customer in a bank statement giving a summary of all the transactions (both deposits and withdrawals) that have gone through the bank account for the period.

❑ **Cheque clearing**: Cheques lodged to a bank account are likely to be drawn on an account held at a different bank. Such cheques have to move through the banking system before the money is 'cleared' or made available. Cheques may take around three working days to clear.

❑ **Bank overdraft**: This is a facility where a business can draw out from its bank more than the amount it has in its current account. Unless prior agreement is reached with the bank for this purpose and a limit is negotiated, cheques drawn by the business may be dishonoured. This means that the payee will not be able to receive the money value of the cheque. An overdraft is classified as a current liability.

❑ **Direct debit:** This is when authority is given by a customer (business) to a specified third party to obtain money directly from the bank. The amount varies and depends on what the third party claims. This arrangement is useful when the amounts to be paid are likely to vary and is commonly used to pay utility and telephone bills. With a direct debit, control over the amount is passed to the third party involved.

❑ **Standing order**: This is an order given to a bank by a customer (business) to pay a specified amount to a named third party at a specified interval. With a standing order the control remains with the customer. In a standing order the amount paid is the same every period.

❑ **Credit transfers**: This is where a customer pays a bill by ordering their bank to transfer a sum of money directly into the account of the business they owe.

❑ **Dishonoured cheque**: This is where a bank refuses to pay the amount of money due to the payee. The cheque is dishonoured or bounced by the bank usually because there are insufficient funds available in the customer's account.

❑ **Bank statement**: This is a copy of the records that exist in the bank's accounting system for the transactions with the business named on the statement.

Illustration 8.1: *A typical bank statement*

First Commercial Bank

Sort code 75:75:10

STATEMENT OF ACCOUNT

ABC Providers Ltd,   Account number: 24684971
Unit 1,
Belton Industrial Estate,   Statement number: 5109
Co. Dublin.   Statement date: 03 Sept 05

Date	Transaction details	Debit	Credits	Balance
1 Sept	Balance forward			6,500.00
1 Sept	CH 500103	500.00		6,000.00
1 Sept	CH 500104	299.00		5,701.00
1 Sept	CH 500109	133.50		5,567.50
1 Sept	CH 500110	24.99		5,542.51
2 Sept	LG 49910		6,780.00	12,322.51
2 Sept	DD Telecom Eireann	425.16		11,897.35
2 Sept	DS IMT32607	2,283.11		9,614.24
2 Sept	CH 50106	394.24		9,220.00
2 Sept	CH 50107	650.00		8,570.00
2 Sept	**Carried forward**			**8,570.00**

Bank statements usually have five columns. The first column shows the date the transaction took place while the second gives a description and/or reference of the transaction. The third shows the amounts debited to the account representing money withdrawn from the account. The fourth shows amounts credited to the account representing amounts lodged to the account. The fifth column represents the balance on the account. If the balance on the statement was overdrawn (the account holder owed the bank money) the figure in the balance column would have 'Dr', 'O/D' or '–' beside it (standing for debit or overdrawn).

Comparison of Business Records with Banking Records

When matching business records with banking records, we are comparing two different entities, recording common transactions in their respective systems. The records are viewed from different perspectives. It is important to understand how the transactions will be recorded in the respective systems. The following example may help to illustrate the point.

Illustration 8.2: *Cash book and bank statement*

On 1 March Mr Topper, a wholesaler of hats, lodges €5,000 in BJC Bank Plc, which he received from selling hats. The opening balance in the bank had amounted to €2,500 at the start of business.

The business' records

In Mr Topper's records he will credit his sales account and debit his cash book (bank column) with €5,000 on 1 March. The cash book in Mr Topper's ledger will appear as follows:

Dr		Cash Book		Cr
		Bank €		Bank €
1 Mar	Bal b/d	2,500		
1 Mar	Sales a/c	5,000		

The bank's records

However, in BJC Bank Plc's accounting system, they will debit their cash account with €5,000 and credit Mr Topper's account with €5,000. This will appear on Mr Topper's statement as follows:

Date	Transaction details	Dr	Cr	Balance
		€	€	€
1 Mar	Bal forward			2,500.00
1 Mar	Lodgement		5,000.00	7,500.00

So a credit balance on Mr Topper's bank statement means that he has money in the bank. This is represented by a debit balance in Mr Topper's own records. It is important to remember that, from the bank's perspective, they owe Mr Topper €7,500. He is a creditor to them and thus they will credit his account every time he lodges monies in this bank account. Obviously when he withdraws cash or pays using cheques, his account in the bank is debited, whereas this transaction in his own records is credited to his cash/bank account.

Differences between cash book and bank statement balances

When the closing balance in the cash book is compared with the closing balance on the bank statement, on the same date, the two balances may differ. The main reason for these differences is timing. We can classify the reasons for differences into two categories.

1. Items that are in the bank statement but are not in the cash book. Examples would include:
    ❑   Automatic payments through the banking system, standing orders, direct debits and credit transfers appear on the bank statement but may not yet be entered into the cash book.
    ❑   The bank charges for its services. The money is taken directly out of the bank account by the bank and notification is through the periodic bank statement. Therefore bank charges may not be entered in the cash book prior to receipt of the statement.
    ❑   Dishonoured cheques.

2. Items that are recorded in the cash book but not appearing in the bank statement. Some of the valid reasons for differences between the two balances are as follows:
    ❑   Cheques written by a business may not have been presented to the bank for payment by the payee. These are referred to as 'un-presented cheques'. These transactions appear in the cash book but not on the bank statement.
    ❑   Lodgements made by a business to the bank might not have been cleared through the banking system before the statement was printed. These transactions appear in the cash book but not on the bank statement.

Preparing a Bank Reconciliation

The aim of undertaking a bank reconciliation is to ensure that the cash book balance in the double entry ledgers of the business is accurate and to obtain evidence of the accuracy from a third party (the bank) through its bank statement. The reconciliation will show that the reasons for the difference between the two balances are valid. If after the reconciliation is carried out the balances are still different, it means that there are errors recorded. It then becomes important to identify the errors so they can be corrected.

The preparation of a bank reconciliation statement should take the following steps:

1. Updating and/or correcting the cash book for items that are in the bank statement but not in the cash book.
2. Preparation of the bank reconciliation statement itself which reconciles an updated cash book with the bank statement balance, concentrating solely on transactions that are recorded in the cash book but not in the bank statement.

Tasks in the bank reconciliation process

Step 1

Each item in the bank statement needs to be traced to the cash book in order to identify all items that appear in the bank statement but are not in the cash book. All such items should then be entered in the cash book and a new updated balance calculated.

Step 2

Each item in the cash book should be traced to the bank statement so as to identify bank deposits and cheques drawn that are not appearing on the bank's statement because the former are awaiting clearance and the latter are yet to be presented to the bank for payment. The bank reconciliation would look as follows:

Bank Reconciliation Statement	€
Balance as per bank statement	xxx
Add outstanding lodgements	xxx
Less un-presented cheques	(xxx)
Balance as per cash book (corrected)	xxx

The reconciliation is always at a specific date. The date does not necessarily have to be the last day of the accounting period or even the last date of a calendar month. Reconciliations could be prepared for the date of the closing balance on a bank statement.

Example 8.1: *Bank reconciliation (basic)*

Ryan and Associates have recorded their bank transactions for the month of August as follows:

Cash Book

	€		€
1 Aug Balance	1,200	5 Aug Cheque 201	525
10 Aug Lodgement 25	150	12 Aug Cheque 202	750
22 Aug Lodgement 26	225	21 Aug Cheque 203	1,250
25 Aug Lodgement 27	1,500	26 Aug Cheque 204	260
31 Aug Lodgement 28	1,750	29 Aug Cheque 205	1,150
		31 Aug Bal c/d	890
	4,825		4,825
31 Aug Bal b/d	890		

In early September they received their bank statement for the month of August as showing:

Bank Statement

Date	Particulars	Dr	Cr	Balance
		€	€	€
1 Aug	Balance			1,200
6 Aug	Cheque 201	525		675
11 Aug	Lodgement 25		150	825
12 Aug	Cheque 202	750		75
23 Aug	Lodgement 26		225	300
26 Aug	Lodgement 27		1,500	1,800
25 Aug	Cheque 203	1,250		550
26 Aug	Cheque 204	260		290
31 Aug	Direct debit (Ins)	125		165
31 Aug	Bank charges	50		115

You are required to:

1. Update the cash book as necessary.
2. Prepare the bank reconciliation statement.

Approach

You are required to carry out two steps when reconciling bank accounts. Firstly, the cash book should be updated and secondly, the actual reconciliation should be prepared.

Preliminary work

Compare and match each item in the cash book with the bank statement

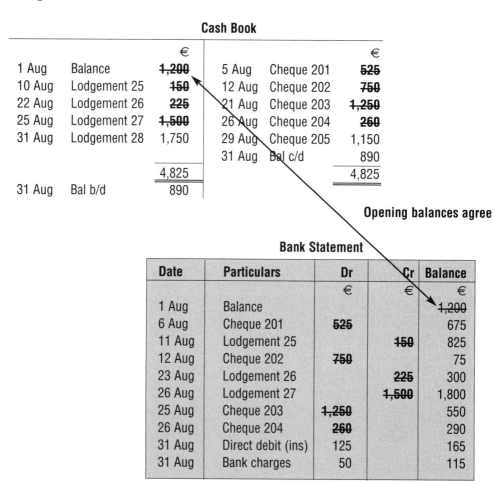

Cash Book

		€			€
1 Aug	Balance	1,200	5 Aug	Cheque 201	525
10 Aug	Lodgement 25	150	12 Aug	Cheque 202	750
22 Aug	Lodgement 26	225	21 Aug	Cheque 203	1,250
25 Aug	Lodgement 27	1,500	26 Aug	Cheque 204	260
31 Aug	Lodgement 28	1,750	29 Aug	Cheque 205	1,150
			31 Aug	Bal c/d	890
		4,825			4,825
31 Aug	Bal b/d	890			

Opening balances agree

Bank Statement

Date	Particulars	Dr	Cr	Balance
		€	€	€
1 Aug	Balance			1,200
6 Aug	Cheque 201	525		675
11 Aug	Lodgement 25		150	825
12 Aug	Cheque 202	750		75
23 Aug	Lodgement 26		225	300
26 Aug	Lodgement 27		1,500	1,800
25 Aug	Cheque 203	1,250		550
26 Aug	Cheque 204	260		290
31 Aug	Direct debit (ins)	125		165
31 Aug	Bank charges	50		115

Step 1: Update the cash book

Identify items on the bank statement omitted from the cash book

Bank Statement

Date	Particulars	Dr	Cr	Balance
		€	€	€
1 Aug	Balance			1,200
6 Aug	Cheque 201	525		675
11 Aug	Lodgement 25		150	825
12 Aug	Cheque 202	750		75
23 Aug	Lodgement 26		225	300
26 Aug	Lodgement 27		1,500	1,800
25 Aug	Cheque 203	1,250		550
26 Aug	Cheque 204	260		290
31 Aug	**Direct debit (Ins)**	**125**		165
31 Aug	**Bank charges**	**50**		115

When Ryan and Associates compared their cash book with the bank statement. They noticed that on 31 August a direct debit was paid to their insurance company and bank charges of €50 were debited on the bank statement. These two transactions were not recorded in their cash book.

Correct the cash book with items identified above

Cash Book

		€			€
1 Sept	Bal b/d	890	1 Sept	Direct debit	125
			1 Sept	Bank charges	50
			1 Sept	Bal c/d	715
		890			890
1 Sept	Bal b/d	715			

Step 1 is now complete but at this point the cash book is showing a Dr balance of €715 while the amount on the bank statement is Cr €115. A bank reconciliation statement is necessary to find out if the difference can be explained or if there are errors in the system.

Step 2: Carry out the bank reconciliation

Identify outstanding items from the cash book not appearing on the statement

Cash Book

		€			€
1 Aug	Balance	1,200	5 Aug	Cheque 201	525
10 Aug	Lodgement 25	150	12 Aug	Cheque 202	750
22 Aug	Lodgement 26	225	21 Aug	Cheque 203	1,250
25 Aug	Lodgement 27	1,500	26 Aug	Cheque 204	260
31 Aug	**Lodgement 28**	**1,750**	**29 Aug**	**Cheque 205**	**1,150**
			31 Aug	Bal c/d	890
		4,825			4,825
31 Aug	Bal b/d	890			

A comparison of the cash book will show that cheque number 205 and lodgement number 28 do not appear on the bank statement. Cheque number 205 is an un-presented cheque, which means that the money has not yet been paid to the payee by the bank. Lodgement number 28 is an un-cleared lodgement, which means that on 31 August the lodgement had not yet gone through to the account.

Carry out the reconciliation with the outstanding items identified from the cash book

A bank reconciliation starts with the closing balance on the bank statement; outstanding lodgements are then added and un-presented cheques are subtracted. The reconciliation should end up with a balance which agrees with the corrected cash book balance. The bank reconciliation for Ryan and Associates reconciles as follows:

Bank Reconciliation

	€
Balance as per bank statement	115
Add outstanding lodgements	
Lodgement number 28	1,750
Less un-presented cheques	
Cheque number 205	(1,150)
Balance as per cash book (corrected)	**715**

As the balances now agree, the original difference can be explained by timing differences and there are no errors in the system. If the balance in the reconciliation disagrees with the corrected cash book, then there are errors in the system and further investigation is required.

It is likely that when a bank reconciliation is being carried out, outstanding items that appeared in a previous reconciliation may well appear in the current bank statement. Example 8.2 outlines such a situation. This example also illustrates errors that can occur. In reality, errors are usually made by the organisation rather than the bank. Banking systems are supposed to have complex controls that help minimise errors by the bank.

Example 8.2: *Bank reconciliation (advanced)*

Sandra Smith runs a travel agency and has recorded her bank transactions for the month of January in her own records as follows:

Cash Book

	€		€
1 Jan Balance	3,560	5 Jan Cheque 3050	225
10 Jan Lodgement 104	890	12 Jan Cheque 3051	195
22 Jan Lodgement 105	720	21 Jan Cheque 3052	2,100
25 Jan Lodgement 106	3,110	26 Jan Cheque 3053	180
31 Jan Lodgement 107	199	29 Jan Cheque 3054	2,250
		31 Jan Bal c/d	3,529
	8,479		8,479
31 Jan Bal b/d	3,529		

In early February she receives her bank statement for the month of January. The bank statement is as follows:

Bank Statement

Date	Particulars	Dr	Cr	Balance
		€	€	€
1 Jan	Balance			5,130
4 Jan	Cheque 3048	1,120		4,010
5 Jan	Cheque 3050	225		3,785
6 Jan	Cheque 3049	450		3,335
11 Jan	Lodgement 104		890	4,225
12 Jan	Cheque 3051	195		4,030
23 Jan	Lodgement 105		720	4,750
26 Jan	Lodgement 106		3,210	7,960
26 Jan	Cheque 3052	2,100		5,860
28 Jan	Cheque 3053	180		5,680
31 Jan	Direct debit	175		5,505
31 Jan	Bank charges	75		5,430

You are required to:

1. Update the cash book as necessary.
2. Prepare the bank reconciliation statement.

Approach

You are again required to carry out two steps or tasks when reconciling bank accounts. This can be achieved as follows:

Preliminary work

Compare and match each item in the cash book with the bank statement

Cash Book

		€				€
1 Jan	Balance	3,560	5 Jan	Cheque 3050	225	
10 Jan	Lodgement 104	890	12 Jan	Cheque 3051	195	
22 Jan	Lodgement 105	720	21 Jan	Cheque 3052	2,100	
25 Jan	Lodgement 106	3,110	26 Jan	Cheque 3053	180	
31 Jan	Lodgement 107	199	29 Jan	Cheque 3054	2,250	
			31 Jan	Bal c/d	3,529	
		8,479			8,479	
31 Jan	Bal b/d	3,529				

Opening balances disagree

Bank Statement

Date	Particulars	Dr	Cr	Balance
		€	€	€
1 Jan	Balance			5,130
4 Jan	Cheque 3048	1,120		4,010
5 Jan	Cheque 3050	225		3,785
6 Jan	Cheque 3049	450		3,335
11 Jan	Lodgement 104		890	4,225
12 Jan	Cheque 3051	195		4,030
23 Jan	Lodgement 105		720	4,750
26 Jan	Lodgement 106		3,210	7,960
26 Jan	Cheque 3052	2,100		5,860
28 Jan	Cheque 3053	180		5,680
31 Jan	Direct debit	175		5,505
31 Jan	Bank charges	75		5,430

As the opening balances disagree, you need to identify items relating to last month and reconcile opening balances

Bank Statement

Date	Particulars	Dr	Cr	Balance
		€	€	€
1 Jan	Balance			5,130
4 Jan	**Cheque 3048**	**1,120**		4,010
5 Jan	Cheque 3050	225		3,785
6 Jan	**Cheque 3049**	**450**		3,335
11 Jan	Lodgement 104		890	4,225
12 Jan	Cheque 3051	195		4,030
23 Jan	Lodgement 105		720	4,750
26 Jan	Lodgement 106		3,210	7,960
26 Jan	Cheque 3052	2,100		5,860
28 Jan	Cheque 3053	180		5,680
31 Jan	Direct debit	175		5,505
31 Jan	Bank charges	75		5,430

On examining the bank statement it is possible that cheques number 3048 and 3049 may have related to last month. The cash book shows the first cheque written in January was cheque number 3050. This implies that cheques numbered 3048 and 3049 were written in December and should have appeared in December's cash book. If Sandra checked December's reconciliation, she would find the two cheques in the list of un-presented cheques. This can be verified by taking the opening balance from the statement of €5,130 and deducting the two cheques (€1,120 + €450). The adjusted balance would be €3,560, which is the same as the opening balance on the cash book. These cheques can be ignored this month.

Step 1: Update the cash book

Identify items on the bank statement omitted from the cash book and any errors made

Cash Book

		€			€
1 Jan	Balance	3,560	5 Jan	Cheque 3050	~~225~~
10 Jan	Lodgement 104	~~890~~	12 Jan	Cheque 3051	~~195~~
22 Jan	Lodgement 105	~~720~~	21 Jan	Cheque 3052	~~2,100~~
25 Jan	**Lodgement 106**	**3,110**	26 Jan	Cheque 3053	~~180~~
31 Jan	Lodgement 107	199	29 Jan	Cheque 3054	2,250
			31 Jan	Bal c/d	3,529
		8,479			8,479
31 Jan	Bal b/d	3,529			

Bank Statement

Date	Particulars	Dr	Cr	Balance
		€	€	€
1 Jan	Balance			5,130
4 Jan	Cheque 3048	~~1,120~~		4,010
5 Jan	Cheque 3050	~~225~~		3,785
6 Jan	Cheque 3049	~~450~~		3,335
11 Jan	Lodgement 104		~~890~~	4,225
12 Jan	Cheque 3051	~~195~~		4,030
23 Jan	Lodgement 105		~~720~~	4,750
26 Jan	**Lodgement 106**		**3,210**	7,960
26 Jan	Cheque 3052	~~2,100~~		5,860
28 Jan	Cheque 3053	~~180~~		5,680
31 Jan	**Direct debit**	**175**		5,505
31 Jan	**Bank charges**	**75**		5,430

Sandra has recorded lodgement number 106 as €3,110 but it appears on the bank statement as €3,210. On further investigation she discovers that the bank statement is correct and she made a mistake entering the figure into the cash book. The transactions and error must be updated in the cash book to complete step 1.

There are two statement items that have no matching cash book entry. On 31 January a direct debit for €175 and bank charges of €75 appear on the bank statement. Up until this time Sandra was unaware of either transaction. These two transactions must be recorded in the cash book.

Correct the cash book with items identified above

Cash Book

		€			€
1 Feb	Bal b/d	3,529	1 Feb	Direct debit	175
1 Feb	Correction to		1 Feb	Bank charges	75
	Lodgement 106	100	1 Feb	Bal c/d	3,379
		3,629			3,629
1 Feb	Bal b/d	3,379			

At this point the cash book is showing a balance of €3,379 while the amount on the bank statement is €5,430. It is necessary to carry out step 2, a bank reconciliation, to find out if the difference can be explained by timing.

Step 2: Carry out the bank reconciliation

Identify outstanding items from the cash book not appearing on the statement

Cash Book

		€			€
1 Jan	Balance	3,560	5 Jan	Cheque 3050	225
10 Jan	Lodgement 104	890	12 Jan	Cheque 3051	195
22 Jan	Lodgement 105	720	21 Jan	Cheque 3052	2,100
25 Jan	Lodgement 106	3,110	26 Jan	Cheque 3053	180
31 Jan	**Lodgement 107**	**199**	**29 Jan**	**Cheque 3054**	**2,250**
			31 Jan	Bal c/d	3,529
		8,479			8,479
31 Jan	Bal b/d	3,529			

A comparison of the cash book will show that cheque number 3054 and lodgement number 107 do not appear on the bank statement. Cheque number 3054 is an un-presented cheque and lodgement number 107 is an un-cleared lodgement.

Carry out the reconciliation with the outstanding items identified from the bank account

The bank reconciliation reconciles for Sandra as follows:

Bank Reconciliation Statement

	€
Balance as per bank statement	5,430
Add outstanding lodgements	
Lodgement 107	199
Less un-presented cheques	
Cheque 3054	(2,250)
Balance as per cash book (corrected)	**3,379**

As the balances now agree, the original difference can be explained by timing differences and there are no further errors in the system.

Dealing with bank overdrafts

A business may find itself short of available cash to fund its activities. It is possible to organise a short-term overdraft facility with the bank. This will allow the business to pay out more than it currently has available. In such circumstances that bank statement will show the balance as a debit balance indicating the overdraft.

Example 8.3: *Bank reconciliation with overdrafts*

While the book-keeper has been on sick leave the receptionist of Kelly Sales has been maintaining the cash book. The February statement has arrived from the bank and while the opening balance agrees with the cash book the closing balance disagrees. The bank has confirmed that the statement is accurate. You have been requested to prepare a bank reconciliation correcting any errors in the cash book you may find.

Cash Book

		€			€
1 Feb	Bal b/d	500	3 Feb	Cheque 19560	1,160
7 Feb	Lodgement 715	2,230	3 Feb	Cheque 19561	54
14 Feb	Lodgement 716	3,100	3 Feb	Cheque 19562	3,380
21 Feb	Lodgement 717	1,870	16 Feb	Cheque 19563	29
28 Feb	Lodgement 718	2,150	17 Feb	Cheque 19564	4,220
28 Feb	Lodgement 719	650	23 Feb	Cheque 19565	1,680
28 Feb	Bal c/d	400	23 Feb	Cheque 19566	37
			23 Feb	Cheque 19567	340
		10,900			10,900
			1 Mar	Bal b/d	400

Bank Statement

Date	Particulars	Dr	Cr	Balance
		€	€	€
1 Feb	Opening balance			500
5 Feb	Cheque 19562	3,380		(2,880)
7 Feb	Lodgement 715		2,230	(650)
8 Feb	Bank interest		13	(637)
9 Feb	Cheque 19561	45		(682)
14 Feb	Lodgement 716		3,100	2,418
19 Feb	DD Telecom	225		2,193
19 Feb	Cheque 19564	4,220		(2,027)
22 Feb	Lodgement 717		1,770	(257)
24 Feb	Dishonoured cheque	98		(355)
25 Feb	Cheque 19563	290		(645)
25 Feb	Cheque 19565	1,680		(2,325)
28 Feb	Bank charges	39		(2,364)

Approach

When the cash book and the bank statement are examined it can be seen that both closing balances are overdrawn. The steps are exactly the same as in previous examples.

Preliminary work

Compare and match each item in the cash book with the bank statement

Cash Book

		€			€
1 Feb	Bal b/d	500	3 Feb	Cheque 19560	1,160
7 Feb	Lodgement 715	2,230	3 Feb	Cheque 19561	54
14 Feb	Lodgement 716	3,100	3 Feb	Cheque 19562	3,380
21 Feb	Lodgement 717	1,870	16 Feb	Cheque 19563	29
28 Feb	Lodgement 718	2,150	17 Feb	Cheque 19564	4,220
28 Feb	Lodgement 719	650	23 Feb	Cheque 19565	1,680
28 Feb	Bal c/d	400	23 Feb	Cheque 19566	37
			23 Feb	Cheque 19567	340
		10,900			10,900
			1 Mar	Bal b/d	400

Bank Statement

Date	Particulars	Dr	Cr	Balance
		€	€	€
1 Feb	Opening balance			500
5 Feb	Cheque 19562	3,380		(2,880)
7 Feb	Lodgement 715		2,230	(650)
8 Feb	Bank interest		13	(637)
9 Feb	Cheque 19561	45		(682)
14 Feb	Lodgement 716		3,100	2,418
19 Feb	DD Telecom	225		2,193
19 Feb	Cheque 19564	4,220		(2,027)
22 Feb	Lodgement 717		1,770	(257)
24 Feb	Dishonoured cheque	98		(355)
25 Feb	Cheque 19563	290		(645)
25 Feb	Cheque 19565	1,680		(2,325)
28 Feb	Bank charges	39		(2,364)

Step 1: Update the cash book

Identify items on the bank statement omitted from the cash book and any errors made

Cash Book

		€			€
1 Feb	Bal b/d	~~500~~	3 Feb	Cheque 19560	1,160
7 Feb	Lodgement 715	~~2,230~~	3 Feb	Cheque 19561	54
14 Feb	Lodgement 716	~~3,100~~	3 Feb	Cheque 19562	~~3,380~~
21 Feb	Lodgement 717	1,870	16 Feb	Cheque 19563	29
28 Feb	Lodgement 718	2,150	17 Feb	Cheque 19564	4,220
28 Feb	Lodgement 719	650	23 Feb	Cheque 19565	1,680
28 Feb	Bal c/d	400	23 Feb	Cheque 19566	37
			23 Feb	Cheque 19567	340
		10,900			10,900
			1 Mar	Bal b/d	400

Bank Statement

Date	Particulars	Dr	Cr	Balance
		€	€	€
1 Feb	Opening balance			~~500~~
5 Feb	Cheque 19562	~~3,380~~		(2,880)
7 Feb	Lodgement 715		~~2,230~~	(650)
8 Feb	**Bank interest**		13	(637)
9 Feb	Cheque 19561	45		(682)
14 Feb	Lodgement 716		~~3,100~~	2,418
19 Feb	DD Telecom	225		2,193
19 Feb	Cheque 19564	~~4,220~~		(2,027)
22 Feb	Lodgement 717		1,770	(257)
24 Feb	**Dishonoured cheque**	98		(355)
25 Feb	Cheque 19563	290		(645)
25 Feb	Cheque 19565	1,680		(2,325)
28 Feb	**Bank charges**	39		(2,364)

There are three errors:

1. Cheque number 19561 was recorded in error in the cash book as €54 as the

statement reads €45. The cash book is over by €9 and a debit of €9 must be entered in the cash book.

2. Cheque number 19563 was recorded in error in the cash book as €29 as the statement reads €290. The cash book is short by €261 and a credit of €261 must be entered in the cash book.

3. Lodgement 717 was recorded in error in the cash book as €1,870 as the statement reads €1,770. The cash book is over by €100 and a credit of €100 must be entered in the cash book.

Also four items appear on the statement and not in the cash book so they must now be entered in the cash book.

Correct the cash book with items identified above

Cash Book

		€			€
1 Mar	Error cheque 19561	9	1 Mar	Bal b/d	400
1 Mar	Bank interest	13	1 Mar	Error cheque 19563	261
1 Mar	Bal c/d	1,101	1 Mar	Error lodge 717	100
			1 Mar	DD Telecom	225
			1 Mar	Dishonoured cheque	98
			1 Mar	Bank charges	39
		1,123			1,123
			1 Mar	Bal b/d	1,101

Step 2: Carry out the bank reconciliation

Identify outstanding items from the cash book not appearing on the statement

Cash Book

		€			€
1 Feb	Bal b/d	500	3 Feb	**Cheque 19560**	1,160
7 Feb	Lodgement 715	2,230	3 Feb	Cheque 19561	54
14 Feb	Lodgement 716	3,100	3 Feb	Cheque 19562	3,380
21 Feb	Lodgement 717	1,870	16 Feb	Cheque 19563	29
28 Feb	**Lodgement 718**	2,150	17 Feb	Cheque 19564	4,220
28 Feb	**Lodgement 719**	650	23 Feb	Cheque 19565	1,680
28 Feb	Bal c/d	400	23 Feb	**Cheque 19566**	37
			23 Feb	**Cheque 19567**	340
		10,900			10,900
			1 Mar	Bal b/d	400

Carry out the reconciliation with the outstanding items identified from the bank account

The bank reconciliation reconciles but it is important to remember that the closing balance on the bank statement is an overdraft and should be treated as a negative figure.

Bank Reconciliation Statement

	€	€
Balance as per bank statement		(2,364)
Add outstanding lodgements		
Lodgement 718	2,150	
Lodgement 719	650	2,800
Less unpresented cheques		
Cheque 19560	1,160	
Cheque 19565	37	
Cheque 19566	340	(1,537)
Balance as per cash book (corrected)		**(1,101)**

The Advantages of Preparing Bank Reconcilations

Practically all businesses prepare bank reconciliations as part of their normal control procedures. The advantages of preparing bank reconciliation statements are as follows:

1. It confirms the accuracy of the bank figure in the company's records.
2. It can help in identifying errors and fraud within the company.
3. It can help identify errors made by the bank which may include overcharging for their services.

Control of Cash and Bank Transactions

Performing bank reconciliations is one form of control that can be used in relation to bank transactions but there is a wider picture that needs to be considered in relation to dealing with both cash and bank transactions. The management and control of cash must be carefully considered to avoid fraud and theft. To minimise the risk of fraud, whenever possible separate authorised persons should carry out the following procedures:

1. *Authorising* payments from cash or bank account.

2. *Recording* cash and bank transactions.
3. *Custody/handling* of cash and cheques.
4. *Reconciling/checking* cash balances and bank statements.

Otherwise a single person dealing with all the above procedures could misappropriate cash and conceal the fact by altering the records. In very small organisations this may be difficult, but one person, no matter how trustworthy, should not be responsible for the entire cash handling cycle.

Dealing with cash

Retailing in particular and many businesses within hospitality and tourism by their nature handle very large volumes of cash on a daily basis. The risks are far greater in such organisations and it is vital that adequate controls are put in place. As a minimum the following should be considered:

❏ All receipts of cash should require the issue of a receipt to the customer, preferably automatically by a cash register or by duplicate pre-numbered receipts.
❏ Cash registers should open only when a sale is rung up; other openings should require a special key held by an authorised staff member.
❏ Cash registers should be locked when authorised users are away from the till.
❏ Takings of cash and cheques should be counted regularly and agreed with totals per the cash register's till roll or other internal record, or with copies of written receipts.
❏ Cash held overnight should be kept in a secure safe box.
❏ Cash and cheque takings should be prepared for lodgement to the bank daily and lodged to the bank by separate persons.
❏ Payments should not be made directly out of cash takings.
❏ Bank statements should be regularly reconciled by persons not involved in recording or handling cash.

Dealing with cheques

Although cheques are considered to be safer and less vulnerable than cash, fraud can still occur. The table below outlines some controls that can be instigated to reduce the risk of fraud occurring.

The above safeguards go some way in protecting a business but management must always be vigilant in dealing with money transactions. Controls should be reviewed regularly to ensure that they are adequate in the current environment.

Controls relating to the receipt of cheques	Controls relating to payments by cheque
❏ All cheques received should be crossed 'A/C payee only'. ❏ Receipts of cheques should be recorded in books by a separate person. ❏ Cheques received should be prepared for lodgement to the bank daily and lodged by another separate person. ❏ Statements/copies of debtors ledger accounts should be sent regularly to debtors, and queries from debtors dealt with by a person independent of the above.	❏ Payments should be made based only on purchase invoices and employee payroll records etc. which have been approved by designated authorised persons. ❏ Cheques should be signed by separate designated, authorised person(s) who have inspected the supporting documentation. ❏ Cheque payments should be recorded in books by a different person. ❏ Statements from creditors/suppliers of their ledger accounts with the business should be received regularly. They should be reconciled with the business' own creditors ledger accounts, and queries followed up by a person independent of the above.

Accounting for Credit Card Payments

A significant proportion of sales payments are received by businesses through credit cards. Today all banks offer their customers credit cards, which are used to purchase goods or services without the need for cash or cheques. When buying goods the customer authorises payment from their credit card account by signing a special voucher or inputting their pin number on a credit card machine used by the vendor. At the end of the day the vendor presents the vouchers either manually or electronically to the credit card company (financial institution) and the total of the vouchers less any commissions is transferred to their account within two days (normally). The vendor deals with the sale in the same way as cash and cheque payments by accounting for the sale immediately. The credit card company provides the credit to the customer. For customers and vendors, credit cards offer greater security as there is less cash in circulation. However, there is a cost for the vendor, as credit card companies tend to charge commission (normally between 1 and 3 per cent of the total sales value). In addition the vendor must pay a rental charge for the credit card machines used to account and communicate the transactions to the bank.

Summary

The balance on the bank column in the cash book should be checked periodically with the closing balance on the bank statement issued by the bank. This is carried out by a two-task process known as a bank reconciliation. The aim of undertaking a bank reconciliation, is to ensure that the bank balance is accurate and to obtain evidence of the accuracy from a third party (the bank). It is important to understand that the bank balance included in the balance sheet is the one stated in the bank account (cash book) and not the one in the bank statement. The bank account (cash book) is part of the double entry process and follows the accounting concepts relevant to preparing final accounts. Bank statements should be regularly reconciled with business records by persons not involved in authorisation, recording or custody procedures.

The following are the main information points covered in this chapter:

❑ Bank reconciliation statements are control mechanisms that check the accuracy of a business' own records relating to banking transactions, as well as checking the accuracy of the bank records of the same.
❑ When matching business records with banking records, we are comparing two different entities recording common transactions in their respective systems. When receiving monies a business will debit their cash book whereas a financial institution for the same transaction will credit the business bank account. The reason for this is that the bank views any customers with a positive balance in their bank accounts as creditors.
❑ We can classify the reasons for differences between the balance in the cash book and the bank statement into two categories:
   — Items in the bank statement that are not in the cash book. These can include standing orders, direct debits and bank charges and interest.
   — Items in the cash book not in the bank statement – outstanding lodgements and un-presented cheques.
❑ The preparation of a bank reconciliation statement should follow the following steps:
   — Updating and/or correcting the cash book for items that are in the bank statement but not in the cash book.

— Preparation of the bank reconciliation statement, which reconciles an updated cash book with the bank statement balance, concentrating solely on transactions that are recorded in the cash book but not in the bank statement.

❏ If the balance in the reconciliation disagrees with the statement then there are errors in the system and further investigations are required.

❏ Adequate controls should be put in place to safeguard money transactions (both cash and cheques) to minimise the risk of fraud.

Review Questions

Question 8.1

The bank account of Ryans Health Gyms for January appears as follows:

Cash Book

		€			€
1 Jan	Bal b/d	12,000	2 Jan	Cheque 5561	8,100
5 Jan	Lodgement 811	7,819	5 Jan	Cheque 5562	4,655
14 Jan	Lodgement 812	5,462	10 Jan	Cheque 5563	650
16 Jan	Lodgement 813	3,240	18 Jan	Cheque 5564	832
28 Jan	Lodgement 814	1,340	26 Jan	Cheque 5565	1,440
31 Jan	Lodgement 815	8,100	31 Jan	Bal c/d	22,284
		37,961			37,961

The company has just received the following bank statement for the month of January:

Bank Statement

Date	Particulars	Dr	Cr	Balance
		€	€	€
1 Jan	Balance			12,000
4 Jan	Cheque 5561	8,100		3,900
5 Jan	Lodgement 811		7,819	11,719
9 Jan	Standing order	850		10,869
12 Jan	Bank charges	20		10,849
14 Jan	Lodgement 812		5,462	16,311
15 Jan	Cheque 5562	4,655		11,656
16 Jan	Lodgement 813		3,240	14,896
20 Jan	Cheque 5564	832		14,064
28 Jan	DD - Telecom	465		13,599
28 Jan	Lodgement 814		1,340	14,939
30 Jan	Credit transfer		1,200	16,139

Required

(a) Update the cash book as necessary.
(b) Prepare a bank reconciliation statement.

Question 8.2

Paddy O'Brien, a restaurateur, is concerned why his bank statement balance and the cash book balance are different. All bank entries on the statement are correct.

Cash Book

		€			€
1 Feb	Bal b/d	4,250	2 Feb	Cheque 2384	689
5 Feb	Lodgement 161	1,550	5 Feb	Cheque 2385	1,250
19 Feb	Lodgement 162	890	10 Feb	Cheque 2386	332
24 Feb	Lodgement 163	1,840	10 Feb	Cheque 2387	780
27 Feb	Lodgement 164	520	10 Feb	Cheque 2388	540
28 Feb	Lodgement 165	700	10 Feb	Cheque 2389	982
			18 Feb	Cheque 2390	214
			26 Feb	Cheque 2391	300
			28 Feb	Bal c/d	4,663
		9,750			9,750

Bank Statement – February

Date	Particulars	Dr	Cr	Balance
		€	€	€
1 Feb	Balance			4,250
4 Feb	Cheque 2384	689		3,561
5 Feb	Lodgement 161		1,550	5,111
9 Feb	DD - ESB	382		4,729
12 Feb	Cheque 2386	332		4,397
13 Feb	Cheque 2388	540		3,857
15 Feb	Credit transfer		640	4,497
18 Feb	Cheque 2389	982		3,515
19 Feb	Lodgement 162		890	4,405
22 Feb	Cheque 2387	870		3,535
24 Feb	Lodgement 163		1,840	5,375
24 Feb	Cheque 2390	214		5,161
26 Feb	Standing order	900		4,261
28 Feb	Lodgement 164		520	4,781
28 Feb	Bank charges	45		4,736

Required

(a) Explain clearly why the balance on a bank statement may not agree with the balance in the accounting system representing bank.
(b) Update the cash book as necessary.
(c) Prepare a bank reconciliation statement.

Question 8.3

The balance in the business accounts representing the bank figure of Break-Away Tours does not agree with the closing balance on the bank statement. You have been provided with the following:

Cash Book

		€			€
1 Oct	Bal b/d	350	5 Oct	Cheque 79965	950
2 Oct	Lodged	1,500	10 Oct	Cheque 79966	840
9 Oct	Lodged	685	11 Oct	Cheque 79967	380
9 Oct	Lodged	300	18 Oct	Cheque 79968	1,250
15 Oct	Lodged	1,425	20 Oct	Cheque 79969	765
22 Oct	Lodged	878	24 Oct	Cheque 79970	845
27 Oct	Lodged	1,260	27 Oct	Cheque 79971	1,021
30 Oct	Lodged	1,320	28 Oct	Cheque 79972	577
30 Oct	Lodged	2,510	28 Oct	Cheque 79973	1,320
			30 Oct	Bal c/d	2,280
		10,228			10,228

Bank Statement

Date	Particulars	Dr	Cr	Balance	
		€	€	€	
1 Oct	Bal b/d			180	Cr
2 Oct	Lodged		650	830	Cr
3 Oct	Lodged		1,500	2,330	Cr
6 Oct	Cheque payment – 79965	950		1,380	Cr
6 Oct	Credit transfer – Smith Ltd		650	2,030	Cr
7 Oct	Cheque payment – 79964	480		1,550	Cr
9 Oct	Lodged		985	2,535	Cr
10 Oct	DD – ESB	870		1,665	Cr
15 Oct	Cheque payment – 79967	380		1,285	Cr
15 Oct	Dividend		925	2,210	Cr
30 Oct	Lodged		1,425	3,635	Cr
22 Oct	Lodged		878	4,513	Cr
23 Oct	DD – Bord Gais	380		4,133	Cr
23 Oct	Cheque payment – 79969	765		3,368	Cr
25 Oct	Cheque payment – 79966	840		2,528	Cr
27 Oct	Lodged		1,200	3,728	Cr
27 Oct	Cheque payment – 79970	854		2,874	Cr
28 Oct	Standing order ref 354	250		2,624	Cr
29 Oct	Cheque payment – 79971	1,021		1,603	Cr
30 Oct	Bank charges	22		1,581	Cr

The bank has assured you that all entries on the statement are correct.

Required

(a) Update the cash book as necessary.
(b) Prepare a bank reconciliation statement.

Question 8.4

The book-keeper of Celtic Ceramics, a small retailer of exclusive pottery, is unable to get the closing balance on the November bank statement to agree with the closing balance on the bank account in the business books.

Bank Statement

Date	Particulars	Dr	Cr	Balance
		€	€	€
1 Nov	Bal b/d			383 Cr
2 Nov	Lodged		864	1,247 Cr
3 Nov	Lodged		1,840	3,087 Cr
6 Nov	Cheque payment – 80265	320		2,767 Cr
6 Nov	Credit transfer – ABC Ltd		950	3,717 Cr
7 Nov	Cheque payment – 80264	632		3,085 Cr
9 Nov	Lodged		888	3,973 Cr
11 Nov	DD – Bord Gais	398		3,575 Cr
15 Nov	Cheque payment – 80267	425		3,150 Cr
16 Nov	Lodged		1,425	4,575 Cr
22 Nov	Lodged		378	4,953 Cr
23 Nov	DD – Ryan Rental	725		4,228 Cr
23 Nov	Cheque payment – 80269	1,465		2,763 Cr
25 Nov	Cheque payment – 80266	1,615		1,148 Cr
26 Nov	Cheque payment – 80263	146		1,002 Cr
27 Nov	Lodged		1,500	2,502 Cr
27 Nov	Cheque payment – 80270	304		2,198 Cr
28 Nov	Standing order ref 006	465		1,733 Cr
29 Nov	Cheque payment – 80271	1,362		371 Cr
30 Nov	Bank charges	43		328 Cr

The bank has assured you that all entries on the statement are correct. The bank reconciliation statement at the end of October is as follows:

Bank Reconciliation Statement Carried out on 31 October

	€	€
Balance per bank statement		383
Add lodgement not processed		864
Less un-presented cheques	632	
	146	(778)
Balance per cash book		469

The following account shows the cash book (bank column) as it appears in the business ledger:

Cash Book

		€			€
1 Nov	Bal b/d	469	5 Nov	Cheque 80265	320
2 Nov	Lodged	1,840	11 Nov	Cheque 80266	1,615
9 Nov	Lodged	728	11 Nov	Cheque 80267	425
9 Nov	Lodged	160	18 Nov	Cheque 80268	1,246
15 Nov	Lodged	1,425	20 Nov	Cheque 80269	1,465
22 Nov	Lodged	378	24 Nov	Cheque 80270	295
27 Nov	Lodged	1,560	27 Nov	Cheque 80271	1,362
30 Nov	Lodged	859	28 Nov	Cheque 80272	266
30 Nov	Lodged	95	28 Nov	Cheque 80273	860
30 Nov	Bal c/d	340			
		7,854			7,854

Required

(a) Update the cash book as necessary.
(b) Prepare a bank reconciliation statement.

Question 8.5

The book-keeper of Barry Retail Solutions is on leave and you have been requested to reconcile the bank statement with the cash book for the month of February. You have been provided with the following data:

Bank Statement						Cash Book					
Date	Details	Dr	Cr	Balance				€			€
		€	€	€	1 Feb	Bal b/d	250	2 Feb	Cheque 96584		766
1 Feb	Balance			320	5 Feb	Lodgement 791	780	5 Feb	Cheque 96585		450
1 Feb	Lodgement 790		730	1,050	19 Feb	Lodgement 792	490	10 Feb	Cheque 96586		966
2 Feb	Cheque 96582	625		425	24 Feb	Lodgement 793	768	10 Feb	Cheque 96587		740
3 Feb	Standing order	500		-75	27 Feb	Lodgement 794	1,020	10 Feb	Cheque 96588		696
4 Feb	Cheque 96584	766		-841	28 Feb	Lodgement 795	1,500	10 Feb	Cheque 96589		760
5 Feb	Lodgement 791		780	-61	28 Feb	Bal c/d	2,705	18 Feb	Cheque 96590		1,200
9 Feb	Cheque 96583	175		-236				22 Feb	Cheque 96591		320
12 Feb	Cheque 96586	966		-1,202				24 Feb	Cheque 96592		500
13 Feb	Cheque 96588	696		-1,898				28 Feb	Cheque 96593		480
15 Feb	Credit transfer		175	-1,723				28 Feb	Cheque 96594		635
18 Feb	Cheque 96589	760		-2,483							
19 Feb	Lodgement 792		490	-1,993			7,513				7,513
22 Feb	Cheque 96587	740		-2,733							
25 Feb	Lodgement 793		768	-1,965							
24 Feb	Cheque 96590	1,200		-3,165							
27 Feb	Cheque 96592	500		-3,665							
27 Feb	DD – Telecom	130		-3,795							
28 Feb	Lodgement 794		1,020	-2,775							
28 Feb	Bank interest	65		-2,840							

Required

(a) Update the cash book account as necessary.
(b) Prepare a bank reconciliation for February.

CHAPTER 9

Accounting for Fixed Assets and Depreciation

Learning Outcomes

By the end of this chapter you will be able to:

❑ Distinguish between capital and revenue transactions, giving examples of each.
❑ Outline the criteria used to distinguish between transactions of a capital and revenue nature.
❑ Apply the correct accounting treatment for both capital and revenue receipts and expenditure.
❑ Outline the effects of an incorrect accounting treatment of capital or revenue transactions.
❑ Outline the nature, purpose and causes of depreciation.
❑ Calculate depreciation using two methods.
❑ Outline the effect of depreciation on the financial statements.
❑ Apply double entry accounting to depreciation.
❑ Account for the disposal of an asset and the related depreciation complications.

Introduction

It is in preparing the final accounts that the importance of distinguishing between capital and revenue transactions becomes most apparent. For example, capital expenditure relates to fixed assets and affects the balance sheet. Revenue expenditure relates to the operating expenses in running the business and affects the profit and loss account. Distinguishing between what are capital and what are revenue transactions, and what criteria should be taken into account in deciding this, is very important. Should for example the purchase of a fixed asset be wrongly recorded as an expense in the profit and loss account, then the net profit figure would be understated and give a misleading impression on the fortunes of the business. Capital expenditure tends to be very significant within the hospitality, tourism and retail sectors. Thus it is important for students of these and related sectors to understand the importance of identifying capital expenditure and accounting for it correctly.

This chapter is essentially about two related topics:

1. Distinguishing between expenditure that relates to fixed assets and is shown in the balance sheet and expenditure that is shown to the profit and loss account.
2. Accounting for fixed assets in accordance with the accruals concept and thus introducing you to depreciation and accounting for depreciation.

Capital and Revenue Expenditure

Capital expenditure is expenditure on the purchase or improvement of fixed assets. It is money spent to add value to fixed assets. It would also include any costs in bringing the assets to their present location and condition.

Examples of capital expenditure include:

❑ Purchase costs of an asset.
❑ Legal costs in acquiring the asset, for example solicitors' fees in acquiring property. Stamp duty in acquiring certain assets.
❑ The cost of transporting the assets to their present location.
❑ Any other costs needed to ensure the fixed assets are ready for use. For example, some assets may need certain atmospheric conditions and thus the cost in setting this up would be part of the cost in buying the asset.
❑ Installation costs including increasing the size of rooms to facilitate new equipment.
❑ Architects' fees for building plans and supervising construction of a building.
❑ Demolition of existing property to begin new construction.

Expenditure needs to be examined to assess if it is capital expenditure. This can be a difficult task. Table 9.1 outlines key questions useful when categorising capital expenditure.

Table 9.1: *Key questions in identifying capital items*

Key questions to address when classifying items as capital are:

❑   Is the item bought for use in the organisation and not for resale at a profit?
❑   Will it be of use in the organisation, or add benefit, for more than one accounting year?
❑   Is it of significant value?

Revenue expenditure is expenditure which does not increase the value of fixed assets but relates to the operating costs of the business. This expenditure is treated as an expense in the profit and loss account.

Examples include:

❑   Any expense category: rent, rates, light and heat, advertising, wages etc.
❑   The cost in bringing these expenses to their present location and condition. For example, the purchase cost of stock for resale would include the cost of transporting the goods as well as any legal fees in acquiring the goods.

Table 9.2: *Capital and revenue classifications*

Transaction	Classification	Reason
Purchase of computer system	Capital	Purchase of an asset
Upgrading of computer system	Capital	Adding value to the asset
Repairs to computer system	Revenue	Not adding value, just repairing
Extension to restaurant premises	Capital	Adding to value of fixed assets
Painting premises for first time	Capital	Adding to value of fixed assets
Repainting of premises	Revenue	Not adding value, only bringing it back to its original state
Purchase of machinery	Capital	Purchase of new asset
Cost of transporting machinery	Capital	Capital costs included transport costs in bringing the asset to its present location and condition
Light and heat bill	Revenue	Business operating expense
Building work to existing premises of which one-third involved repairs and two-thirds involved building an extension to the property	1/3 Revenue 2/3 Capital	Not adding value Adding value to the asset
Cost of rebuilding warehouse wall that had fallen down	Revenue	Repair/not adding value

Cost of machinery for use in a factory is considered capital expenditure but the oil used to run the machine is considered revenue expenditure. The machinery is capital because it will benefit a company for a number of years, is of significant value and is not bought to resell for profit. Delivery, installation and initial testing costs are also considered as capital expenditure. The oil is a cost associated with running the asset. This is a very clear example but there are many other examples which are less clear and rely on management's judgement; and where there is opportunity for judgement there is opportunity to get things wrong.

Consider this

The cost of a van is classified as capital expenditure but the petrol to use the van is considered revenue expenditure. Why are tax and insurance considered capital expenditure in the first year but not in subsequent years? If spotlights are added, is this capital or revenue expenditure? If a company logo is painted onto the van, would the cost be considered capital or revenue expenditure? If the engine of the van needs replacement, is this a capital cost?

Table 9.3: *Illustration of capital and revenue for a vehicle*

Transaction	Classification	Reason
Purchase of van	Capital	Purchase of asset
Purchase of petrol for van	Revenue	Running expense
Initial tax and insurance on van	Capital	Required to ensure van can be used
Tax and insurance on van thereafter	Revenue	Not adding value to the asset
Spotlights	Capital	Adding value to the asset
Company logo painted on van	Subjective	A case can be argued either way
Replacement engine	Revenue	Maintaining the asset not adding value

Effects of incorrect treatment of capital and revenue expenditure

Should capital expenditure be incorrectly treated as revenue expenditure (for example the purchase of a machine is treated as an expense in the profit and loss account because it was categorised as repairs to machinery), the effects on the final accounts are as follows:

1. In the profit and loss account, expenses will be overstated and thus profit will be understated.
2. In the balance sheet, fixed assets and total assets will be understated as well as capital being understated. (Remember, if profit falls, then capital falls.)

Should revenue expenditure be incorrectly treated as capital expenditure (for example, if repairs to machinery are treated as capital expenditure because the accountant felt they added value to the machine), then the effects on the final accounts are as follows:

1. In the profit and loss account, expenses are understated and thus profit is overstated.
2. In the balance sheet, fixed assets are greater and capital is greater because profit has increased.

Distinguishing between capital and revenue expenditure can be a subjective process despite the guidelines laid out by the accounting and taxation bodies. Where this subjectivity exists there are opportunities for management and owners of businesses to manipulate the figures and create false and misleading accounting statements.

Did You Know?

A survey of the lodging industry in the United States by Schmidgall et al. in 1996 revealed how hotel companies distinguish between capital and revenue expenditure, and the criteria they use in deciding whether an item of expenditure was to be treated as capital or revenue.

The research found that the general criteria used to support capitalisation (to put on the balance sheet) were:

❏   Did the cost add value to the fixed assets?
❏   Were the costs incurred as part of hotel renovations?
❏   Did the expenditure exceed a certain amount?
❏   Did the item of expenditure have a useful life exceeding one year?
❏   How were similar items treated in the past?

Despite these criteria the survey identified many grey areas in deciding whether an item of expenditure is capital or revenue. The following examples taken from the survey show the level of subjectivity in deciding on typical items of expenditure relating to hotel operations.

Rekeying rooms/		
Replacing master keys	74% revenue	26% capital
Pool replastering	65% capital	35% revenue
Pool filters	74% revenue	26+% capital
Reupholstering	59% revenue	41% capital
Repairs & major overhauls of equipment	55% revenue	45% capital
Boiler retubing	54% revenue	46% capital

In similar research by McCormack and O'Donoghue (1999) relating to the Irish hotel sector, significant confusion was identified relating to items of expenditure and the criteria used in deciding whether to capitalise. The following summary findings were recorded:

1. 40% of respondents felt that there were abuses in classifying expenditure into capital or revenue.
2. Some respondents felt that larger companies tended to favour capitalisation wherever possible.
3. Areas such as repairs and renovations were the most subjective.
4. 50% of respondents felt that there was a need for more precise guidelines in this area.

The research concluded by recommending more precise guidelines to be issued to companies from the international accounting standards committee. These guidelines should be limited in number but have a weighting of importance attached to help all financial controllers make these decisions in a more uniform manner.

It is important to remember that a company's eagerness to show strong profits (companies seeking investors) can help even further to blur the distinction between capital and revenue expenditure. The same applies when a company prefers to show its more impoverished side (submitting accounts for tax purposes).

Did You Know?

America On-line (AOL) was fined $3.5 million (May 2000) and was forced to restate its accounts for 1995 to 1997. This was due to the fact that the company treated a promotional expense of $385 million as an asset. It was a clear case of overstating profits. In fining the company for misleading accounts the audit regulators commented that no one ever seems to reduce profit in error. All the 'errors' happen to increase profit. AOL used the excuse that the promotional expense was made up of tangible items, such as disks, which were given away free. The auditors stated that as the disks were never going to be returned and thus it was clearly P&L related expenditure.

Source: The Business Eccountant, 21 May 2000

Capital and revenue receipts

Revenue receipts include receipts from sales of products and services. In addition revenue receipts come from other sources such as commissions, or rents where part of the business premises is sublet.

Capital receipts are from the sale of fixed assets. If a business sells a motor vehicle (original cost of €12,000) for €1,000 then the €1,000 is classified as a capital receipt. A capital receipt is not recorded in the profit and loss account. The €1,000 is recorded in the bank account (debit) and credited to a sale of fixed asset (disposal) account, which calculates whether the business made a profit or loss on the sale. The profit or loss on the sale of the vehicle is recorded in the profit and loss account. This computation will be explained later on in this chapter. At this stage it is sufficient to know that a capital receipt is not recorded in the profit and loss account.

Fixed Assets and Depreciation

Fixed assets are items of significant value, bought for use in a business over a number of years and not with the intention of resale for profit. A fixed asset bought today will not be valued the same in one year's time or in five years' time. Depreciation is a measure of the wear and tear or loss in value of an asset over its life. The difference between the cost of a fixed asset and the amount received when it is sold is called depreciation. Assets such as plant, equipment, motor vehicles and furniture are all assets that lose value over time due to wear and tear, economic factors, such as inadequacy and obsolescence, or the simple passing of time. Depreciation is the measure of this loss in value and must be treated as an expense in the profit and loss account.

Example 9.1: *Asset depreciation*

A large supermarket chain purchased a delivery truck for €80,000 and sold it four years later for €5,000. Calculate the depreciation on the vehicle?

Approach

The vehicle has depreciated by €75,000 (€80,000 - €5,000) and this loss in value should be reflected in the accounts as an expense over the four years that the asset was in use.

Another way to view depreciation is that all fixed assets cost money to purchase. This is a cost to the business and thus must appear in the profit and loss account as an expense. Also, fixed assets over their life will earn revenues for the business and, in accordance with the accruals/matching concept, the cost of the assets should be set against the revenues earned by the assets over the asset's life. Each year the asset will appear in the balance sheet at its reduced book value (net book value), while the reduction, called depreciation, is treated as an expense in the profit and loss account.

Fixed assets must be depreciated in accordance with the accruals and prudence concepts, except non-depreciable land which under normal economic conditions appreciates in value. The only other reason for not depreciating fixed assets would be where the depreciation charge and accumulated depreciation charge are immaterial, in other words, they would not reasonably influence the decisions of the user of the accounts.

Causes of depreciation

The main causes of depreciation can be categorised into four types:

1. **Physical deterioration** including the wear and tear on assets used in the business such as motor vehicles, machinery and equipment. The more they are used the greater the level of wear and tear and thus the greater the level of depreciation.
2. **Economic factors** such as obsolescence, where a certain type of asset, for example office equipment such as computers could become obsolete as new and more powerful computers become available to the business. This would happen even though the existing computer is in good working order. Inadequacy is also an economic factor that causes depreciation. When a business grows, certain assets such as machinery and equipment become inadequate for the size and volume of activity that the business is presently servicing. Hence these assets will be replaced due to their inadequacy.

3. **Time**: This would refer to assets that have a legal life. Examples would include a lease agreement to rent a property for twenty years. Thus the value of the lease reduces as each year goes by. Ultimately the lease is worthless at the end of its life.
4. **Depletion**: This is where a business has a wasting asset such as mines, gas and oil fields. The more raw materials you extract from these assets the less the assets have to offer until they are depleted.

Calculation of Depreciation

Depreciation is simply the sales proceeds of the asset less its original cost. When an asset is bought and sold in one period the difference between the sales price and cost price of the assets equals depreciation, which is treated as an expense, as the sales proceeds would generally be less than original cost.

Most fixed assets, however, are purchased and used for more than one accounting period and an attempt must be made to calculate and charge depreciation to each year that the asset is used. Remember each year that the asset is in use means we have not sold it yet and therefore cannot calculate the true depreciation rate. Thus we must estimate the depreciation rate.

There are two main methods of calculating/estimating depreciation:

1. Straight-line method.
2. Reducing-balance method.

The straight-line method

The straight-line method of calculating depreciation is a simple approach that results in the same amount of depreciation being written off each year for the expected life of the asset.

The formula for this method is:

$$\frac{\text{Cost of Asset} - \text{Estimated residual value}}{\text{Estimated life of the asset}} = \text{Annual depreciation charge}$$

The numerator represents the estimated amount of depreciation, which must be divided and charged to the profit and loss account over the estimated life of the asset.

Residual value is what the business would get for the asset on the open market at the end of its life. It is an estimate and is often estimated at zero.

Example 9.2: *Straight-line depreciation*

A health and fitness centre purchased equipment with an estimated life of eight years for €90,000. It is estimated that the residual value of the assets at the end of eight years is a scrap value of €2,000. Calculate the annual depreciation charge to the profit and loss account using the straight-line method.

Approach

The annual depreciation charge is €11,000 per annum. This is found by taking €90,000 cost and deducting the €2,000 scrap value and dividing by the eight years. Thus over the eight years €11,000 per annum will be charged to the profit and loss account in the form of depreciation. At the end of the first year the asset will be shown in the balance sheet at a net book value of €79,000 after depreciation has been deducted.

The straight-line method ensures that depreciation on the asset is the same each year and is popular due to its simplicity. The amount to be provided for in relation to depreciation is calculated by the formula above. In some questions a specified percentage may be applied. If an asset is to be depreciated over four years, you could be told to depreciate by 25 per cent per annum straight-line. If an asset is to be depreciated over five years, you could be told to depreciate by 20 per cent per annum straight-line. The percentage approach will give you the same result as the formula approach when there is no residual value.

The reducing-balance method

The reducing-balance method of depreciation results in a reduced amount of depreciation being written off each year. Under this method, depreciation is calculated based on a fixed percentage of the cost of the asset in its first year. In the second and later years the same percentage is used but it is based on the reducing balance (i.e. the cost less depreciation already charged). The formula used to calculate the fixed percentage is as follows:

$$R = 1 - \sqrt[n]{s/c}$$

Where:

R = the depreciation rate to be applied.

n = the estimated life of the asset.

s = the estimated residual or scrap value of the asset at the end of its life.

c = the cost of the asset

The reducing-balance method results in a much higher level of depreciation in the first few years of an asset's life, which in reality is when the majority of depreciation takes place for most assets. Thus it would be considered a suitable method for assets such as motor vehicles, which have high depreciation levels in early years and lower levels in later years.

Example 9.3: *Reducing-balance depreciation*

Star Videos purchased a computer system costing €10,000 three years ago. The accountant has advised the business to depreciate the asset at a rate of 40 per cent of the reducing balance. Calculate the depreciation charge for the first three years.

Approach

		€
Year 1	Original cost	10,000
	Depreciation charge to P&L for the first year	
	40% of €10,000 the original cost	4,000
	Net book value balance sheet end of year 1	6,000
Year 2	Depreciation charge to P&L for the second year	
	40% of €6,000 the net book value at end year 1	2,400
	Net book value balance sheet end of year 2	3,600
Year 3	Depreciation charge to P&L for the third year	
	40% of €3,600 the net book value at end of year 2	1,440
	Net book value balance sheet end of year 3	2,160

Accounting for Depreciation

When depreciation is calculated as outlined above, the amount calculated is not the actual amount of depreciation but is a best estimate of what depreciation has occurred. In accounting, when actual amounts are not known, the estimated amount is entered in a special account called a 'provision account'. A provision is an adjustment made in the accounts at the end of a period to take into account costs that have been incurred but not yet accounted for as the true value is not known. Provisions are also used in accounting for liabilities that are likely to occur in the future.

The annual charge for depreciation is recorded as follows in the books of account of a business:

	Account	Amount
DEBIT	P&L account	The annual depreciation charge
CREDIT	The provision for depreciation account*	The annual depreciation charge

* Sometimes called the accumulated depreciation account.
   Each group of fixed assets will have its own accumulated depreciation account.

Regarding the balance sheet, fixed assets are disclosed as follows:

> Cost – Accumulated Depreciation = Net Book Value

Example 9.4: *Accounting for depreciation*

Returning to the health and fitness centre in Example 9.2, the approach in accounting for depreciation can be illustrated. Equipment with an estimated life of eight years was purchased for €90,000. It is estimated that the residual value of the assets at the end of eight years is a scrap value of €2,000. The annual depreciation charge amounts to €11,000.

Show the accounting entries and the effect on the final accounts for the first three years.

Approach

YEAR 1

Dr		Equipment Account			Cr
		€			€
Yr 1	Bank a/c	90,000	Yr 1	Bal c/d	90,000
Yr 2	Bal b/d	90,000			

Dr		Bank Account			Cr
		€			€
			Yr 1	Equipment a/c	90,000

Dr		**Profit and Loss account**			**Cr**
		€			€
Yr 1	Provision dep a/c	11,000			

Dr		**Provision for Equipment Account**			**Cr**
		€			€
Yr 1	Bal c/d	11,000	Yr 1	P&L a/c	11,000
			Yr 2	Bal b/d	11,000

The final accounts of year 1 would appear as follows:

<table>
<tr><td>

P&L extract for first year

Less expenses

Provision depreciation equipment €11,000

</td><td>

Balance sheet as at end year 1

Fixed assets	*Cost*	*Deprec.*	*NBV*
Equipment	€90,000	€11,000	€79,000

</td></tr>
</table>

YEAR 2

Dr		**Equipment Account**			**Cr**
		€			€
Yr 1	Bank a/c	90,000	Yr 1	Bal c/d	90,000
Yr 2	Bal b/d	90,000	Yr 2	Bal c/d	90,000
Yr 3	Bal b/d	90,000			

Dr		**Profit and Loss Account**			**Cr**
		€			€
Yr 2	Provision Dep a/c	11,000			

Dr		**Provision for Equipment Account**			**Cr**
		€			€
Yr 1	Bal c/d	11,000	Yr 1	P&L a/c	11,000
			Yr 2	Bal b/d	11,000
Yr 2	Bal c/d	22,000	Yr 2	P&L a/c	11,000
		22,000			22,000
			Yr 3	Bal b/d	22,000

The final accounts of year 2 would appear as follows:

P&L extract for second year
Less expenses
Provision depreciation equipment €11,000

Balance sheet as at end year 2			
Fixed assets	*Cost*	*Deprec.*	*NBV*
Equipment	€90,000	€22,000	€68,000

€11,000 end year 1
plus €11,000 year 2

YEAR 3

Dr   **Equipment Account**   **Cr**

		€			€
Yr 1	Bank a/c	90,000	Yr 1	Bal c/d	90,000
Yr 2	Bal b/d	90,000	Yr 2	Bal c/d	90,000
Yr 3	Bal b/d	90,000	Yr 3	Bal c/d	90,000
Yr 4	Bal b/d	90,000			

Dr   **Profit and Loss Account**   **Cr**

		€			€
Yr 3	Provision dep a/c	11,000			

Dr   **Provision for Equipment Account**   **Cr**

		€			€
Yr 1	Bal c/d	11,000	Yr 1	P&L a/c	11,000
			Yr 2	Bal b/d	11,000
Yr 2	Bal c/d	22,000	Yr 2	P&L a/c	11,000
		22,000			22,000
			Yr 3	Bal b/d	22,000
Yr 3	Bal c/d	33,000	Yr 3	P&L a/c	11,000
		33,000			33,000
			Yr 4	Bal b/d	33,000

The final accounts of year 3 would appear as follows:

P&L extract for third year
Less expenses
Provision depreciation equipment €11,000

Balance sheet as at end year 3			
Fixed assets	*Cost*	*Deprec.*	*NBV*
Equipment	€90,000	€33,000	€57,000

€22,000 end year 2
plus €11,000 year 3

Note: The asset is shown at its book value after accumulated depreciation has been deducted. The historic cost and accumulated depreciation are shown purely for information and it is the net book value of fixed assets that is the important figure which we add to current assets to get the total assets of the business. Thus fixed assets are shown in the balance sheet at their net book value.

The approach used above can be summarised using the steps set out in Table 9.4 below.

Table 9.4: *Steps in accounting for depreciation*

1. Enter opening balances where necessary and update the fixed asset account with any transactions that have occurred during the period.
2. Balance the fixed asset account(s).
3. Calculate the annual depreciation and account for it by:
   — Crediting the depreciation account.
   — Debiting the profit and loss account.
4. Balance the depreciation account(s).
5. If required, show balance sheet extract by taking the closing balances from the fixed asset and the depreciation accounts.

Depreciation method and policy

When dealing with depreciation, a number of decisions must be made. The first decision is on the method of depreciation. The two methods outlined above, straight line and reducing balance, are the most common in operation. The rates of depreciation applied vary depending on the nature of the asset being depreciated and the policy of management.

Did You Know?

The following approach to fixed asset depreciation has been adopted by Boots Plc. 'Depreciation of tangible fixed assets is provided to write off the cost or valuation, less residual value, by equal instalments over their expected useful economic lives as follows':

- ❏ Freehold land, not depreciated.
- ❏ Freehold and long leasehold buildings, over not more than 50 years.
- ❏ Computer equipment including software, 3 to 8 years.
- ❏ Motor cars, 4 or 5 years.
- ❏ Other motor vehicles, 3 to 10 years.
- ❏ Fixtures and plant, 3 to 20 years.

Source: Annual Report Boots PLC

Having decided on the method and rate of depreciation, the next decision relates to the policy of applying depreciation. There are two main choices:

1. Depreciate on the value of assets held at the end of the accounting year.
2. Depreciate on the basis of one month's ownership equals one month's depreciation.

Depreciating 'on the value of assets held at the end of the accounting year' is the simplest to operate. It allows for a full year's depreciation in the year the asset is bought and no depreciation in the year sold.

Depreciating 'on the basis of one month's ownership equals one month's depreciation' is more accurate but more complex. This requires depreciation to be included for each month the asset was owned. There are more calculations and workings involved.

Did You Know?

Tottenham Hotspur capitalise (treat as a fixed assets) the acquisition cost of their players in the balance sheet and amortise (depreciate) those assets over their respective contracts. The following is their amortisation policy regarding this human asset:

'The costs associated with the acquisition of players' registration and coaching staff are capitalised as intangible fixed assets. These costs are fully amortised over their useful economic lives in equal annual installments over the period of their respective contracts.'

Source: Annual Report Tottenham Hotspur Plc

Accounting for the Disposal of an Asset

Fixed assets are not normally purchased with the intention to resell for a profit. However, when an asset is sold there may be a difference between the written down value (net book value) of the asset and the proceeds of the sale. This results from the fact that depreciation was estimated and a provision was maintained. When the sale or disposal of an asset occurs there will be a profit or loss on sale recorded if the amount provided for as depreciation is different from the actual depreciation that occurred. This is quite complex and a disposal or sale of asset account is opened to account for the transactions. Example 9.5 outlines the procedure.

Example 9.5: *Disposal of a fixed asset*

Alpha Hotels maintains furniture assets at cost, depreciating at a rate of 10 per cent per annum using the straight-line method. The company has a policy of depreciating assets in existence at the year-end rather than depreciating assets on a month-by-month basis. The following is extracted from the balance sheet at 31 December 2003:

	Cost	Accumulated depreciation	NBV
Furniture	€200,000	€122,000	€78,000

New furniture was purchased for €30,000 on 5 May 2004. Furniture, originally costing €18,000 when purchased in March 2000, was sold for €8,000 on 31 May 2004.

You are required to show:

1. The furniture account for 2004.
2. The provision for depreciation account for 2004.
3. The disposal of furniture account.
4. Extracts from the profit and loss account and balance sheet for 2004.

Approach

❏ It must be noted that the hotel's policy is to depreciate based on assets in existence at the year-end. This is the same policy as giving a full year's depreciation in the year of purchase and none in the year of sale.

❏ In this example the hotel has already acquired furniture and equipment costing €200,000 prior to 2004. During 2004, the hotel buys new furniture and sells some old furniture.

❏ The accounts would appear as follows (it is important to note that assets sold are taken out of the asset account at original cost, as they are recorded at that value in the account):

Dr		Furniture Account			Cr
		€			€
1/1/04	Bal b/d	200,000	31/5/04	Disposal a/c	18,000
5/5/04	Bank a/c	30,000	31/12/04	Bal c/d	212,000
		230,000			230,000
1/1/05	Bal b/d	212,000			

Dr		Provision for Depreciation Account				Cr
		€				€
31/5/04	Disposal a/c	7,200	1/1/04	Bal c/d		122,000
	(18,000 x 10% x 4 years)		31/12/04	P&L a/c		21,200
31/12/04	Bal c/d	136,000		(212,000 x 10%)		
		143,200				143,200
			1/1/05	Bal b/d		136,000

The opening balance in the provision for depreciation account represents the depreciation already charged on the furniture the company owned up to the beginning of this year.

Dr		Furniture Disposal Account				Cr
		€				€
31/5/04	Furniture a/c	18,000	31/5/04	Provision dep		7,200
			31/5/04	Bank a/c		8,000
			31/5/04	P&L a/c (loss)		2,800
		18,000				18,000

As the business has sold an asset then they must also dispose or take out of the depreciation account the depreciation on the asset they no longer have. This is calculated as the original cost of the asset multiplied by the annual depreciation rate multiplied by the number of years in use. In this case it is four years, giving a full year's depreciation in 2000 and none in 2004, the year of sale. We must also charge to the profit and loss account the depreciation for the year based on assets in existence at the year-end (balance c/d in furniture account of €212,000). This amounts to €21,200 (€212,000 x 10 per cent).

As it is a fixed asset that is sold we must separately calculate a profit or loss on the sale and transfer the amount involved to the profit and loss account, either adding to or deducting from the gross profit. A disposal or sale of asset account is used, which shows the cost of the asset sold and the depreciation charged on the asset thus far. This gives us a net book value for the asset. If the sales proceeds are less than this, then the business has made a loss; if the sales proceeds are greater than the net book value of the assets sold, then the business has made a profit on the sale.

Extracts from the Profit and Loss Account

Expenses	€
Provision for furniture depreciation	21,200
Loss on sale of furniture and equipment	2,800

Extracts from the Balance Sheet

	Cost	Accumulated depreciation	NBV
Furniture and equipment	€212,000	€136,000	€76,000

The approach used above can be summarised using the four steps set out in Table 9.5.

Table 9.5: *Steps in fixed asset disposal*

1. Transfer the *original cost* of the asset sold from the fixed asset account to the disposal account:
   — Credit the fixed asset account.
   — Debit the disposal account.
2. Transfer the *amount depreciated on the asset sold* from the depreciation account to the disposal account:
   — Debit the depreciation account.
   — Credit the disposal account.
3. Account for the proceeds of the sale:
   — Credit the disposal account with the proceeds from the sale.
4. Find the difference in the disposal account and transfer it to the profit and loss account as the profit or loss on the sale.

Depreciation Policy and the Effect on Net Profit

The depreciation policy of a business directly affects the level of net profit. For example, should a company decide to depreciate its assets worth €2,500,000 over ten years on a straight-line basis then it would charge depreciation in the profit and loss account of €250,000. However, should the directors decide that the life of its assets is closer to twenty years then the amount of depreciation charged in the profit and loss account will amount to €125,000. Thus profit would be €125,000 greater due to the change in estimate of the life of the asset.

Estimating the life of an asset can be a subjective process and with it comes the pressure to ensure that profits are maximised. This happens when asset lives used in the depreciation calculation are too optimistic.

Did You Know?

Ryanair Plc depreciate aircraft over a 20–23-year period. However, Aer-Lingus depreciate their aircraft over an 18–20-year period. Depreciation amounts to about 15 per cent of the operating expenses of Ryanair. This is a very significant item of expense and would be even greater if they applied a more prudent estimate on the life of their aircraft. Ryanair also estimate the residual values of their aircraft to be 15 per cent of cost (Aer Lingus estimate residual value at 10 per cent). GPA (Guinness Peat Aviation), before they were taken over by General Electric, depreciated their aircraft over 23 years using a residual value of 15 per cent. The higher the estimates of residual value and life of the asset the lower the amounts of depreciation in the accounts and the higher the profit figure.

FRS 15 Tangible Fixed Assets states that, other than for non-depreciable land, the only grounds for not depreciating fixed assets are that the depreciation charge and accumulated depreciation figures are immaterial (i.e. they would 'not reasonably influence' the decisions of a user of account). Hotel companies tend to avail of this clause with regard to the depreciation charge on their property and fixed plant assets. This is due to the high maintenance costs they incur in the up-keep of their properties and as the properties have an estimated long life and a high residual value (due to the upkeep of the assets) they can claim that the depreciation charge and accumulated depreciation would not be material. **Jury's Plc** availed of this exemption in 1993, a year in which they made a small operating profit. However, the estimated residual values and useful lives of these assets must be reviewed at the end of each reporting period and revised if expectations are significantly different. If it is revised, the assets should be depreciated over the revised remaining economic life. At the end of accounting period 31 December 2002, Jury's revised their estimates and proceeded to account for depreciation on their building and fixed plant assets depreciating their core building over a 50–125 year period.

This change ensures that their depreciation policy is in line with the requirements of FRS 15, which stated that 'subsequent expenditure that maintains or enhances the previously assessed standard of performance of an asset does not negate the need to charge depreciation'.

Xtra-vision the video rental chain was floated on the ISEQ index in 1989. Some financial commentators questioned their depreciation policy regarding video tapes. Xtra-vision depreciated their video tapes over 30 months whereas some commentators felt a more accurate life of a rental video tape was 6 months. The effect was to reduce the depreciation charges in the profit and loss account and obviously increase profit.

British Airport Authority (BAA) between 1988 and 1990 changed the estimated life of its terminals from 16 to 50 years and its runways from 23.5 to 100 years. This had a dramatic effect not alone on its balance sheet values but also on reported profits.

Summary

The distinction between capital and revenue expenditure is very important. The bank account does not distinguish between capital and revenue transactions. The profit and loss account does, and therein lies one of the main reasons why cash balances and profit levels differ. Another reason for differences between profits and cash levels is the fact that in accordance with the accruals concept and FRS 15, businesses must provide for depreciation on their fixed assets. Depreciation is an estimate of the loss in value of an asset and appears as an expense in the profit and loss account but will not appear in the bank/cash account as it is a non-cash item.

The main information points covered in this chapter are as follows:

❏ Capital expenditure is expenditure on the purchase or improvement of fixed assets. It is money spent to add value to fixed assets and appears in the balance sheet.
❏ Revenue expenditure is expenditure which does not increase the value of fixed assets but relates to the operating costs of the business. This expenditure is treated as an expense in the profit and loss account.
❏ Should capital expenditure be treated as revenue expenditure, then profit, fixed assets and capital would be understated.
❏ Should revenue expenditure be treated as capital expenditure, then profit, fixed assets and capital would be overstated.
❏ The distinction between capital and revenue expenditure is one of the main reasons why there is a difference between net profit and the bank account balance at the year-end.
❏ Depreciation is a measure of the wear and tear or loss in value of an asset over its life. The difference between the cost of a fixed asset and the amount received when it is sold is called depreciation.
❏ Depreciation can be caused by a number of factors including wear and tear to the asset, economic factors, time and depletion.
❏ There are two methods in calculating/estimating depreciation: straight-line method and reducing-balance method. The straight-line method is simple and easy to calculate. The reducing-balance method would be considered more accurate as it results in greater estimates of depreciation in the early years of the asset's life.
❏ The process of accounting for depreciation requires a provision for depreciation account to be set up for each type of asset.
❏ The process of accounting for the sale of fixed assets and the depreciation complication requires the use of a disposal account.
❏ It is important to be aware of the subjective nature of estimating depreciation and its resulting effects on profit and asset levels.

Review Questions

Question 9.1

(a) Distinguish between capital and revenue expenditure giving examples of each.
(b) Discuss criteria that might be used in classifying expenditure as either capital or revenue.

Question 9.2

Classify the following transactions as either capital or revenue:

1. Purchase of new van.	
2. Cost of road tax for new van.	
3. Cost of painting firm's name on new van.	
4. Purchase of stock for re-sale.	
5. Carriage inwards on stock for re-sale.	
6. Carriage costs on sales.	
7. Legal costs of collecting debts.	
8. Legal costs in relation to acquiring a new premises.	
9. Costs of installing new machine.	
10. Installing security equipment.	
11. Roof repairs.	
12. Fitting partitions in the shop.	
13. Installing a security hut.	
14. Wages.	
15. Fire insurance premium.	
16. Carriage costs on bricks for the security hut.	
17. Cost of altering the interior of new van to increase capacity.	
18. Purchase of replacement engine for existing van.	

Question 9.3

Briefly describe the effects of the following on the profit and loss account and balance sheet of a business:

(a) Purchase of fixed assets amounting to €25,000 treated as an expense in the profit and loss account.
(b) Repairs to motor vehicles amounting to €5,000 treated as capital expenditure.

Question 9.4

The Hilda Hotel took delivery of a new computerised reservation system in January 2003, the beginning of its financial year. The list price of the whole system was €25,000; however, the hotel was able to negotiate a price with the supplier of €22,000. This did not include a fee of €2,000 to install and test the system. A cash discount was also agreed with the supplier of 6% (not including the installation fee) should the business pay within 10 days of receipt and installation. The hotel took advantage of this discount. A maintenance agreement was entered into with a sister company of the supplier costing €800 and the extra insurance charge for the equipment was agreed with the hotel's insurance company at €200. An extra charge of €1,000 was agreed with the supplier to train staff on the new system.

Required

Calculate the capital cost of acquiring the new reservation systems.

Question 9.5

(a) Explain what is meant by depreciation.
(b) What is the purpose of a depreciation charge in the accounts of a business?
(c) Which of the following costs should be included as part of the capital cost of fixed assets?
   – Original cost of the asset.
   – Delivery costs of the asset.
   – The legal costs in acquiring the asset.
   – Repairs to the asset.
   – Installation costs of the asset.
   – VAT on the cost of the asset.
   – Wages of maintenance staff.

Question 9.6

Joseph Smith has just purchased a taxi licence and is in the process of setting up as a taxi driver. He is seeking advice on how to account for his business. Joseph has purchased a car costing €20,000. He estimates that the car will be used for four years, after which he will sell it for €4,800.

Calculate the depreciation charge for motor vehicles in the profit and loss account for each year using:

(a) The straight-line method and
(b) The reducing-balance method using a depreciation rate of 30%.

Question 9.7

Star Travel depreciates office equipment at the rate of 20% straight-line method based on assets in existence at the year-end, which is 31 December. The following is extracted from the company's balance sheet as at 31 December 2003:

	Cost	Accumulated depreciation	NBV
Office equipment	€100,000	€50,000	€50,000

During the year 2004 the company purchased two new items of office equipment costing €25,000 and €35,000.

Required

Show the asset and provision for depreciation accounts for the year 2004 as well as extracts from the profit and loss account and balance sheet.

Question 9.8

The Fine Food Retailing Company has just set up business. The owner has opted for a policy of depreciating equipment at 10% per annum and fixtures at 12.5% per annum using the straight-line method. Depreciation is to be charged on assets in existence at the year-end (31/12), thus charging a full year's depreciation even though the asset may only have been bought half-way through the year.

The following transactions in assets have taken place over 2003 and 2004:

Date	Transaction
1/1/03	Bought equipment €22,000 and fixtures €30,000.
1/10/03	Bought equipment €10,000.
1/7/04	Purchased fixtures €5,000.
1/10/04	Part of the equipment bought on 1 January 2003 was sold for €5,000 (originally cost €8,000).

Required

(a) Separate asset accounts for equipment and fixtures for both 2003 and 2004.
(b) The provision for depreciation accounts for both 2003 and 2004.
(c) The disposal of equipment account for 2004.
(d) Extracts from the profit and loss account and balance sheet for 2003 and 2004.

Question 9.9

Logic Smart Ltd, a small transport company, has a financial year-end on the 31 December 2003. At the beginning of the year the company had balances on the vehicles account of €256,000 and on the provision for depreciation account of €135,000.

On 1 April 2003 the company purchased a new delivery van for €56,000. On 30 June 2003 the company sold a vehicle (which originally cost €40,000 when purchased on 1 February 2000) for €8,500. On 1 July 2003, the company purchased a second-hand truck for €25,000.

The company provides for depreciation, using the reducing-balance method, on fixed assets held at the end of its financial year at a rate of 40% per annum.

Required

(a) The vehicles account for 2003.
(b) The provision for depreciation of vehicles account for 2003.
(c) The disposal account.
(d) Profit and loss extracts for 2003.
(e) Balance sheet extracts as at 31 December 2003.

Question 9.10

Fast Print began operations in January 2003 retailing stationery items as well as providing fast and efficient photocopying services. The first photocopying machine was purchased costing €100,000 on 5 January 2003. As business expanded quickly, a second photocopying machine was purchased on 1 September 2003 costing €220,000. Unfortunately, in July 2004 the first machine became very unreliable and management decided to sell it. It was sold for €45,000 on 30 July 2004. A replacement machine was purchased on 1 August for €130,000.

The owner depreciates the machines at 30% per annum straight line, using the basis of one month's ownership means one month's depreciation.

Required

(a) The machinery account for 2003 and 2004.
(b) The provision for depreciation account for 2003 and 2004.
(c) The disposal account.
(d) Profit and loss extracts for 2003 and 2004.
(e) Balance sheet extracts for 2003 and 2004.

CHAPTER 10

Accounting for Provisions, Prepayments and Accruals

Learning Outcomes

By the end of this chapter you will be able to:

- ❑ Explain the concept of prudence and the need for provisions.
- ❑ Explain bad debts and the accounting treatment necessary.
- ❑ Outline the nature and purpose of providing for bad debts and discounts and their effects on the financial statements.
- ❑ Apply double entry accounting to provisions.
- ❑ Explain the need for accruals and prepayments.
- ❑ Illustrate the accounting treatment for accruals and prepayments.
- ❑ Demonstrate the effect accruals and prepayments have on the final accounts.

Introduction

This chapter is primarily about the period end adjustments necessary before the preparation of the final accounts of a business. At the end of an accounting period certain adjustments are made to the accounts before the final accounts can be prepared. These adjustments relate to accounting for accruals, prepayments and provisions, and are a result of two accounting concepts, namely accruals and prudence. Accounting for accruals and prepayments is related to the accruals concepts whereas accounting for provisions is related to the prudence concept. This chapter will begin with an overview of these key concepts before focusing on their application.

Key Accounting Concepts

The prudence concept

The intention of the prudence concept is to see that all asset values and profit figures are realistic rather than optimistic or pessimistic. The essence of the concept is to insist that revenue or profit should not be accounted for until the business is virtually certain to get it, but that a loss in an asset's value is accounted for as soon as it is probable or likely. The ability to reasonably measure the asset or liability is also necessary to ensure the reliability of the accounts. Ultimately the prudence concept requires that in preparing financial statements, gains or losses, assets and liabilities should be neither overstated nor understated.

This concept requires that:

1. One should never anticipate profits. This can be explained by asking when a company accounts for a sales transaction. A sales transaction should only be accounted for when ownership of the goods passes from the company to the buyer and not when the goods were originally ordered. To account for the transaction at the order stage would be imprudent. This is related to the realisation concept outlined in Chapter 3.

2. One must provide for all possible losses. If a company knows that next year it will incur losses on a part/section of the business then it should provide for those losses *now*. To provide for something is to account for it now. In other words show it as a loss/expense in the profit and loss account. However, a provision should only be recognised and accounted for when the following criteria apply:
    — It is probable that a transfer of economic benefits will have to occur.
    — A reasonable estimate of the amount involved can be made.

A good example of the prudence concept is with regard to bad debts. If a company becomes aware just prior to the year-end that a debtor is likely to go into liquidation and cease trading, then prudence requires a provision to be made in the accounts for this future loss.

> A provision is an adjustment made to the accounts to allow for a transaction or event that is likely to occur in the future.

Table 10.1 summarises the important points of both the prudence and accruals concepts.

Table 10.1: *The prudence and accruals concepts*

The prudence concept

The prudence concept has two elements:

1. That one should never anticipate profits.
2. Provide for all possible losses. If a company knows that next year it will incur losses on a part/section of the business, then it should provide for those losses now. One should only provide for a loss when the amount is measurable and it is probable or likely to occur.

The intention of the prudence concept is to see that all asset values and profit figures are realistic rather than optimistic or pessimistic. The essence of the concept is to insist that revenue or profit not be accounted for until the business is virtually certain to get it, but that a loss in an asset value is accounted for as soon as it is probable or likely.

The accruals/matching concept

The accruals concept requires two things:

1. When calculating profit, expenses are matched against related revenues.
2. Profit is the difference between revenues earned (not necessarily received) and expenses charged (not necessarily paid).

See Chapter 6 for more detail on the accruals concept.

Bad Debts and Provision for Bad Debts

Bad debts

A bad debt is a debt where you are almost certain that you will not receive the monies or assets owed to you. For example, you sell goods on credit to Gary Dunne worth €1,000. The credit period is 30 days but after 60 days you investigate and realise that Gary has left the country and is unlikely to return. The likelihood is that you will never receive this €1,000 and thus you should treat it as a loss or expense and charge it to the profit and loss account.

The accounting treatment for bad debts is as follows:

Action	Account	Reason/explanation
DEBIT	Bad debts accounts	This is an expense account (like rent, rates etc.) which is charged to the profit and loss account.
CREDIT	The individual debtor account	In the above example, Gary Dunne has a debit balance signifying he is a debtor and owes us €1,000. By crediting his account we cancel and close his account and thus the overall debtors figure is reduced.

Bad debts recovered

Occasionally, a debt that had been written off as bad will be paid and therefore should be treated as a bad debt recovered. A separate account known as a bad debt recovered account should be opened. There are two transactions involved: firstly, the bad debt must be reinstated and secondly, the payment must be accounted for.

The accounting treatment for bad debts recovered is as follows:

Action	Account	Reason/explanation
DEBIT	The individual debtor's account	The amount involved must be reinstated in the individual debtor's account.
CREDIT	Bad debts recovered account	This is a revenue account which will be added to gross profit in the profit and loss account.
	Then	
DEBIT	Bank account	This recognises the receipt of the money.
CREDIT	The individual debtor account	By crediting the individual debtor's account the debt is cleared by the payment.

Provision for bad debts

The prudence concept helps ensure the information given in the accounts provides a complete and realistic representation of what occurred. The essence of the prudence concept is that the figures for assets and liabilities recorded in the accounts are realistic and reliable. Where businesses have high levels of credit sales in the profit and loss account and high debtor balances in the balance sheet, it is always likely (even after writing off *actual* bad debts that have occurred during the accounting period) that a certain percentage of debtors will not pay up in the future. If this is the norm then a business, acting prudently, should make a provision for this loss now, to ensure debtors are shown at a realistic level and profits are not overstated.

Example 10.1: *Provision for bad debts*

A department store, D & A Stores, provides credit which can be applied for by customers who must pass strict credit risk assessment checks. D & A has a trade debtors figure at the end of its financial year amounting to €56,410. From past experience the sales ledger/credit sales manager knows that the business will not receive the full €56,410. The amount received may average at 98 per cent of the amount outstanding.

In this case the D & A may provide for bad debts at 2 per cent of debtors amounting to €1,128 (€56,410 x 2 per cent).

It is important to remember this provision may be on top of any bad debts that came to light during the accounting period. Thus bad debts and provision for bad debts are not the same.

There are two types of provision that can be created for bad debts:

1. A general provision is as described above, where a percentage is applied to the total debtors and not against individual accounts.
2. A specific provision relates to an individual account where there could be some concern about the future payment of the debt but not enough certainty to write off the debt.

Accounting for bad debt provisions

Once the estimate of the likely level of bad debts has been agreed then the double entry procedure to create the provision is as follows:

Action	Account	Reason/explanation
DEBIT	P&L account	This is the process of charging to the P&L account the *estimate* of the *possible* loss in future revenue.

CREDIT	Provision for bad debts	This account can appear in the balance sheet as a current liability (credit), although the normal process is to deduct it from debtors in current assets.

It is important to remember that this is a provision for an estimate of a possible future loss. It is by no means certain that these bad debts will actually go bad. It is just a process of showing debtors in current assets at a more realistic figure and the resulting effect on profit. Should some debtors actually 'go bad' in the future then we treat them as bad debts in the normal way and at the end of the year a new provision for bad debts is estimated.

Example 10.2: *Creating a provision for bad debt*

Gibson Retailing Ltd have a financial year-end 31 December. At 31 December 2002 the total figure for debtors amounted to €150,000 after accounting for bad debts during the year. Management now think it is prudent to provide for bad debts to the amount of 1.5 per cent of the debtors figure based on past experience. Show the transactions required to create the relevant provision and the effect on the balance sheet and profit and loss account

Approach

Dr		Provision for Bad Debts Account			Cr
		€			€
31/12/02 Bal c/d		2,250	31/12/02 P&L a/c		2,250
			1/1/03 Bal b/d		2,250

Dr	Profit and Loss Account (31 December 2002)		Cr
	€		€
Provision for bad debts (created)	2,250		

Balance Sheet Extract (31 December 2002)

Current assets	€	€
Debtors	150,000	
Less provision for bad debts	(2,250)	147,750

Example 10.3: *Accounting for an increase in the provision for bad debt*

At 31 December 2003 total debtors for Gibson Retailing amounted to €200,000. During the year some debtors amounting to €10,000 were written off as bad, but this was not accounted for and their balances are included in the total debtors figure of €200,000. At 31 December 2003 management decided to maintain the provision for bad debts at the level of 1.5 per cent of debtors. Prepare the relevant accounts showing extracts from the balance sheet and profit and loss account for 2003.

Approach

Dr	Total Debtors Account			Cr
	€			€
31/12/03 Total debtor balances	200,000		Bad debts a/c	10,000
		31/12/03	Bal c/d	190,000
	200,000			200,000

Dr	Bad Debts Account		Cr
	€		€
31/12/03 Debtors	10,000	31/12/03 P&L a/c	10,000

Dr	Provision for Bad Debts Account		Cr
	€		€
		1/1/03 Bal b/d	2,250
31/12/03 Bal c/d (1.5% of €190,000) 2,850		31/12/03 P&L a/c	600
	2,850		2,850

Explanation

	€
New provision	2,850
Old provision	2,250
Difference therefore	600 increase required

Profit and Loss Account (31 December 2003)

	€		€
Bad debts (written off)	10,000		
Provision for bad debts (increase)	600		

Balance Sheet Extract (31 December 2003)

Current assets	€	€
Debtors	190,000	
Less provision for bad debts	(2,850)	187,150

Notes

❑ In the above example we had to reduce the debtor balance by the debts written off as bad before calculating a new provision for bad debts. Thus the provision for bad debts is based on 1.5 per cent of the total debtors after bad debts are written off.

❑ The new provision for bad debts amounts to €2,850. Management feel that a more realistic value for debtors in the balance sheet would be (€190,000 – €2,850) €187,150. It is important to remember that we already created a provision last year amounting to €2,250. In 2002 we already reduced profit by €2,250 and correspondingly debtors by €2,250. In 2003 although we reduce debtors by €2,850 we only need to reduce profit by the amount of the increase in the provision of €600. Thus only the increase in provision for bad debts is charged to profit. However, in the balance sheet we always deduct the full amount from debtors to show debtors at their realisable amount.

If there is a decrease in the provision for bad debts, then the profit and loss account is credited (add to gross profit) with the amount of the decrease and debtors in the balance sheet is reduced by the amount of the new provision.

Example 10.4: *Accounting for a decrease in the provision for bad debts*

At 31 December 2004 the total trade debtors for Gibson Retailing amounted to €170,000. Management wish to maintain the provision for bad debts to the amount of 1.5 per cent of debtors. Prepare the relevant accounts showing extracts from the balance sheet and profit and loss account for 2004.

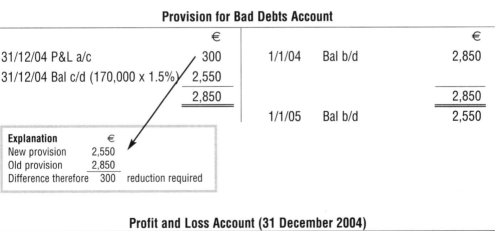

Provision for Bad Debts Account

	€			€
31/12/04 P&L a/c	300	1/1/04	Bal b/d	2,850
31/12/04 Bal c/d (170,000 x 1.5%)	2,550			
	2,850			2,850
		1/1/05	Bal b/d	2,550

Explanation	€
New provision	2,550
Old provision	2,850
Difference therefore	300 reduction required

Profit and Loss Account (31 December 2004)

	€		€
		Provision for bad debts (reduced)	300

Balance Sheet Extract (31 December 2004)

Current assets	€	€
Debtors	170,000	
Less provision for bad debts	(2,550)	167,450

Provisions for bad debts can be either general, as in the examples above where an agreed percentage of debtors was provided for, or specific. A specific provision occurs when a provision is made for non-payment of a specific account(s). This could occur if a customer was identified as being likely to go into receivership or cease business without clearing outstanding debts. The full amount likely to be 'lost' should be provided for by crediting the provision for bad debts account and debiting the profit and loss account.

Provision for Discounts

Often a business will offer customers the option of a discount for early payment. Goods may be sold with 30 days before payment is due, but if the customer pays within say 10 days, a discount is granted. For businesses offering discounts for early payment, it is likely that some of the debtors at the end of a period will receive a discount for early payment. Following the prudence concept, a provision for discount should be provided for. The accounting treatment is similar to that for bad debts.

Example 10.5: *Accounting for a provision for discount*

The accounts of Electrical Sales Ltd are being finalised for the year ended 31 December 2004. Outstanding debtors total €100,000. The provision for bad debts account currently has a balance of €5,500. Management wish to maintain the provision for bad debts at 5 per cent of debtors and wish to introduce a provision for discount of 1 per cent.

Provision for Bad Debts Account

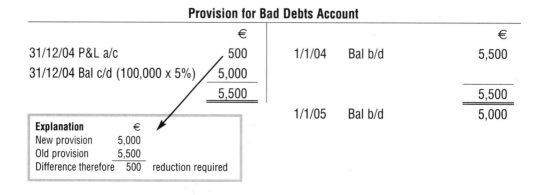

	€			€
31/12/04 P&L a/c	500	1/1/04	Bal b/d	5,500
31/12/04 Bal c/d (100,000 x 5%)	5,000			
	5,500			5,500
		1/1/05	Bal b/d	5,000

Explanation	€	
New provision	5,000	
Old provision	5,500	
Difference therefore	500	reduction required

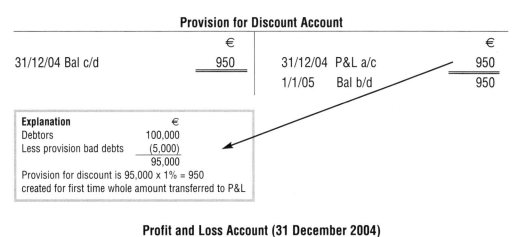

Provision for Discount Account

	€			€
31/12/04 Bal c/d	950	31/12/04	P&L a/c	950
		1/1/05	Bal b/d	950

Explanation

	€
Debtors	100,000
Less provision bad debts	(5,000)
	95,000

Provision for discount is 95,000 x 1% = 950
created for first time whole amount transferred to P&L

Profit and Loss Account (31 December 2004)

	€		€
Provision for discount (created)	950	Provision for bad debts (reduced)	500

Balance Sheet Extract (31 December 2004)

Current assets	€	€
Debtors	100,000	
Less provision for bad debts	(5,000)	
Less provision for discount	(950)	94,050

As can be seen from the above example the provision for discounts is calculated based on the debtors figure, net of the provision for bad debts, and both provisions are deducted from debtors in the balance sheet.

Accruals and Prepayments

Special adjustments known as accruals and prepayments are necessary at the end of a period to ensure the financial statements comply with the accruals concept.

The key points relating to the accruals concept are:

1. When calculating net profit, expenses should be matched against related revenues. In other words, expenses should be matched on a time basis.
2. Net profit is the difference between revenues earned (not necessarily received) and expenses charged (not necessarily paid). Expenses in the profit and loss account should represent the total benefit derived from the service during the year, not just the amount that was paid for.

If some expenses have not been billed for (invoiced) prior to the accounting year-end, the organisation should estimate the amount outstanding for the year and put a special adjustment, known as an accrual, in the accounts to comply with the accruals concept. If part of an expense already paid includes some amount relating to a future period, an adjustment known as a prepayment should be made.

Accrued expenses

An accrued expense represents a cost unaccounted for by a business for services rendered and is unpaid by the accounting period end. For example, a business' accounting year-end is 31 December and at that date it has not been billed for electricity for November and December. The electricity bill will be received and paid in January. For a business, this is a service that has been used during the accounting period and is unaccounted for at the year-end and hence an adjustment should be made to take account of the amount relating to the current year not yet paid. The adjustment is both an expense and a liability at the year-end.

When calculating the profit for the year, we include the expenses charged or services rendered during the year irrespective of whether they have been paid. We would include as expenses in the profit and loss account any electricity used up irrespective of whether we paid for it. Any unpaid element for which service has been rendered we show as a current liability (called accruals) in the balance sheet.

Example 10.6: *Accounting for an accrual*

Video Express pays its telephone bill every two months in the middle of the third month. The accounting year-end is 31 December. The following telephone bills were received relating to the year 2002 and the dates they are paid:

Bill period	Amount paid	Date paid
	€	
Jan/Feb	700	15/3/02
March/April	600	15/5/02
May/June	500	15/7/02
July/Aug	200	15/9/02
Sept/Oct	500	15/11/02
Nov/Dec	600	**15/1/03**
	3,100	

Show how the telephone account, profit and loss account and balance sheet are affected by the accrual.

Approach

The amount charged to the company and used in the accounting period is €3,100 but the amount paid by 31 December 2002 is only €2,500. There is an accrual of €600. In accounting for this we charge €3,100 as an expense to the profit and loss account as the amount of services charged to us for the year. We also show the €600 as a current liability that will be paid shortly in the new accounting year. The telephone account would look as follows:

Telephone Account 2002

		€			€
15 Mar	Bank	700			
15 May	Bank	600			
15 July	Bank	500			
15 Sept	Bank	200	31 Dec	P&L a/c	3,100
15 Nov	Bank	500			
31 Dec	Bal c/d	600			
		3,100			3,100
			1 Jan	Bal b/d	600

Note: The closing balance is a credit balance and thus comes down on the credit side representing a liability.

Profit and Loss Account for the Year 2002

Expenses	€		€
Telephone	3,100		

Balance Sheet Extract

Current liabilities	€
Accruals	600

Should the charge for telephone in 2003 amount to €3,600 and the bi-monthly payments amount to €600 on 15 January, €900 on 15 March, €700 on 15 May, €400 on 15 July, €500 on 15 September and €600 on 15 November, the telephone account would look as follows:

Telephone Account 2003

		€			€
15 Jan	Bank	600	1 Jan	Bal b/d	600
15 Mar	Bank	900			
15 May	Bank	700			
15 July	Bank	400			
15 Sept	Bank	500	31 Dec	P&L a/c	3,600
15 Nov	Bank	600			
31 Dec	Bal c/d	500			
		4,200			4,200
			1 Jan	Bal b/d	500

Notes

1. The first payment represents the amount charged for November/December 2002. Although this is paid in 2003 it has already been charged to the profit and loss account in 2002.
2. The company owes €500 for telephone at the year-end and this will be recorded as a current liability in the balance sheet.

Prepaid expenses

A prepayment is effectively an amount paid during the accounting period for a service which has not been provided by the accounting year-end. For example, a business' accounting year-end is 31 December and annual insurance was taken out on 1 November. At the year-end (31 December) the business will have paid ten months' insurance in advance to the end of the following October. This is a service which is paid for but not yet received at the year-end and an adjustment should be made to take account of this payment relating to a future period.

Example 10.7: *Accounting for a prepayment*

Shop Local, a retail outlet, has decided to rent an adjoining unit. An agreement is reached to pay €3,000 a quarter, payable in advance commencing on 1 May. The business' year-end is 31 December. The following are the details of rent charged and paid during the year:

Bill period	Amount paid	Date paid
	€	
May, June, July	3,000	01/05/03
Aug, Sept, Oct	3,000	01/08/03
Nov, Dec, Jan	3,000	01/11/03

Show how the rent payable account, profit and loss account and balance sheet are affected by the prepayment.

Approach

Rent is €3,000 per quarter or €1,000 per month. As the rent commenced on 1 May, Shop Local got eight months' benefit from the unit in 2003. The amount paid by the company at the end of 2003 amounts to €9,000, but €1,000 of this relates to January in the next accounting year. There is a prepayment of €1,000. In accounting for this, we charge as an expense to the profit and loss account €8,000 as the amount of rent charged to us for the year ended 31 December 2003. However, €9,000 has been credited from the bank account. Thus we also show as a current asset the €1,000 prepaid as at 31 December 2003 (the landlord owes the business €1,000).

The relevant accounts are as follows:

Rent Account 2003

		€			€
1 May	Bank	3,000			
1 Aug	Bank	3,000	31 Dec	P&L a/c	8,000
1 Nov	Bank	3,000	31 Dec	Bal c/d	1,000
		9,000			9,000
1 Jan	Bal b/d	1,000			

Note: The closing balance is a debit balance and thus comes down on the debit side representing an asset.

Profit and Loss Account for the Year 2003

Expenses	€		€
Rent	8,000		

Balance Sheet Extract

Current asset	€
Prepayment	1,000

If the rent is paid on time each quarter in 2004, the rent payable account would look as follows:

Rent Payable Account 2004

		€			€
1 Jan	Bal b/d	1,000			
1 Feb	Bank	3,000	31 Dec	P&L a/c	12,000
1 May	Bank	3,000			
1 Aug	Bank	3,000			
1 Nov	Bank	3,000	31 Dec	Bal c/d	1,000
		13,000			13,000
1 Jan 05	Bal b/d	1,000			

Accrued and prepaid revenue

Just as accruals and prepayments relate to expenses, they can also relate to revenues receivable by the business. For example, sales revenue not yet received (accrual) is reflected in the trading account as credit sales and in the balance sheet as debtors. Sometimes a business may have other forms of revenue, such as rent receivable if they choose to rent out excess space.

Example 10.8: *Accounting for an accrued/prepaid revenue*

The Break-Away Hotel rents out part of its premises to a newsagent/convenience shop for which it charges an annual rent of €30,000 paid quarterly in advance. The business' year-end is 31 December and the following are the details of rent charged and paid during the year:

Bill period	Amount due	Amount received	Date paid
	€	€	
Jan/Feb/March	7,500	7,500	01/01/02
April/May/June	7,500	7,500	01/04/02
July/Aug/Sept	7,500	7,500	01/07/02
Oct/Nov/Dec	7,500	9,500	01/10/02
	30,000	32,000	

Show how the rent receivable account, profit and loss account and balance sheet are affected by the prepayment.

Approach

The amount the company charged its tenant in the accounting period is €30,000 but the amount received by 31 December 2002 is €32,000. There is a prepayment of €2,000. In accounting for this, we add to gross profit €30,000 as the amount of rent earned for the year. However, €32,000 has been debited to the bank account as the tenant has overpaid his rent account. In this case we also show as a current liability the €2,000 prepaid by the tenant at 31 December 2002. In other words, we owe the tenant €2,000 at 31 December 2002.

The relevant accounts are as follows:

Rent Receivable Account

	€			€
31 Dec P&L a/c	30,000	1 Jan	Bank	7,500
		1 Apr	Bank	7,500
		1 July	Bank	7,500
31 Dec Bal c/d	2,000	1 Oct	Bank	9,500
	32,000			32,000
		1 Jan	Bal b/d	2,000

Note: The closing balance is a credit balance and thus comes down on the credit side representing a liability for the business.

Profit and Loss Account for the Year 2002

	€		€
Expenses		Gross Profit	
		Rent receivable	30,000

Balance Sheet Extract

Current liability	€
Rent receivable prepayment	2,000

Summary

From this chapter we can see how the accruals and prudence concepts really influence the calculation of profit and the balance sheet of a business. The main information points from this chapter are as follows:

❑ The prudence concept requires that in accounting for transactions, businesses should never anticipate profits and should provide for all possible losses if they are probable and measurable. The objective of the prudence concept is to show assets, profit and capital at realistic levels.

❑ A bad debt occurs when a debtor fails to pay what is owed and the business believes they will never receive these monies. This is a loss to the business and must be treated as an expense in the profit and loss account.

❑ Provision for bad debts is where a business tries to show its debtors at realistic (collectable) levels and thus management should estimate the amount of debts that could 'go bad' and provide for this now.

❑ An accrual represents monies owed by a business for services rendered to it which remain unpaid by the accounting period end. In accounting for accruals, the profit and loss account is debited with the full charge relating to the period (including the accrual) and the accrual is shown in the balance sheet at the period end under current liabilities.

❑ A prepaid expense is effectively an amount paid during the accounting period for a service which will be provided in the next accounting period. In accounting for prepayments, although the amount is paid, it should not appear in the profit and loss account as an expense as it does not relate to the accounting period. The prepayment is shown in the balance sheet as a current asset.

❑ Accruals and prepayments also apply to 'other income' generated by a business. Accruals relating to income are shown as current assets whereas prepayments are shown as a current liability in the balance sheet.

Question 10.1

A provision for bad debts has been maintained at a level of 5% of debtors. As the marketing manager has proposed introducing a cash discount to customers, the finance manager is considering introducing a provision for discount on debtors.

(a) Why would a provision be carried in the accounts?
(b) Explain the term 'provision for bad debts'.
(c) If end of year debtors amounted to €320,000, what provision for bad debts should be carried?
(d) If the previous year's provision for bad debts had amounted to €16,340 and using the figures calculated in '3.' above, show the effects on the profit and loss account.
(e) If the finance manager introduced a provision for discount of 2.5%, what provision should be carried in the accounts and what effect would it have on the profit and loss account?
(f) Show the balance sheet extract covering debtors and both provisions.

Question 10.2

A business started trading on 1 January 2002. During the year to 31 December 2002 the business wrote off bad debts as follows:

	Amount
	€
F. Flanagan	500
G. Dunne	236
A. Kearns	425
C. White	125
	1,286

Debtors at the year-end amounted to €56,750 and management decided to make a provision for bad debts amounting to 3% of the closing debtors figure.

Required

(a) The bad debts account.
(b) The provision for bad debts account.
(c) Relevant extracts from the profit and loss account and balance sheet.

Question 10.3

The following data relates to the debtors and provision policy of a company, Dublin DIY Providers, for five years:

2001   Debtors on 31 December 2001 amounted to €150,000. Management wish to create a provision for bad debts of 5% of debtors at the end of year.

2002   Bad debts during the year amounted to €35,000. During the year, €5,000 previously written off was paid. Debtors on 31 December 2002 amounted to €160,000 after bad debts were written off. Provision is to be maintained at 5% of debtors.

2003   During the year bad debts were written off amounting to €47,000. Debtors on 31 December 2003 amounted to €168,000 after the above debts were written off. It was decided to write off additional bad debts of €8,000. Provision is to be maintained at 5% of debtors.

2004   Bad debts during the year amounted to €34,000. Debtors on 31 December 2004 amounted to €158,000 after the above debts were written off. As well as the 5% provision for bad debts, management plan on introducing a provision for discount on debtors of 3%.

2005   Bad debts during the year amounted to €25,000. Debtors on 31 December 2005 amounted to €170,000 after the above adjustments. Both provisions are to be maintained.

Show for each year from 2001 to 2005 the affects of the above on:

(a) Profit and loss account.
(b) Balance sheet.

Question 10.4

PBD Ltd prepares annual accounts on the 31 December each year. The opening balance on the provision for bad debts was €14,000 at 1 January 2001. Bad debts written off during the year amounted to €7,750. Debtors at 31 December 2003 stood at €240,000. Provision for bad debts is to be maintained at 5% of debtors at the end of year. As the company introduced a discount for early payment during 2003, management have decided to provide a new provision for discount, at a level of 3% of debtors at the end of year.

Debtors at 31 December 2004 were €270,000. Bad debts written off during the year amounted to €4,500. Management has decided to write off a further €2,500 as bad at 31 December 2004. One customer's account has been identified as being particularly high risk and it has been decided to make a specific provision of €6,000 against it. A general provision of 5% of remaining debtors is to be carried. Provision for discount on debtors is to be maintained at 3%.

Prepare the following accounts for the years ended 31 December 2003 and 2004:

(a) Bad debts account.
(b) Provision for bad debts account.
(c) Provision for discount on debtors account.
(d) Relevant extracts from the balance sheets as at the year-end dates.

Question 10.5

The financial year-end of E. Mangan is 31 December 2005. For each of the following expense items you are required to prepare the ledger accounts showing the amount to be charged to the profit and loss account and any amounts to be transferred to the balance sheet at 31 December 2005:

1. Insurance: paid €1,560 in June. The profit and loss charge for the year is €1,200.
2. Rent: paid rent in January €300, April €300, July €300 and November €800. The annual charge for rent is €1,200.
3. Motor expenses: paid during the year €560 and at the end of the year owed €100.
4. General expenses: paid during the year €700 and owed at the year-end €50.
5. Rental income: Mangan sub-lets part of his premises at an annual rent of €1,000. During the year he received four payments in March, June, September and December of €300 each.

CHAPTER 11

Preparing Final Accounts, Including Period End Adjustments

Learning Outcomes

By the end of this chapter you will be able to:

❑ Prepare the final accounts of a single owner organisation, taking into account adjustments such as depreciation, bad debts and bad debt provisions, accruals and prepayment adjustments.
❑ Be aware of how the calculation of profit requires management to estimate a number of figures and that this can be a subjective process.

Introduction

This chapter focuses on the preparation of the final accounts of a business. It brings together all the learning points covered in the previous chapters, including capital and revenue distinctions, depreciation, the need for provisions, accruals and prepayments and applies them in the preparation of the final accounts of a single owner organisation. The chapter concentrates on the final accounts of a sole trader organisation, as it is the most simplistic form of business organisation. Although there are no official statistics, it is estimated that the sole trader organisation is the most common type within the hospitality, tourism and retail sectors. An illustration of the final accounts is provided and explained followed by a comprehensive example.

The Final Accounts (with adjustments)

The final accounts below are broadly similar to those outlined in Chapter 6 'Preparing Financial Statements – An Introduction'. The key difference is that the adjustments for depreciation, provision for bad debts, accruals and prepayments are now applied to the final accounts. The illustration outlined below shows the accounts of a sole trader.

Illustration 11.1: *Final accounts with adjustments*

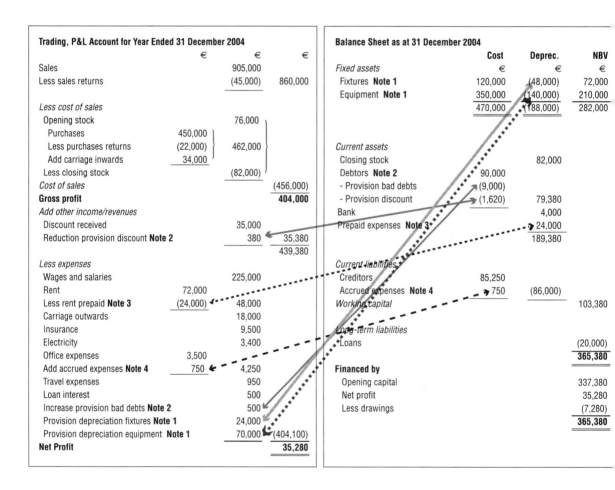

Note 1: Provision for depreciation

Provision for depreciation is charged in the profit and loss account each year and added to the accumulated depreciation in the balance sheet. In the case of fixtures, a rate of 20 per cent per annum straight line was applied. The profit and loss entry appears under the expenses category and the €24,000 amount is simply 20 per cent of the original cost of €120,000. The accumulated (total) depreciation figure appearing in the balance sheet of €48,000 represents two years' depreciation. Presumably the fixtures are two years old. The same applies to depreciation on equipment. The 'net book value' figure is the original cost less the accumulated depreciation. *Revise the depreciation section in Chapter 9 if you need further explanation.*

Note 2: Provision for bad debts and discount

The provision for bad debts must be reassessed while preparing the final accounts. In this illustration the provision for bad debts was adjusted to €9,000. This indicates that the provision for bad debts is maintained in this organisation at 10 per cent of debtors. Debtors in the balance sheet amount to €90,000 and the new provision is carried in the balance sheet at €9,000. The figure entered in the profit and loss account is the amount by which the provision increased or decreased. In this case the provision was increased by €500 and is shown in the expenses section.

The provision for discount (if carried) must also be reassessed while preparing the final accounts. In this illustration the provision for discount was adjusted to €1,620. The calculation for this would have been 2 per cent of debtors once the provision for bad debts was deducted. The new provision of €1,620 is carried in the balance sheet. The profit and loss account contains the amount by which the provision increased or decreased. In this case the provision was reduced by €380 and is shown in the other income/revenues section.

Note 3: Prepaid expenses

Prepaid expenses reflect expenditure that was accounted for this year but relates to a future year. In this illustration €24,000 of the €72,000 cost of rent was prepaid. The €24,000 is reduced from the rent expenditure in the profit and loss account and appears as a current asset in the balance sheet.

Note 4: Accrued expenses

Accrued expenses relate to expenditure that was outstanding at end of the accounting period for which the business received a benefit during the accounts period. In this illustration €750 of office expenses was outstanding and had not been accounted for at the end of the accounting year. The €750 is added to office expenses in the profit and loss account and appears as a current liability in the balance sheet

A Comprehensive Example

The following example takes into account all the learning points covered to date and applies them to the preparation of the trading, profit and loss account and balance sheet.

Example 11.1: *Final accounts with adjustments*

Joseph Healy operates a sole trader business retailing goods to customers via a mail order catalogue. The business delivers goods directly to the customer's door step and offers a number of valued customers credit. From the following trial balance you are required to prepare the trading, profit and loss account for the business of Joseph Healy for the year ended 30 June 2004 and a balance sheet at that date.

Trial Balance as at 30 June 2004

	Dr €	Cr €
Purchases	154,000	
Sales		350,000
Creditors		30,000
Debtors	25,000	
Bad debt	1,200	
Marketing and sales	10,420	
Office expenses	5,600	
Insurance	6,700	
Discounts	900	1,000
Carriage inwards	5,000	
Stock as at 1/7/03	5,000	
Wages and salaries	90,000	
Motor expenses	5,600	
Rates	4,600	
Light and heat	4,678	
Provision for bad debts (1/7/03)		300
Premises	154,000	
Furniture and equipment	60,500	
Depreciation provision furniture and equipment (1/7/03)		4,000
Motor vehicles	40,000	
Depreciation provision vehicles (1/7/03)		3,200
Bank	4,200	
Loan from D. Heavin (to be repaid 2009)		120,000
Drawings	22,500	
Capital		91,398
	599,898	**599,898**

Additional information:

1. Stock was counted and valued at 30 June 2004 at €6,000.
2. Insurance includes €1,000 of cover that relates to the year to 30 June 2005.
3. Bad debts of €1,000 included in debtors in the trial balance is to be written off.
4. Wages owing at 30 June 2004 amounted to €5,000.
5. Provision for bad debts is to be maintained at a level of 3 per cent of debtors after all bad debts are written off.
6. It is the policy of the business to depreciate furniture and equipment at 10 per cent per annum straight-line method and motor vehicles at 20 per cent per annum straight-line method. There is no depreciation on premises.
7. Interest on the loan is charged at €6,000 for the year. This has not been paid by 30 June 2004.

You are required to:

(a) Prepare a trading and profit and loss account for the year to 30 June 2004.
(b) Prepare a balance sheet at that date.

Solution to comprehensive example

Trading, Profit and Loss Account for Year Ended 30 June 2004

	€	€	€
Sales			350,000
Less cost of goods sold			
Opening stock		5,000	
Purchases	154,000		
Carriage Inwards	5,000	159,000	
Closing stock		(6,000)	(158,000)
Gross profit			192,000
Add other income/gains			
Discount received			1,000
Less expenses			
Bad debts **Note 1**	1,200		
Add additional bad debts	1,000	2,200	
Marketing and sales		10,420	
Office expenses		5,600	
Insurance **Note 2**	6,700		
Less prepayment	(1,000)	5,700	
Discount allowed		900	
Wages/salaries **Note 3**	90,000		
Add accrual	5,000	95,000	

Motor expenses		5,600	
Rates		4,600	
Light and heat		4,678	
Provision for bad debts **Note 4**		420	
Depreciation – F. & E. **Note 5**		6,050	
Depreciation – vehicles **Note 5**		8,000	
Loan interest **Note 6**		6,000	(155,168)
Net profit			37,832

Balance Sheet as at 30 June 2004

	Cost	Accumulated depreciation	NBV
	€	€	€
Fixed assets			
Premises	154,000		154,000
Furniture and equipment **Note 5**	60,500	10,050	50,450
Motor vehicles **Note 5**	40,000	11,200	28,800
	254,500	21,250	233,250
Current assets			
Stock		6,000	
Debtors (25,000 - 1,000) **Note 1**	24,000		
Less provision for bad debts **Note 4**	(720)	23,280	
Prepayments **Note 2**		1,000	
Bank		4,200	
		34,480	
Current liabilities			
Creditors	30,000		
Accruals (5,000 + 6,000) **Note 3/6**	11,000	(41,000)	
Net current assets			(6,520)
Long-term liabilities			
Loan			(120,000)
			106,730
Financed by			
Opening capital			91,398
Net profit			37,832
Drawings			(22,500)
			106,730

Note 1: Bad debts

The bad debts in the trial balance of €1,200 have already been recorded and debtors have already been adjusted by this figure. Point 3 in the question tells us that more debts are to be written off as bad amounting to €1,000, increasing the bad debts figure in the profit and loss account to €2,200. The debtors figure in the trial balance has not been adjusted for the extra €1,000 bad debts and so in the balance sheet we deduct €1,000 from debtors.

Note 2: Insurance prepaid

Point 2 in the question tells us that a portion of the insurance paid relates to the *next* accounting period. This should not be charged to the profit and loss account for this year as it relates to next year. Insurance is prepaid and thus we deduct from insurance the amount prepaid and show it as a current asset, as the insurance company owes the business insurance cover relating to next year.

Note 3: Wages and salaries accrued

In point 4 we are told that at the end of the year the business owes €5,000 in respect of wages and salaries. This charge of €5,000 relates to work done within the accounting period and so should be included as part of wages and salaries in the calculation of profit for the year. The figure for wages and salaries in the trial balance represents the amount of wages actually paid out of the bank account. The figure in the profit and loss account should represent the amount of wages charged during the period. This would include the €5,000 unpaid. Because this €5,000 charge is unpaid at the year-end it is included as an accrual in the balance sheet under current liabilities.

Note 4: Provision for bad debts

In the trial balance the provision for bad debts is €300. This tells us that the business in past periods provided for bad debts to the tune of €300 and this has been deducted from net profit in past periods. In point 5 we are told that the provision is to be maintained at 3 per cent of debtors. This figure amounts to €720 (3 per cent of €24,000). Thus there is an increase of €420. In the balance sheet we deduct from debtors €720 to show debtors at a more realistic figure. In the profit and loss account we only charge as an expense the increase in provision of €420, as we have already deducted in past periods the other €300 from profits.

Note 5: The provision for depreciation

Figures in the trial balance relate to depreciation charged to the profit and loss account in previous years. It is the accumulated depreciation charged up to the beginning of this year. In point 6 we are told the business' policy on depreciation and thus we calculate the annual depreciation charge as follows:

— Furniture and equipment 10 per cent straight line. This is 10 per cent multiplied by the cost of the furniture and equipment of €60,500 = €6,050.
— Motor vehicles 20 per cent straight line. This is 20 per cent multiplied by the cost of the vehicles of €40,000 = €8,000.

In the balance sheet we deduct from the cost of the assets the accumulated depreciation on the assets. For furniture and equipment this amounts to (€4,000 + €6,050) €10,050 and for motor vehicles (€3,200 + €8,000) €11,200.

Note 6: Loan interest accrued

The cost of a loan is the interest charged on the loan and this is an expense in the profit and loss account. The interest charged on the loan for the year amounts to €6,000; however, it is unpaid at the year-end. This is an unpaid expense and thus should be included in expenses in the profit and loss account and classified as an accrued expense in the balance sheet under current liabilities.

Profit as an Estimate

At this stage it should be clear that the calculation of profit requires management to estimate certain figures and thus an element of profit is based on management's subjective opinions. Should management be under extreme pressure to show an improved profit figure then the temptation is there to exercise their judgement on certain issues in a very optimistic way to ensure profit is maximised. For example:

❑ Management ignoring the need to provide for bad debts to ensure profit and assets (debtors) are recorded at higher levels.
❑ Management estimating long lives on their assets ensuring a lower depreciation charge in the profit and loss account. Again the result is higher profits and higher asset levels. For example, if a piece of equipment cost a business €100,000 and management decide its estimated life is ten years, then the annual depreciation charge in the profit and loss account is €10,000. However, should management decide on an estimated life of twenty years then the annual depreciation charge

would fall to €5,000. This could significantly improve profits.
- ❏ Sometimes accruals need to be estimated. Again a subjective judgement can be an opportunity to show an improved profit figure.
- ❏ The many subjective decisions in distinguishing between capital and revenue expenditure can result in profit being created.

Even at this stage in accounting it is important to appreciate that profit is, in many respects, an opinion and one should judge a profit figure based on the assumptions that underlie the calculation of that profit.

Summary

In this chapter we have dealt solely with the preparation and presentation of the final accounts of a sole trader organisation bringing together all the learning points covered in the previous chapters, including capital and revenue distinctions, depreciation, provisions, accruals and prepayments. From this section we can see how the accruals and prudence concepts really influence the calculation of profit and the balance sheet of a business. It is also important to be aware of the subjective process involved in estimating depreciation and providing for possible future losses such as bad debts and how this can allow management in some respects to be 'creative' when calculating the monthly or annual profit figure.

Review Questions

Question 11.1

Gary Dunne has been operating as a sole trader for the past ten years. Gary sells power tools both for cash and on credit. From the following trial balance you are required to prepare a trading, profit and loss account for the year ended 31 January 2003 and a balance sheet at that date.

	Dr €	Cr €
Purchases	102,763	
Sales		330,231
Carriage inwards	10,152	
Wages and salaries	78,456	
Motor expenses	12,356	
Rent	59,400	
Rates	12,456	
Insurance	15,000	
Sundry expenses	4,520	
Light and heat	12,564	
Stock as at 1/2/02	10,900	
Drawings	12,300	
Debtors	50,309	
Creditors		36,000
Bank	18,000	
Office furniture	56,000	
Office fittings	40,000	
Equipment	70,120	
Provision for depreciation office furniture		20,000
office fittings		24,000
equipment		35,610
Bad debts	560	
Capital		98,715
8% loan to be repaid 2008		21,300
	565,856	565,856

The following additional information is available at 31 January 2003:

1. Stock counted at 31 January 2003 was valued at €12,000.
2. Wages and salaries accrued at 31 January 2003 amounted to €2,300.
3. Rent prepaid at 31 January 2003 amounted to €4,000.
4. Provide for depreciation on a straight-line basis as follows: office furniture 12.5%, office fittings 10% and equipment 10%.
5. Provide for bad debts amounting to €1,000.

Question 11.2

From the following trial balance of Marc Donald, who operates a heath and fitness centre, you are required to prepare a trading, profit and loss account for the year ended 31 December 2002 and a balance sheet at that date.

	Dr €	Cr €
Wages and salaries	102,763	
Motor expenses	20,000	
Rent	40,152	
Rates	15,689	
Purchases	150,456	
Sales		397,148
Carriage inwards	8,900	
Bad debts	1,200	
Provision for bad debts as at 1/1/02		900
Insurance	15,000	
Marketing and sales expenses	4,520	
Office expenses	5,200	
Sundry expenses	2,900	
Furniture and fittings	85,300	
Plant and equipment	80,309	
Provision for depreciation as at 1/1/02		
Furniture and fittings		42,560
Plant and equipment		35,420
Light and heat	6,879	
Stock as at 1/1/02	15,600	
Drawings	40,000	
Debtors	40,000	
Capital		80,000
7% loan (repayable 2005)		50,000
Cash	1,160	
Creditors		20,000
Bank		10,000
	636,028	636,028

The following additional information is also available as at 31 December 2002:

1. Stock counted at 31 December 2002 was valued at €10,250.
2. Wages and salaries accrued at 31 December 2002 amounted to €10,250.
3. Insurance prepaid amounted to €3,000.
4. Provide for depreciation on a straight-line basis as follows: furniture and fittings 12.5%, plant and equipment 10%.
5. A debtor, F. Gant, who had arranged corporate membership for his staff, has been declared bankrupt and the business has decided to write off the debt as bad amounting to €1,000.
6. The provision for bad debts is to be increased to 5% of debtors.

Question 11.3

The trial balance detailed below was extracted on the 31 August 2003, the financial year-end of a retailing business owned by Robert Casey.

Trial Balance at 31 August 2003

	Dr €'000	Cr €'000
Administration costs	177	
Bank		7
Capital		400
Carriage out	38	
Cost of sales	2,295	
Creditors		168
Debtors	270	
Discount allowed	33	
Discount received		27
Drawings	18	
Equipment (cost €820,000)	520	
Fixtures and fittings (cost €450,000)	210	
Provision for bad debts (1/9/2002)		14
Stock (31/8/2003)	75	
Rent payable	90	
Rent receivable		36
Repairs	18	
Returns in	65	
Sales		3,335
Wages and salaries	178	
	3,987	3,987

Additional information:

1. Equipment is to be depreciated at a rate of 20% per annum straight line.
2. Fixtures and fittings are to be depreciated at a rate of 25% per annum reducing balance.
3. Administration costs due and unpaid at 31 August 2003 amount to €9,000.
4. Rent receivable of €3,000 is due from a tenant and remains unpaid on the 31 August 2003.
5. A provision for bad debts of 5% of year-end debtors is to be maintained and a new provision for discount on debtors of 2% is to be created.

Required

(a) A trading, profit and loss account for year ended 31 August 2003.
(b) A balance sheet as at 31 August 2003.

Question 11.4

The trial balance detailed below was extracted on 30 April 2004, the financial year-end of a business owned by Sam Wilson. Sam is operating a medium-sized frozen food retail and distribution business. In addition to customers visiting the retail outlet, Sam supplies some hotels and restaurants in the area.

Trial Balance at 30 April 2004

	Dr	Cr
	€'000	€'000
Administration costs	118	
Bank		5
Capital		390
Carriage inwards	24	
Carriage outwards	18	
Creditors		112
Debtors	185	
Discount allowed	22	
Discount received		15
Drawings	12	
Equipment (cost €820,000)	350	
Furniture and fittings (cost €450,000)	140	
Provision for bad debts (1/5/2003)		9
Purchases	1,580	
Rent payable	60	
Rent receivable		24
Repairs	12	
Returns in	42	
Returns out		25
Sales		2,320
Stock (1/5/2003)	77	
Utility costs	15	
Vehicles (cost €320,000)	120	
Wages and salaries	125	
	2,900	2,900

Additional information:

1. Stocks at the close of business on 30 April 2004 were valued at €75,000.
2. No adjustment has been made for goods of €4,000 taken by Sam for his own personal use.

3. Equipment is to be depreciated at a rate of 10% per annum straight line.
4. Furniture and fittings are to be depreciated at a rate of 30% per annum reducing balance.
5. Vehicles are to be depreciated at a rate of 25% per annum straight line.
6. Rent receivable of €3,000 is due from a tenant and remains unpaid on 30 April 2004.
7. Administration costs due and unpaid at 30 April 2004 amount to €9,000.
8. Utilities costs due and unpaid at 30 April 2004 amount to €1,000.
9. Repair costs include the sum of €2,000 relating to repairs carried out on Sam's private property.
10. Rent payable by Sam has been prepaid on 30 April 2004 by €8,000.
11. Bad debts of €10,000 is to be written off.
12. A provision for bad debts of 5% of year-end debtors is to be maintained and a new provision for discount on debtors of 2% is to be created.

Required

(a) The trading, profit and loss account for year ended 30 April 2004.
(b) The balance sheet as at 30 April 2004.

CHAPTER 12

The Legal Forms of Organisation

Learning Outcomes

By the end of this chapter you will be able to:

❑ Compare and contrast the characteristics of the various legal forms of business organisations.
❑ Outline the advantages and disadvantages of each form of legal organisation.
❑ List and explain the procedures and requirements associated with the different legal forms of business organisations.
❑ Outline the legal and administrative requirements of company status.

Introduction

The legal form of organisation is one of the first decisions an entrepreneur must take. The type of legal organisation assumed by a business is normally a function of the amount of finance required and the size of the business. Once established, the legal form of organisation affects a business in the following ways:

❑ The taxation requirements of a business.
❑ The legal requirements.
❑ The audit and financial requirements.
❑ The sources of finance available.

The types of legal organisation available to an organisation are:

1. Sole proprietorships.
2. Partnerships.
3. Companies.
4. Not for profit organisations.

In Chapter 1 the different legal forms of organisation were introduced. This chapter will now go into greater detail on this area, focusing on the characteristics, advantages and disadvantages of each.

Sole Trader Organisations

The sole trader legal form of organisation comes into being when an individual sets up in business and starts to trade in their own name. The individual is the sole owner of the business. A sole trader can also register a business name such as John Ryan trading as Ryan & Sons. The sole trader option is often adopted by businesses in the hospitality and services area. There are also many small retail outlets operating as sole traders.

The advantages of being a sole trader

❑ The simplicity and ease with which one can set up in business.
❑ The lack of legal controls and constraints. However, sole traders do have a legal requirement under tax law (in particular, self-assessment, VAT and PAYE/PRSI regulations) to keep proper books and records for inspection by the Revenue Commissioners.
❑ Privacy, as the accounts of sole proprietorships are not required to be published unlike the accounts of companies.

The disadvantages of being a sole trader

❑ A sole trader is not protected by limited liability. Limited liability means that if the business fails, the only loss the owners incur is the amount that was invested in the business. In other words, a sole trader has unlimited liability and is liable personally for all the debts of the business and personal assets may be lost.
❑ Sourcing finance can be more difficult with only one owner.
❑ The rates of tax on profits for sole traders are higher than for companies, as profits are taxed under income tax rules whereas for companies, profits are taxed according to corporation tax rules.

Partnerships

A partnership can be described as an association of persons carrying on business in common with a view to making a profit. The agreement between the persons can be in a verbal or written format.

Most partnership agreements tend to be written and partners usually draft a 'Deed of Partnership'. The Deed of Partnership would normally contain the following information:

- The name of the partnership.
- The date the partnership commenced.
- The planned duration of the partnership.
- The rules governing the retirement or admittance of partners.
- The capital subscribed and rules regarding the distribution of profits.
- Cheque signing regulations.

There are two types of partnership in Ireland: a general partnership, which is regulated through the Partnership Act of 1890, and a limited partnership, regulated through the Limited Partnerships Act of 1907. In a general partnership each partner contributes an agreed amount of capital and is an agent of the partnership and thus has full liability for all the debts of the partnership. General partnerships are quite common, especially amongst professional firms such as solicitors and accountants in Ireland. Under the terms of the Limited Partnership Act of 1907 a limited partnership must consist of at least one general partner who shall be liable for all the debts and obligations of the partnership and at least one limited partner. A limited partner is a partner who shall not be liable for the debts and obligations of the partnership beyond the amount they contribute. Thus their liability is limited to what they have invested in the business. Limited partners may not take an active role in the running of the business. The number of limited partnerships registered in Ireland is small by comparison to general partnerships.

The advantages of partnerships

- Simplicity and ease with which one can set up in business.
- The general lack of legal controls and restrictions compared to limited liability companies.
- Partners often have a blend of skills and experience, which can help to create a more effective organisation.

❑   Partnerships have greater access to capital due to the fact that there is a greater pooling of resources and borrowing capacity.
❑   Privacy, as the accounts of partnerships are not required to be published to the general public but are required for tax purposes.

The disadvantages of partnerships (in addition to sole proprietorship disadvantages)

❑   Partnerships can be unstable and break up over relatively minor issues.
❑   As in sole traders, partnerships are not protected by limited liability.
❑   Each partnership is liable for the debts of the partnership: 'joint and several' liability.
❑   The life of the partnership can be limited by agreement or by the life of the partners.
❑   Profits are taxed at income tax rates.

'The figures are between myself, God and the Revenue Commissioners'

Source: *The Irish Times*, October 2004

Privacy is a major factor in influencing the decision on whether to incorporate or not. In Ireland the advantages of limited liability and the current tax rates ensure many businesses incorporate. At present the tax on company profits is 12.5 per cent, whereas for sole proprietorships and partnerships it can go as high as 42 per cent. This in itself is reason enough for many businesses to incorporate. However, many sole traders/partnerships stay as they are and one of the main advantages they give is privacy. The quote above from *The Irish Times* was made by Fionn MacCumhaill, a hotelier, who owns 7 hotels (300 beds) in Dublin and operates within a partnership legal form of organisation

Limited Liability Companies

A company is a corporate body which has a legal existence quite separate from the owners (shareholders). Limited liability companies can have a perpetual life since ownership is represented by shares that are transferable. This ensures that companies can exist beyond the lives of their original owners. This is unlike sole traders or partnerships, where the business ceases to exist on the death of the owners or partners. Many Irish companies have been in existence for over 100 years. Thus a company is a business entity created by law that is capable of entering into contracts, incurring liabilities and carrying out business. The liability of its owners is limited to what they have invested and what they owe the company.

Formation of a company

The formation of a limited company is handled by solicitors who draft the necessary legal documents that form its make-up. These documents are then registered with the companies registrar whereupon a certificate of incorporation is issued to the company. The company is now registered and can commence trading.

Did You Know?

According to estimates from the Revenue Commissioners the number of self-employed persons (sole proprietorship and partnerships) amounts to 215,000. The number of company returns made in 2002 amounted to 86,570. The Revenue Commissioners do not distinguish between sole traders and partnerships from a tax perspective as they view each partner in a partnership as self-employed.

The main legal documents required are:

- ❑ Memorandum of association.
- ❑ Articles of association.
- ❑ Statement of nominal share capital.
- ❑ Statutory declaration of compliance with all the requirements of the relevant companies acts.
- ❑ List of persons who have consented to be directors.
- ❑ Form of consent to act as directors from those who have agreed to be directors.

The first two documents are the main documents representing the company. In many respects they represent the 'body and soul' of the company.

- ❑ **Memorandum of association**: This document governs the relationship between the company and the external environment. It is in effect the company's constitution. It sets out for the public the basic facts relating to the company. It must include data such as:

- Company name (with Ltd as the last word in the title).
- Location of registered office.
- The objectives of the company.
- A limited liability clause.
- The authorised share capital of the business.
- The signatures of subscribers (usually the directors) with their addresses and the number of shares they are taking in the company.

❑ **Articles of association**: The articles govern the internal workings of the company. They form a contract between the company and the shareholders, defining their respective rights and duties. In effect they are a set of rules and regulations defining the rights, responsibilities and powers of shareholders and directors. The articles would deal with issues such as the rights attached to shares, procedures at shareholders' meetings, appointment/retirement and powers of directors. A company may draw up its own articles or it may use a model set of articles set out in table A of the Companies Act 1963. Articles of association can be changed from time to time by a special resolution of the shareholders, i.e. with the approval of 75 per cent of those voting.

Types of company

There are four types of company one can choose from. The most popular are private companies, of which there are approximately 130,000 in Ireland.

Private limited companies
A private limited company is a company that has between two and fifty shareholders that have restrictions on the transfer of their share, but are protected by limited liability.

Key characteristics are:

1. Between two and fifty shareholders (minimum of two).
2. Business can commence immediately on incorporation.
3. The right of transfer of shares is restricted as there is no market in which to actively trade the shares.
4. The company is prohibited from inviting the public to subscribe for its shares or debentures.
5. Accounts must be audited each year. Companies with annual sales of less than €1,500,000 are exempt from this requirement to have an audit. Many small companies avail of this exemption as it translates directly into a cost saving. However, some small companies still commission an audit, as it can provide some protection against fraud, and financial institutions require audited accounts in

assessing finance applications. In a survey by MORI (1999) on behalf of the ACCA a majority of lending bankers said that they were less likely to offer loans to companies who refused to commission an audit.

6. All companies must file their annual accounts whether audited or not with the companies registrar. This ensures that a company is less private than a sole trader or partnership. Small and medium sized companies can avail of an exemption to file abridged accounts. These accounts are for public consumption and can be viewed at the companies registration office or through an on-line search at http://www.cro.ie.

7. Generally private companies are formed to ensure their owners benefit from limited liability.

Public limited companies (Plc)

A public limited company is a company that has a minimum of seven shareholders that are protected by limited liability. Shares are freely transferable as they can be traded publicly and are quoted on a stock exchange.

Key characteristics are:

1. A minimum of seven shareholders is required for incorporation. There is no maximum limit.

2. Shares are freely transferable. In other words, a market exists to buy and sell the shares.

3. Shares and debentures of Plcs may be quoted on the stock exchange (subject to permission by the stock exchange authorities).

4. Though incorporated, a Plc cannot commence business until the registrar of companies issues a Trading Certificate to commence business. This cannot happen until €38,092 of share capital has been subscribed.

5. Accounts must be audited each year and a copy filed with the companies registration office (CRO) where they are available for public inspection.

6. Generally public companies are significantly larger than private (although this is not always the case) and they tend to have more of an international dimension.

7. Generally public companies are formed to raise capital from the public.

It is important to understand the difference between a private and public company. Table 12.1 outlines the key differences of both types of company.

Table 12.1: *Private versus public comparison*

	Private	Public
	Ltd	*Plc*
Number of shareholders	2–50	Minimum of 7
Right of transfer	Limited	Not restricted
Public subscription	Prohibited	Not prohibited
Level of information required to be made available to the public	Limited	Very detailed
Stock exchange	Not quoted	May be quoted

Companies limited by guarantee

This is a company where the members usually do not provide money/capital on its formation but guarantee to pay its debts up to a certain limit in the event that the company goes into liquidation. Usually the sum is a nominal amount. This method of incorporation is used by non-profit making organisations such as clubs, charities and societies.

Unlimited companies

An unlimited company is one which ensures its members can be personally liable for the debts and liabilities of the business. This liability can be totally unlimited or limited to a certain figure. Although this is a big disadvantage, unlimited companies have the following advantages:

1. The right to reduce issued capital without court permission.
2. Exemption from filing accounts (privacy advantage).

Did You Know?

The following numbers of companies were registered with the Companies Registration Office (CRO) in 2003:

Private limited companies	130,303
Public limited companies	1,021
Unlimited companies	2,870
Companies limited by guarantee	10,688

Source: Companies Report 2003

Advantages of limited liability company status

1. The investor's liability is limited. However, the Companies Act 1990 has somewhat tightened up this area. Now there *will* be personal liability for all or part of a company's debts if a director is a party to carrying on the business of the company in a fraudulent or reckless manner, and they can become disqualified from becoming a director of another company for five years. Civil and criminal liability is imposed on directors where a company fails to keep proper books of account which the court considers has contributed to the company's inability to pay all of its debts.
2. Companies tend to have greater access to capital.
3. The business continues despite the death or incapacity of the investors.
4. Profits are taxed at the corporation tax rate of 12.5 per cent (2004). This is nearly incentive enough for businesses to incorporate as the profits of sole traders and partnerships are taxed at income tax rates of up to 42 per cent (2004).

Disadvantages of limited liability company status

1. Limited companies are more regulated than either partnerships or sole traders.
2. It is more difficult to withdraw money from a company for directors than it is for a sole trader or partnership. Generally, drawing money from a company has to be by way of a salary or bonus which will be subject to PAYE. With a sole trader/partnership you can have drawings throughout the year and pay the tax later. Shareholders not directly employed in a company can only receive moneys through dividends.
3. Once incorporated, companies must file their accounts with the companies registrar and hence there is a lack of privacy compared to sole proprietorship and partnership legal forms of organisation.

Did You Know?

❑ During 2003 nearly 14,800 companies were struck off the companies registrar for failing to file company returns for 2001 in the Republic of Ireland.
❑ During 2003 there were 40 instances of auditor reports highlighting the failure of companies to 'keep proper books of accounts'.
❑ In 2003 there was a three-fold increase in the number of reports and complaints of corporate misconduct received by the office of corporate enforcement within the CRO.
❑ A total of 5 persons were disqualified from acting as directors of

> companies for 5 years due to being convicted on an indictment for an offence in relation to the company, or acts of fraud and dishonesty under section 160 of the Companies Act 1990.
> ❑ In 2003 there were a total of 1,242 liquidations notified to CRO. By the end of 2003 there were 341 companies in receivership.
>
> Source: Companies Report 2003

Legal requirements for limited companies

The main legal requirements are contained in the Companies Acts 1963, the Companies (Amendment) Act 1983, the Companies (Amendment) Act 1986 (which introduced the EC 4th Directive to corporate reporting), the Companies Act 1990, Company Law Enforcement Act 2001 and Companies (Auditing and Accounting) Act 2003.

The administration of limited liability companies

The majority of companies in Ireland are small private companies where the shareholders and managers/directors are the same persons. However, in large companies where there are many shareholders obviously not all can be involved in running the company. Each year at the annual general meeting the shareholders can vote and appoint directors to run the company on their behalf. In this case there is a clear division between the owners and directors/stewards of the company. Each year the directors report back to the shareholders in terms of their stewardship of the company. Their annual report includes a profit and loss account and balance sheet. If the company performed well and made profits then part of those profits can be given to the shareholders in the form of dividends. Part of the profits can also be retained in the company for investment and expansion. The annual report also includes a report from the company auditors who state whether the accounts show a true and fair view of the affairs of the company. An audit is a legal requirement under the Companies Act 1963 and the auditors are employed by the shareholders to report on whether the accounts in the annual report give a true and fair view of the financial performance of the company.

Companies are legally required to carry out the following:

❑ Keep proper books of accounts that properly record and explain a company's transactions and form the basis of the final accounts of the company for the period. These accounts and records must also be audited by an independent auditor on behalf of the shareholders. The auditor's report states whether the accounts show a true and fair view and is included in the annual report presented at the AGM by the directors.

❑   All limited companies must register with the companies registrar in Dublin Castle. The companies registration office keeps a file on each company which includes its annual accounts, names of directors, location of business, business name etc. Anyone can issue a search to get details of all companies both public and private.

❑   Each company must hold an AGM once in every calendar year. An AGM must be held within nine months of the end of each accounting period. At each AGM the profit and loss account and balance sheet of the company must be presented to the shareholders. The Companies Acts along with financial reporting standards (FRS) set out the format for the presentation of these accounts as well as information that must be presented. Other issues dealt with at an AGM are the elections of directors to the board.

❑   The company must legally keep what are called statutory books which include the following:
  – Register of shareholders.
  – Register of debenture holders.
  – Register of assets given as security.
  – Register of directors and secretaries.
  – Register of directors' interests in ordinary shares and debentures.
  – Minute books of directors' meetings and general meetings.
  – Record of declarations by directors of interests in company contracts.

It must be remembered that a company is a separate legal person and where the company is acting unlawfully or is negligent in any way, it is the company that is sued not the shareholders. Thus the maximum amount any shareholders (not acting as directors) can loose is the amount they have invested in the business. Such is limited liability.

Other Types of Legal Organisation

The three types of business organisation discussed above (sole traders, partnerships and limited companies) are primarily business organisations that are established for the purpose of making a profit. However, there are organisations which are established to achieve some goal or goals other than making a profit. These companies are frequently referred to as 'not for profit organisations'. This does not mean that the companies in question never make a profit. It simply means that the making of a profit is not their primary goal. Examples would include the following:

1.   Co-operatives.
2.   State sponsored enterprises.
3.   Charities.

Tourism State Sponsored Enterprises

Failte Ireland, the National Tourism Development Authority, was established under the Tourism Development Authority Act 2003. It brings together and builds on the functions previously discharged by Bord Failte and CERT. Failte Ireland provides strategic support to develop and sustain Ireland as a high-quality and competitive tourist destination. Its mission is 'to increase the contribution of tourism to the economy by facilitating the development of a competitive and profitable tourism industry'. Failte Ireland works in strategic partnership with tourism interests to support the industry's efforts to be more competitive and more profitable and to help individual enterprises to improve their performance.

Table 12.2: *Comparison of ownership classification*

	Sole Proprietorships	Partnerships	Limited liability Companies
Ownership	1 person	2–20	Private: 2–50 Public: minimum 7 but no maximum limit
Financial	Set up costs minimal	Set up costs minimal	Legal fees and stamp duty apply
	No restriction on distribution of profit or cash withdrawal	Profits distributed in agreed proportions	Distribution of profits restricted under company law
	No legal requirement to prepare accounts except under tax law	No legal requirement to prepare accounts except under tax law	Accounts must be prepared and registered with the Companies Registrations Office
	No audit fees	No audit fees	Audit fees
Legal	No limited liability	No limited liability except for limited partners under the Limited Partnership Act 1907	Limited liability
	No real legal restrictions except tax law	Must obey Partnership Acts	Restricted under companies acts and accounting regulations
Taxation	Profits taxed at income tax rates 42% & 20%	Profits taxed at the income tax rates of 42% and 20%	Profits taxed at corporation tax rates 12.5%

Summary

Establishing the legal form of organisation is one of the first decisions an entrepreneur must take and a knowledge of the financial, legal and taxation aspects relating to this decision is very important. Generally small, one-person businesses begin as a sole proprietorship and, as they develop and grow, they choose a limited liability company format. This is normally in the form of a private company and, as the business expands and requires new sources of capital, it may need to develop into a public limited company.

The main information points covered in this chapter are:

❑ The legal form of organisation affects the taxation, legal, audit and financial requirements of a business. Table 12.2 briefly summarises the main characteristics of each.

❑ The sole trader legal form of organisation comes into being when an individual sets up in business and starts to trade in their own name. The individual is the sole owner of the business.

❑ The advantages of sole proprietorship status are privacy, lack of regulation, simplicity and ease in set up. Its disadvantages include unlimited liability for the owner and difficulty sourcing finance.

❑ A partnership can be described as an association of persons carrying on business in common with a view to making profit. The agreement between the persons can be in a verbal or written format.

❑ A company is a business entity created by law that is capable of entering into contracts, incurring liabilities and carrying out business. The liability of its owners is limited to what they have invested in the company.

❑ The formation of a limited company is handled by solicitors who draft the necessary legal documents that are then registered with the companies registrar before trading can take place. The main documents are known as the memorandum and articles of association.

❑ The majority of companies in Ireland are small private companies where the shareholders and managers/directors are the same persons. However, in large companies where there are many shareholders, obviously not all can be involved in running the company.

❑ Each year at the annual general meeting (AGM) the shareholders can vote and appoint directors to run the company on their behalf. In this case there is a clear division between the owners and directors/stewards of the company. At each AGM the directors report back to the shareholders on their stewardship of the company.

❑ All companies (except companies with a turnover of less than €1.5 million) are legally required to have their accounts audited.

❑ The main advantages of limited liability company status are actual limited liability, generally having greater access to capital, perpetual life and profits taxed at corporation tax rates. Its main disadvantages are the level of regulation and lack of privacy, as the accounts of all companies are available for public inspection.

Review Questions

Question 12.1

Describe each of the following:

(a) Sole trader.
(b) Partnership.
(c) Private limited company.
(d) Public limited company.

Question 12.2

What are the advantages and disadvantages of being a sole trader?

Question 12.3

(a) What do you understand by the term 'limited liability'?
(b) Why would a company choose to have 'unlimited liability'?

Question 12.4

List and explain the similarities and differences between a private limited company and a public limited company.

CHAPTER 13

The Regulatory Framework of Accounting

Learning Outcomes

By the end of this chapter you will be able to:

- Outline the elements that make up the regulatory framework of accounting.
- Understand the role of the accounting standards board and accounting standards.
- Outline the role of accounting concepts and have an understanding of the main accounting concepts and their application in financial accounting.
- Outline the essence and importance of the Statement of Principles as issued by the ASB in influencing the financial reporting standard setting process.
- Demonstrate an understanding of the main information points relating to FRS 18 Accounting Policies.
- Demonstrate an awareness of the increasing importance of international financial reporting standards.

Introduction

'Every company in the country is fiddling its profit. Every set of published accounts is based on books which have been gently cooked or completely roasted.'

Ian Griffiths, *Creative Accounting*, 1987

There are significant moves in the business world towards a more ethical climate. Abuse in the provision of financial statements in the latter part of the last century has brought about the need to enforce more rigorous regulation of business practices. The term regulation implies the imposition of rules and requirements. In an accounting context this would relate to the preparation and presentation of reports, and statements for third parties. This level of regulation in financial reporting relates primarily to limited liability companies, as they are legally required to prepare and present their accounts to the companies registrar for public inspection.

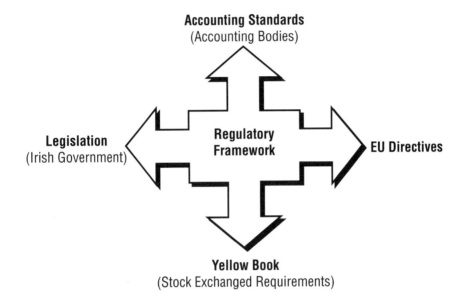

The objective of an accounting regulatory framework is to ensure adequate relevant disclosure, objectivity and comparability of accounting information to external users of financial reports. Accounting and the preparation of accounting financial statements and reports is regulated through the following:

1. The government, through the relevant legislation. In Ireland this relates to the Companies Acts of 1963 to 2003 and the various Companies (Amendment) Acts of which 1983 and 1986 are the most important. The Company Acts provide regulation for companies alone.
2. Regulation through the European Union. The EU issues directives to its member states to help ensure greater harmony in the presentation of financial statements. An EU directive requires the government of each member state to incorporate that directive into their laws. The EU's 4th Directive concerned the preparation and presentation of the accounts of companies and this was made law in Ireland through the Companies (Amendment) Act 1986.
3. The stock exchange listing requirements (yellow book) for listed, publicly quoted companies.

4.   The accounting standards issued by the ASB.

This chapter is primarily concerned with the role of accounting concepts that have developed over the years and accounting standards issued by the accounting bodies as part of the regulation process.

The Role of Accounting Standards

In the UK the accounting profession began to make recommendations about accounting practices as early as 1942. These recommendations were issued with the sole purpose of reducing the wide range of diverse accounting methods then in operation. Each method of accounting could lead to the presentation of a completely different profit figure. Thus there was no unifying code of practice in preparing and presenting accounting information. The recommendations made by the accounting profession did not, however, solve the situation as they were not mandatory.

In the 1960s there was a surge of public criticism of financial reporting methods. This was due to a number of cases which highlighted the subjective nature of accounting. In essence individuals and companies relied on the work of professional accountants for take-over and investment decisions. This work was subsequently found to be flawed due to the choice of accounting treatments allowed at the time. One such case involved General Electric Company (GEC).

Case Scenario – General Electric Company (GEC)

In 1967 GEC was successful in a takeover bid of Associated Electrical Industries (AEI). Before the takeover AEI, produced a profit statement for the year which included 10 months' actual results and 2 months' of forecast sales and expenses. They estimated a profit of £10 million. GEC's takeover bid was influenced by this level of profitability. However, after the takeover, GEC reported the company actually made a loss of £4.5 million. According to GEC auditors the difference was mainly due to judgements made regarding provisions for estimated losses and amounts of stock to be written off.

The response of the accounting profession to this level of subjectivity and lack of uniformity in accounting practice was to set up the Accounting Standards Committee (ASC). The committee consisted of members from the accounting bodies. It issued a total of 25 Statements of Standard Accounting Practice (SSAPs) dealing with a variety of topics in an attempt to reduce the level of subjectivity and variety in accounting practice. Once an accounting standard was issued, any material deviation from the standard by any company in the preparation and presentation of their accounting reports was to be disclosed in that report. SSAPs were also enforced by company law, as compliance with standards implied truth and fairness in the accounts. The financial statements of companies are required through the 1963 Companies Act to give a 'true and fair view'.

In 1990 the ASC was replaced by the Accounting Standards Board (ASB) following a review of the standard setting process. The ASB agreed to adopt the existing SSAPs and update and review where necessary. The accounting standards issued by the ASB are called Financial Reporting Standards (FRSs) of which to date the ASB have issued 27. Some of these FRSs have replaced SSAPs (for example FRS 18 replaced SSAP 2).

In November 1997 the ASB issued a third category of standard for smaller businesses called Financial Reporting Standard for Smaller Entities (FRSSE). The reason for this was that the ASB felt that smaller companies should not have to follow the very detailed rules in the existing FRSs and SSAPs. Thus the FRSSE is a collection of some of the rules in all the other standards (SSAPs and FRSs) that small companies can choose to comply with or not.

The ASB also issued Urgent Issue Task Force (UITF) abstracts, which are intended to be in force while a new standard is being prepared or an existing standard amended. UITFs are compulsory and carry the same weight as FRSs.

The ASB's consultative process before issuing an FRS is as follows:

Step 1:   The issue of working drafts for discussion (DD).
Step 2:   After the discussion period a Financial Reporting Exposure Draft (FRED) is issued.
Step 3:   After consideration of feedback on the exposure draft an FRS is published.

For up-to-date information on the ASB and the various standards and UITFs in issue consult www.asb.org.uk.

Table 13.1: *Accounting standards – key terms*

ASC	Accounting Standards Committee (in existence up to 1990)
ASB	Accounting Standards Board (in existence from 1990 onwards)
IASC	International Accounting Standards Committee (in existence from 1973 onwards)
SSAP	Statements of Standard Accounting Practice (issued by ASC) *Originally 25 issued, currently 11 enforced*
FRS	Financial Reporting Standard (issued by ASB) *Currently over 27 enforced*
FRSSE	Financial Reporting Standard for Smaller Entities (issued by ASB) *Regulations for small companies – one standard enforced*
UITF	Urgent Issue Task Force Abstracts (issued by ASB) *In force while new standard is being prepared or existing amended*
FRED	Financial Reporting Exposure Draft (issued by ASB) *Issued during the process of preparing a new FRS*
IAS	International Accounting Standard (issued by IASC)
IFRS	International Financial Reporting Standard (issued by the IASC) have taken over from IAS.

Accounting Concepts and their Role

Modern accounting is based on certain concepts and conventions that have developed over the years. These concepts are broad basic assumptions which form the basis of the financial accounts of a business. They help ensure transactions are recognised and measured on a uniform basis. The accounting policies of a business are based on these generally accepted accounting concepts. An understanding of accounting is not possible without understanding the role and essence of these concepts.

Although we have covered most of these concepts already in the text the following is a summary:

The business entity concept

This concept states that the business is separate from the owner. Thus the items recorded in a firm's accounting records and books are limited to the transactions that affect the firm and will not concern themselves with the private transactions of the owner. The only transactions between the business and the owner that are recorded in the business records are:

1. The owner investing resources (usually cash) in the business.
2. The owner taking out resources (usually cash or stock) from the business for their own use (termed drawings).

The dual aspect concept

This concept states that there are two aspects of accounting: one represented by the assets of the business and the other by the claims against them (capital and liabilities). This concept states that these two aspects will always be equal.

The money measurement concept

The assets of the business must be measured in some uniform way. Obviously this has to be in some monetary form. It follows that some assets of the business cannot appear on the balance sheet of a company because to put a monetary value on them would be too subjective. The most obvious example is the human asset of a good work force or an excellent management team. These assets cannot appear on the balance sheet as it is very difficult if not impossible to put an objective monetary value on them. An example of an exception to this rule can be found where sporting clubs purchase their playing staff.

The realisation concept

The concept clarifies when a business accounts for a transaction and thus the related profit or loss on the transaction. For example, when is a sale a sale, or when is a purchase a purchase? When do we account for expenses? There are three clear stages in the life of a transaction:

1. The order stage.
2. The transfer of goods and acceptance of liability by the purchaser.
3. The payment or cash stage.

Obviously, if some businesses account for sales on the basis of orders received and other businesses account for sales based only on cash received, then there is no point in comparing the businesses' performances as they recognise sales and profits at different periods. The realisation concept holds to the view that a transaction should be accounted for at the transfer of goods and acceptance of liability stage, *not* at the order stage. Effectively the realisation concept tells us when to recognise the profit or loss on a transaction. It states that profits or losses on transactions can only be accounted for when realisation has occurred. A number of criteria have to be observed before realisation can occur. The most critical of these is that goods or services have been provided to a buyer who accepts liability for them and the monetary value of the goods or services has been established. Ultimately it is essential that all businesses account for transactions on the same basis. The realisation concept is very much a part of the prudence concept below.

The cost/current value concept

In presenting financial statements a measurement basis must be chosen for each category of asset and liability. The choice is:

❑   **Historical cost**: This is where the asset is valued at its initial transaction cost. This may be subsequently re-measured if the recoverable amount of the asset is lower than cost.
❑   **Current value**: This is where the asset is valued based on its current value at the time it was acquired. Assets and liabilities measured on the current value basis are carried at up-to-date current values and thus will be re-measured frequently. Re-measurement, however, will only be recognised if there is sufficient evidence that the monetary values of the asset/liability have changed and the new amount can be measured with sufficient reliability. For example, once a business has decided to apply current values to its property assets then they will be constantly re-measured on the basis of an independent valuer's assessment.

The going concern concept

The going concern concept requires that in preparing the accounts we assume the business will continue into the foreseeable future. This ensures the basis of measuring and valuing assets and liabilities will remain at either cost or current value. If the accounts were to be prepared on the basis that the business was to be sold or about to go into liquidation, then an alternative basis for valuing the assets would have to be considered, including the break-up values for assets. Thus unless the business entity is in liquidation or the directors have no alternative but to cease trading, then the going concern basis will apply and all assets and liabilities will be valued at historic cost or current value, whichever is appropriate.

The accruals concept

The calculation of profit is based on the accruals concept, which requires that the effects of transactions should be accounted for when they occur and are included in the statements for the periods they relate to. Knowledge of this concept is essential in understanding the net profit figure and the differences between cash and profit.

The accruals concept requires two things:

1. When calculating net profit, expenses should be matched against related revenues. Thus in the trading account, if 100 units are sold in January then only the cost of 100 units is deducted in calculating gross (trading) profit. In the profit and loss section only the expenses for January are deducted when calculating net profit for January. In the trading account of a product-based company, purchases are matched to sales on a unit basis. In the profit and loss account expenses are matched on a time basis. For a service company all expenses are matched on a time basis.
2. Net profit is the difference between revenues earned (not necessarily received) and expenses charged (not necessarily paid). Thus net profit is worked on a transactions basis, i.e. if a transaction occurs it should be accounted for irrespective of whether cash has passed hands. Thus revenues and expenses are accounted for as soon as an invoice has been issued and liability has been accepted. For businesses that buy and sell on credit, sales and purchases in the trading account will be a mixture of cash and credit transactions. Also, expenses that relate to a period will be deducted from sales in the calculation of net profit for that period whether those expenses are paid or not. Any unpaid expenses will also be shown in the balance sheet under liabilities.

The prudence concept

The intention of the prudence concept is to see that all asset values and profit figures are realistic rather than optimistic or pessimistic. The essence of the concept is to insist that revenue or profit should not be accounted for until the business is virtually certain to get it, but that a loss in an asset's value is accounted for as soon as it is probable or likely. The ability to reasonably measure the asset or liability is also necessary to ensure the reliability of the accounts. Ultimately the prudence concept requires that, in preparing financial statements, gains or losses, and assets and liabilities should not be overstated or understated.

This concept requires that:

1. One should never anticipate profits. This can be explained by asking, when does a company account for a sales transaction? A sales transaction should only be accounted for when ownership of the goods passes from the company to the buyer and not when the goods were originally ordered. To account for the transaction at the order stage would be imprudent. This is related to the realisation concept outlined above.
2. One must provide for all possible losses. If a company knows that next year it will incur losses on a part/section of the business then it should provide for those losses *now*. To provide for something is to treat it as a loss *now*. In other words, show it as a loss/expense in the profit and loss account. However, a provision should only be recognised and accounted for when the following criteria apply:
    ❏   It is probable that a transfer of economic benefits will occur.
    ❏   A reasonable estimate of the amount involved can be made.

A good example of the prudence concept is with regard to bad debts. If a company becomes aware, just prior to the year-end, that a debtor is likely to go into 'liquidation' and cease trading, then prudence requires a provision in the accounts for this likely future loss.

The consistency concept

The consistency concept requires that when a business has decided on an accounting treatment for an item it will account for all similar items in the same way. The objective of the consistency concept is to ensure that accounts are comparable. Consistency arose due to the belief that if accounts are not prepared on a consistent basis using similar accounting policies and assumptions, then any comparison will not only be meaningless but also misleading. However, the consistency concept is not rigid and should the directors feel that the 'truth and fairness' of the accounts are impaired by rigidly sticking to the particular accounting policy, they can change it, but the reason for the change and the effect of the change must be explained.

FRS 18 has reconsidered the consistency concept and downgraded it from being a fundamental accounting concept. Now consistency, although important, should not be allowed to prevent improvements in accounting and consequently it can be ignored if a new accounting policy is more appropriate than that used previously.

The materiality concept

The materiality concept recognises that some transactions are not sufficiently important to waste time and effort in ensuring the correct accounting treatment. For example, a hotel company purchases a cleaning machine which has an estimated life of five years for €60. Should a company treat this as a fixed asset and depreciate accordingly or write it off as an expense in the period purchased. In this case the €60 cost implies this is not a material item and thus should be written off as an expense in the period purchased?

Information is considered material if its omission or misstatement could influence the economic decisions of the various users of account. What represents a material value will differ from business to business, as some businesses can fix their materiality level at €1,000 and others at €200. The deciding factor is if the cost of accounting for a transaction in the correct manner is greater than the value of the transaction, then the amount in question would not be considered material.

The substance over legal form concept

The concept states that if the legal aspect of a transaction is different to the substance of the transaction then the substance of the transaction takes precedence over the legal form. In other words, we account for the substance (economic reality) of the transaction, not the legal aspect of it.

For example, a hotel leases its premises from a property company on a long-term lease. The legal aspect of this transaction is the hotel company does not own the property and should not show the property as an asset in its balance sheet. Thus any lease payments are just treated as expenses in the profit and loss account. The substance of the transaction is, however, that because the company has the property on a long-term lease and, most likely, has the option to renew the lease, then in substance it has the use of the asset for the majority of its life. Thus the company should account for it as if it owned the asset, showing it as a fixed asset (leasehold property) and showing the liability (the future amount of lease payments) in the long-term liabilities section of the balance sheet. This concept helps to restrict companies from window dressing their balance sheet through the use of 'off balance sheet finance'.

SSAP 2, published in 1971, identified four fundamental accounting concepts from the list above. These were accruals, prudence, materiality and going concern. These were to be the most important concepts that formed the bedrock of accounting. The accounting policies of a business are based on these generally accepted accounting concepts. Accounting policies are those principles, bases, conventions, rules and practices applied by an entity that specify how the effects of material items are to be reflected in the financial statements. Before a company determines the accounting policies that are relevant to its circumstances it must have regard to both the fundamental accounting concepts and accounting bases in existence.

Note: Accounting bases are the methods that have been developed for expressing or applying fundamental accounting concepts to financial transactions. Accounting bases lay out the choice of acceptable ways to account for a transaction. An accounting policy is where a company chooses one of these bases to account for a specific transaction type. As more FRSs are developed the choice of accounting bases will diminish.

SSAP 2 was replaced by FRS 18 Accounting Policies (see below) in December 2000. This came about when the ASB issued its Statement of Principles in December 1999. The Statement of Principles is not an accounting standard but underpins all of the accounting standards issued and to be issued in the future. It effectively lays out the objectives of financial statements and the qualitative characteristics of financial information. It focuses on the *elements of financial statements*, how these elements are *recognised* and *measured* and how this information should be *presented*. It is an accounting framework which lays the basis for all other accounting standards. Many of its principles especially those relating to the elements of financial statements and the recognition and measurement of these elements have been discussed in Chapters 2, 3 and 10 of this text.

The following is a summary of both the Statement of Principles and FRS 18:

Statement of Principles for Financial Reporting

The ASB published in December 1999 its Statement of Principles for financial reporting. Its main purpose is to provide a framework from which the ASB can develop and review its accounting standards. It sets out the principles that the ASB believe should underlie the preparation and presentation of financial statements that are required to give a true and fair view.

The statement had a total of eight chapters dealing with the following areas:

1. The objectives of financial statements

This chapter outlines the objectives of financial statements which is to provide information about the financial performance and financial position of an enterprise that is useful to a wide range of users for assessing the stewardship of management, and for making economic decisions. This objective can usually be met by focusing on the needs of present and potential investors. *This was covered in detail in Chapter 1.*

2. The reporting entity

This chapter identifies two main forms of business entity: single entities and groups. It states that an entity should prepare and publish financial statements if there is a legitimate demand for that information and the entity is a cohesive economic unit. It also states the boundary of the reporting entity is determined by the scope of its control. *This text is primarily concerned with single entity businesses.*

3. The qualitative characteristics of financial information

This chapter identifies four principal qualitative characteristics classified as follows:

- Relevance.
- Reliability.
- Comparability.
- Understandability.

4. The elements of financial statements

This chapter sets out and discusses the definitions of the elements of financial statements namely:

- Assets: rights or other access to future economic benefits controlled by an entity as a result of past transactions or events.
- Liabilities: obligations of an entity to transfer economic benefits as a result of past transactions or events.
- Ownership interest: the residual amount found by deducting all of the entity's liabilities from all of the entity's assets.
- Gains: increases in ownership interest not resulting from contributions from owners.
- Losses: decreases in ownership interest not resulting from distributions to owners.

The elements of financial statements were covered in detail in Chapters 2 and 3.

5. Recognition in financial statements

This section focuses on what is required to recognise a transaction that creates or increases assets and liabilities, gains and losses. In order to recognise, and thus include in the accounts, any transaction that affects any of the elements of financial statements, there must be evidence of its existence so that it can be measured as a monetary amount with sufficient reliability. *Recognition in financial statements was covered in Chapter 3 when dealing with the money measurement and realisation concepts.*

6. Measurement in financial statements

This chapter provides an overview of issues relevant to the measurement of assets and liabilities recognised in the balance sheet and the associated effects of gains and losses. Its main points are:

❑ In preparing financial statements, the measurement basis of historic cost or current cost needs to be selected for each category of asset and liability.
❑ An asset or liability measured using historic cost is recognised at its initial transaction cost. If measured on current value basis it is recognised at its current value at the time it was acquired.
❑ Re-measurement will occur if it is necessary to ensure that assets measured at historic cost are carried at the lower of cost and the recoverable amount. For assets measured at current value, re-measurement will occur to ensure that assets and liabilities are carried at up-to-date values.
❑ Re-measurement will only be recognised if there is sufficient evidence that the monetary value of the asset or liability has changed and the new value to the asset/liability can be measured with sufficient reliability.

Measurement in financial statements was discussed in Chapters 3 and 10 when dealing with the cost/current value, going concern, accruals and prudence concepts.

7. Presentation of financial information

In presenting information in financial statements the objective is to communicate clearly and effectively and thus meet the objectives of Chapter 1 in the Statement of Principles. This chapter focuses on the way in which the information on financial performance (profit and loss), financial position (balance sheet) and cash flow information is presented. It lays out the following:

❑ The presentation of information on financial performance should focus on the components of that performance and the characteristics of those components. For example, their nature, cause, function, stability, risk, reliability and predictability.

❑ The presentation of information on financial position should focus on the type and function of assets and liabilities held and the relationships between them.

❑ The information on cash flow should be presented in a way that distinguishes between those cash flows that are a result of operating activities and those that are from other activities.

8. Accounting for interests in other entities

This chapter focuses on accounting for interests in other entities and how these interests should be fully reflected in the financial statements of the entity that has the interest and exerts the influence.

FRS 18 Accounting Policies

The Statement of Principles laid the way for the issue of FRS 18 Accounting Policies, which deals with how accounting policies are selected, applied and disclosed. The standard defines what accounting policies are and distinguishes them from estimation techniques such as depreciation methods or ways of evaluating bad debts.

According to the ASB, the objective of FRS 18 is to ensure that for all material items:

❑ An entity adopts the accounting policies most appropriate to its particular circumstances for the purpose of giving a true and fair view.

❑ The accounting policies adopted are reviewed regularly to ensure that they remain appropriate and are changed when a new policy becomes more appropriate to the entity's particular circumstances.

❑ Sufficient information is disclosed in the financial statements to enable users to understand the accounting policies adopted and how they have been implemented.

The standard states that accounting policies are those principles, bases, conventions, rules and practices applied by an entity that specify how the effects of material items are to be reflected in the financial statements. Any material item must firstly be:

❏ *Recognised* in the financial statements as assets, liabilities, gains, losses or changes to shareholders' funds.

❏ The *measurement* basis for the transaction must be selected. This monetary value can be chosen from two broad categories: current value or historic value.

❏ The *presentation* of the information in the financial statements must enable the users to understand the policies adopted.

Should there be any changes to any one of the three bases (recognition, measurement and presentation) then there is deemed a change of accounting policy and that change, and the effect of the change, must be reported in the financial statements. This is in contrast to a change of an 'estimate' or estimation technique where none of the three elements is affected and thus not required to be reported in the accounts. The following illustrations should make the distinction clearer.

Illustration 13.1: *Accounting policy change*

❏ The loan interest previously charged to the profit and loss is now added to the cost of the assets as per FRS 15.

❏ In this transaction there is a change in recognition, as the transaction was treated as an expense and is now treated as an asset. The measurement basis is unchanged; however, the presentation is changed as the item is now in the balance sheet and not in the profit and loss account. This would be considered a change of accounting policy and reported as such.

Illustration 13.2: *Accounting estimate change*

❏ A change from depreciating on the reducing balance method to the straight-line basis.

❏ In this transaction there is no change to either the recognition, the presentation or the measurement basis (as we are still depreciating assets valued at either historic cost or current value) and thus this change would not be considered a change in accounting policy but rather a change in estimating technique. In this case the change is not required to be reported in the financial statements.

The reason for this distinction is to provide information for external users. A change in accounting policy is required to be reported in such a way that the users of accounts will understand the nature and effect of the change on the financial statements. A change in estimating techniques is not required to be reported in the financial statements.

FRS 18 states that accounting policies should be adopted that enable a company's financial statements to give a true and fair view. Out of all the accounting concepts the standard chooses two, going concern and accruals, for their pervasive role in selecting policies. FRS 18 replaced SSAP 2, which identified four fundamental concepts – going concern, accruals, prudence and consistency – as part of the foundations of accounting. FRS 18 downgrades the influence of both the prudence concept (now desirable) and the consistency concept.

The standard gives clear disclosure requirements about accounting policies and when changes occur in accounting policies. It also states that an entity should judge the appropriateness of its accounting policies against the following objectives:

❑ **Relevance**: will it influence the economic decisions of the users of accounts?
❑ **Reliability**: is it reliable and does it reflect the substance of the transaction?
❑ **Comparability**: is it capable of being compared with similar information about the entity in past periods or similar information about other entities?
❑ **Understandability**: can it be understood by the users of financial statements?

Note: These are qualitative characteristics of financial information as outlined in the Statement of Principles.

International Financial Reporting Standards

In 1973 the International Accounting Standards Committee (IASC) was formed with the object of harmonising standards on a worldwide basis as many countries had accounting associations that issued their own accounting standards. The IASC issue their own International Financial Reporting Standards (IFRSs), which replace their earlier International Accounting Standards (IASs). In most cases compliance with FRSs ensures automatic compliance with IFRSs. In 2005 all listed companies worldwide will be obliged to follow IFRSs and this will extend to all private companies by 1 January 2007. This requirement and its implications will be dealt with later in the text. For more information on IFRSs refer to www.iasc.org.uk.

Summary

The following are the main information points covered in this chapter:

❑ The objective of an accounting regulatory framework is to ensure adequate relevant disclosure, objectivity and comparability of accounting information for external users of financial reports. Accounting and the preparation of accounting financial statements and reports is regulated by the following:

- The government, through the relevant legislation. In Ireland this relates to the Companies Acts of 1963 to 2003 and the various Companies (Amendment) Acts of which 1983 and 1986 are the most important.
- Regulation through the European Union. The EU issues directives to its member states to help ensure greater harmony in the presentation of financial statements.
- The stock exchange listing requirements.
- The accounting standards issued by the accounting bodies.

❑ The accounting bodies created the ASB which issues FRSs to help regulate the practice of accounting and financial reporting. To date they have issued 27 financial reporting standards.

❑ Modern accounting is based on certain concepts and conventions that have developed over the years. These concepts are broad basic assumptions which form the basis of the financial accounts of a business. They help ensure transactions are recognised and measured on a uniform basis. The accounting policies of a business are based on these generally accepted accounting concepts.

❑ Accounting policies are those principles, bases, conventions, rules and practices applied by an entity that specify how the effects of material items are to be reflected in the financial statements. Before a company determines the accounting policies that are relevant to its circumstances it must have regard to both the fundamental accounting concepts and accounting bases in existence.

❑ The Statement of Principles as published by the ASB sets out the principles that the ASB believe should underlie the preparation and presentation of financial statements that are required to give a true and fair view. It underpins all of the accounting standards issued and to be issued in the future.

❑ FRS 18 Accounting Policies deals with how accounting policies are selected, applied and disclosed. The standard defines what accounting policies are and distinguishes them from estimation techniques such as depreciation methods or ways of evaluating bad debts.

❑ In 2005 all listed companies throughout the world will be obliged to follow IFRSs and this will extend to all private companies by 1 January 2007.

Review Questions

Question 13.1

Outline the different elements that provide the Regulatory Framework for Accounting.

Question 13.2

Outline the role of accounting standards and briefly outline the process the ASB undertakes in developing accounting standards.

Question 13.3

Outline the role of accounting concepts and discuss the following concepts:

(a) Accruals.
(b) Realisation.
(c) Materiality.
(d) Substance over form.

Question 13.4

Discuss the relationship between the prudence and realisation concepts.

Question 13.5

State the purpose of the Statement of Principles for Financial Reporting and give a brief summary of the eight chapters involved.

Question 13.6

With reference to the Statement of Principles for Financial Reporting, outline what is meant by 'recognition in financial statements' and list the accounting concepts that support it.

Question 13.7

With reference to the Statement of Principles for Financial Reporting, outline what is meant by 'measurement' in financial statements and list the accounting concepts that support it.

Question 13.8

With reference to FRS 18, contrast accounting policies with estimation techniques.

CHAPTER 14

Company Accounts

Learning Outcomes

By the end of this chapter you will be able to:

❑ Outline how companies are financed, distinguishing between the various types of share capital and debt capital and their associated costs in terms of dividends and interest on debt.
❑ Explain the purpose of the appropriation account.
❑ Prepare the final accounts of a company.
❑ Distinguish between the internal final accounts and the final accounts for publication of limited liability companies.
❑ Show an awareness of the format and terminology of published accounts including the notes to the accounts and the requirements of FRS 3.

Introduction

Part of Chapter 12 focused on the financial, legal, taxation and administration aspects of companies. This chapter builds on that theory and also applies the period-end adjustments covered in Chapters 9, 10 and 11 to the preparation of financial statements for companies.

This chapter will concentrate on the following:

❑ How limited companies are financed.
❑ The preparation of the final accounts of companies.
❑ The publication of company accounts and reports.

The Financing of Companies

Companies are normally financed through a combination of the following:

1. The contributions of the owners (share capital).
2. Loans that the company acquires.

Share capital

Share capital represents what has been invested in the company by the owners or shareholders. A person invests or buys ownership of a company by purchasing shares in that business.

Share capital can have the following meanings:

Authorised share capital: This is the maximum amount of shares (as stated in the memorandum and articles of association of the company) a company is entitled to issue. This maximum amount can, however, be increased at a general meeting of the company. The authorised share capital is shown in a note to the accounts.

Issued share capital: This is the amount of authorised share capital actually issued and allotted to shareholders. If all of the authorised share capital was issued then the authorised and issued share capital would be the same.

Called-up capital: This is the amount of capital payment which has actually been demanded by the company. This applies only where shares are issued and are payable by instalments rather than in full on application. Thus where 100,000 shares of €1 each have been issued and only 75 cent per share has been called up, the called-up capital is €75,000. This is the amount that appears in the balance sheet.

Paid-up capital: This is the amount of the called-up capital that has been actually paid over to the company by the shareholders. Thus in the example above if only €60,000 has been paid up, the shareholders owe the company €15,000 and should pay immediately. These calls in arrears would appear as a current asset in the balance sheet of a company showing the amounts owed to the company from shareholders.

Un-called capital: This is the amount of capital that shareholders agree to pay if they are called upon to do so. Thus in the above example, the un-called capital amounts to €25,000 and this would be shown in a note to the accounts.

Share premium: When shares are issued they have a nominal value. This is the value or denomination the company chooses for its shares. It may be €1, €1.50, €2.00 or €0.50. This is a meaningless value. The true value of the shares is the market value. Thus if a company issues 1,000 shares with a nominal value of €1 and they receive €3 per share, then the shares have been issued at a premium of €2 per share. The company will debit their bank account with €3,000, credit a share capital account with the nominal value of the shares €1,000 and credit a share premium account with €2,000, representing the premium obtained for the shares. The share capital account is always credited with the nominal value of the shares.

A shareholder's reward for investing in the company comes in the form of a dividend. A dividend is a share of the profits made by the company. The directors of the company decide the amount of profits to be retained in the business for expansion and the balance is given as dividends to the shareholders. The shareholders cannot propose a dividend higher than the one proposed by the directors, but they can propose a lower one, although this action is quite rare. Should the directors propose no dividend then the shareholders are powerless to alter the decision apart from having the power to appoint new directors for the following year.

There are two types of shares:

— *guaranteed first to get a dividend (get preference).*

1. **Preference shares**: These get an agreed, fixed rate of dividend each year. This dividend is paid before any ordinary share dividends are paid. Preference shareholders generally take less risk than ordinary shareholders and thus are not considered the real owners of the business and do not vote on company resolutions such as the appointment of directors etc. In the case of the company going into liquidation they will be repaid their investment before the ordinary shareholders are paid, if there are any monies left in the company. Thus preference shareholders take less risk than ordinary shareholders and can demand a fixed rate of dividend each year out of company profits.
2. **Ordinary shares**: Holders of ordinary shares are the real owners of the business as each share carries voting rights and a right to a share of the profits of the business after preference share dividends are paid. Ordinary shareholders receive the remainder of the total profits available for dividend and, in the case of liquidation, are the last to receive any payments of cash and as a result will generally receive no repayment of capital.

Dividends are generally expressed as a percentage of the share capital. For example, a dividend of 5 per cent of 100,000 shares with a nominal value of €2 each will amount to €10,000. A shareholder holding 10,000 shares will receive €1,000 as their dividend.

Example 14.1: *Dividend calculation*

A company is financed by 100,000 5 per cent preference shares of €1 each and 100,000 ordinary shares of €2 each. Calculate the dividend payable out of profits for the following years, assuming an ordinary dividend of 10 per cent in years one and two and 7 per cent in years three and four.

Approach

	Year 1	Year 2	Year 3	Year 4
	€	€	€	€
Net profit after tax	30,000	26,000	20,000	24,000
Less preference dividend (100,000 x €1 x 5%)	5,000	5,000	5,000	5,000
ordinary dividend (100,000 x €2 x 10%)	20,000	20,000	14,000	14,000
Retained profits	5,000	1,000	1,000	6,000

Loan capital

The term loan capital refers to the loans acquired by a company. Loans can be acquired in two ways:

1. Approaching your bank in the normal way.
2. The company issuing its own loans/debentures.

The term debenture is used when a company seeks people or other companies to lend it money. In return the loan providers will get debenture certificates on which will be stated the annual interest rate and the repayment date. For a public limited company this debenture certificate is a marketable instrument, which can be sold on to other investors. For example, if a holder of a debenture wants to get their money back before the repayment date, then they can go to the stock exchange and sell the debenture in a similar way to selling shares. This option of liquidity makes debentures popular for investors. Debentures can be secured against the assets of the company. Obviously investors may require security before giving a company a loan and thus these debentures are termed mortgage debentures. Unsecured debentures, whose interest rate would be higher to compensate the investor for the lack of security, are termed simple or naked debentures.

The Final Accounts of Companies

All the accounting concepts, principles and techniques we have met so far in dealing with sole traders also apply to partnerships and limited companies. However, there are a number of differences that need to be taken into account when preparing the trading, profit and loss account and balance sheet of a company.

The following is an illustration of the final accounts of a limited company with notes following, explaining the different terms and headings.

Illustration 14.1: *Final accounts with adjustments*

Trading, Profit and Loss and Appropriation Account for the Year Ended 30 June 2005

	€	€
Sales		250,000
Less cost of goods sold		
Opening stock	28,500	
Add purchases	175,000	
Less closing stock	(50,000)	
Cost of sales		(153,500)
Gross profit		96,500
Less expenses		
Motor expenses	4,000	
Directors remuneration **Note 1**	18,000	
Rates	10,000	
Wages and salaries	26,000	
Light and heat	9,000	
Audit fees **Note 2**	5,000	
Depreciation – equipment	4,000	
Depreciation – vehicles	4,600	
Amortisation of intangibles **Note 9**	2,000	(82,600)
Net operating profit		13,900
Debenture interest **Note 3**		(2,500)
Net profit before tax		11,400
Corporation tax **Note 4**		(3,000)
Net profit after tax		8,400
Transfer to reserve **Note 5**	(5,000)	
Dividend **Note 6**	(3,000)	(8,000)
Retained profit for the year		400
Add retained profit b/f* **Note 7**		17,100
Retained profit c/f ** **Note 7		17,500

* "b/f" represents brought forward from previous periods.
** "c/f" represents carried forward to future periods.

Balance Sheet as at 30 June 2005

	Cost	Deprec/ amort.	NBV
Fixed assets			
Tangible assets **Note 8**	€	€	€
Premises	122,000	0	122,000
Equipment	40,000	(10,400)	29,600
Motor vehicles	23,000	(10,800)	12,200
	185,000	(21,200)	163,800
Intangible assets **Note 9**	42,000	(2,000)	40,000
Investments **Note 10**			30,000
Current assets			
Stock		50,000	
Debtors		45,500	
Bank		6,300	
		101,800	
Current liabilities **Note 11**			
Creditors	10,100		
Corporation tax **Note 4**	3,000	(13,100)	
Net current assets			88,700
Long-term liabilities			(25,000)
			297,500
Capital and reserves			
Ordinary share capital **Note 12**			200,000
Reserves			
Share premium **Note 13**			50,000
General reserve **Note 5**			30,000
Retained profit **Note 7**			17,500
Shareholders' funds **Note 14**			297,500

Trading, profit and loss account

There are no differences between the trading account of a sole trader/partnership and a company. The main differences between the two types of business come when focusing on the profit and loss account. These differences are:

Note 1: Directors' remuneration

Since only companies have directors, the expense of paying them is found only in the company accounts. Directors are employees of a company, appointed by the shareholders and charged with running the company on their behalf. Any remuneration (salaries, bonuses, incentives) must be shown in the profit and loss account in accordance with the Companies Acts. Directors' remuneration cannot be omitted or mixed in with other figures such as general wages and salaries.

Note 2: Audit fees

As stated earlier, auditors are employed and legally required to assess whether proper accounting records are being kept and to give their opinion as to whether the accounts show a true and fair view. This is a expense that the company must pay and thus is recorded in the profit and loss account.

Note 3: Debentures and debenture interest

Debentures are a form of long-term loan that many companies use. A debenture can be described as a fixed-interest loan taken out for a specified period. The interest rate is fixed for the period of the loan and assets of the company may be used as security for the loan. Therefore a debenture represents an amount of money borrowed and will appear as a long-term liability in the balance sheet. Interest payable for the use of money borrowed is an expense and therefore interest on debentures will be shown in the profit and loss account as an expense

Profit and loss appropriation account

Previous profits + this years profits – Dividends.

The profit and loss appropriation account is prepared to show how profits are to be divided up or distributed. In the accounts of a sole trader no division is required, as the owner gets everything. For a partnership an appropriation account is required, as the profits must be divided amongst the various partners. For a company, the directors must decide on how the profits after tax are to be appropriated. In other words, how much is to be given to shareholders in the form of dividends and how much is to be retained in the business.

Note 4: Corporation tax

Each company resident in the state must pay corporation tax on its profits. The rates of corporation tax in the Republic of Ireland are 12.5 per cent for trading profits and 25 per cent for non-trading profits. Corporation tax in Ireland is due and payable on an instalment basis with the first instalment due one month before the company's accounting year-end and the outstanding instalments due after the year-end. Hence a company will not have paid its full corporation tax liability by the year-end. Thus this corporation tax liability will also be shown in the balance sheet under creditors due within one year. It is beyond the scope of this text to go into detail regarding corporation tax, its calculation and payment schemes and hence, unless specifically stated, this text will assume that corporation tax is not fully paid by the year-end.

Note 5: Transfer to reserve

This is where the directors decide that a certain amount of profit should be put aside and retained in the company and not given as dividend. Hence they propose a transfer of profits to a reserve account. These reserves can be of a general nature or a specific nature, showing the specific reason why this amount of profit was retained. Examples would include a fixed-asset replacement reserve, which is a fund set aside to replace fixed assets. Retained profits and reserves are the same thing, i.e. profits that have not been distributed as dividends, although there is nothing stopping the company from paying dividends out of these reserves at some future date. These reserves would appear in the balance sheet under capital and reserves.

Note 6: Dividends

We have already discussed dividends in detail. However, there is a distinction between interim dividend and the final dividend proposed by a business. The interim dividend is based on the half-yearly accounts, which, if they show good profits, will prompt the directors to propose a dividend half-way through the year. This dividend will generally have been paid by the year-end. The final/proposed dividend represents any extra dividend the directors propose based on the full year's accounts. This dividend is normally decided upon and proposed after the balance sheet date and thus will not have been paid (only proposed) by the year-end. The current treatment for proposed dividends is that they are deducted from profits after tax in the appropriation account and shown as a current liability in the balance sheet. However, FRS 21 Events After the Balance Sheet Date removes the requirement to report dividends proposed after the balance sheet date in the profit and loss account and instead requires disclosures in the notes to the financial statements. The FRS is mandatory for accounting periods beginning on or after 1 January 2005 for all entities other than those applying the FRSSE. This accords with the now generally accepted view that dividends declared after the balance sheet date should not be reported as liabilities. The government has announced a parallel change in the law to take effect in 2005. Thus most companies will only show proposed dividends as a note to the accounts in accounting periods beginning on or after 1 January 2005.

Note 7: Retained profits

These are the profits that have not been distributed as dividends and are thus retained in the company. The retained profits brought forward from last year (€17,100) represent all the profits retained in the business since the company started. Retained profits carried forward (€17,500) represents all the profits retained in the business including this year's profits. Retained profits carried forward will be shown in the balance sheet under capital and reserves.

The balance sheet

The balance sheet is presented in a similar way to the balance sheet of the sole proprietor with a number of exceptions. The format chosen for presentation also follows closely one of the formats suggested by the Companies Act. The general differences between the balance sheet of a sole proprietorship and a company are as follows:

Note 8: Fixed assets
These are generally shown under two categories, tangible fixed assets and intangible fixed assets. Examples of tangible fixed assets are land and buildings, motor vehicles, plant and equipment, fixtures and fittings. These assets are normally presented in the balance sheet at net book value with a note to the accounts showing the cost and accumulated depreciation figures.

Note 9: Intangible assets
Intangible fixed assets are assets that do not have a physical existence such as rights, licences, patents and trademarks, and the goodwill of a business.

FRS 10 Goodwill and Intangible Assets requires:

❑ Purchased goodwill and intangibles should be capitalised as assets in the balance sheet.
❑ Internally generated goodwill should not be capitalised.
❑ Goodwill should be calculated as the excess of the price paid less the total fair value of the assets acquired.
❑ Purchased goodwill and intangibles should be amortised (i.e. depreciated) over their useful economic life. If, however, they are regarded as having an indefinite useful economic life, then they should not be amortised.

Note 10: Investments
If a company has any investments or is part-owner of another company, then these investments are shown in the balance sheet under this category at cost.

Note 11: Creditors
These are classified into those repayable within twelve months (current liabilities) and those payable in greater than twelve months (long-term liabilities). Creditors

payable within twelve months would also include some new items such as corporation tax due along with the more usual items such as trade creditors, accruals and bank overdraft. Creditors payable in greater than twelve months would include the amounts payable in greater than twelve months of long-term loans and debentures.

Note 12: Share capital and share premium

Share capital is valued in the balance sheet at its nominal value, which is the nomination (i.e. €1 shares or €2 shares) they were given when the company was set up. The market value of the shares is what the shares are worth if they were sold now. However, the shares are shown at their nominal value in the balance sheet. If the company issues shares and they are purchased for above their nominal value, then the shares are recorded at their nominal value in the share capital account and the premium is recorded in a share premium account.

Note 13: Capital reserves and revenue reserves

Reserves are profits that have been reinvested in the business and are classified as follows:

Capital reserves are reserves that are not available for distribution in the form of dividend to shareholders. Example of capital reserves would be:

❑ The share premium account, which would in fact be termed a capital reserve as this reserve has occurred because shares were issued at a price greater than the nominal value.

❑ Revaluation reserve, which occurs when land and property assets are re-valued. This creates a notional profit, as it will only be realised in cash form when the property is sold. Until then this notional profit will not appear in the profit and loss account but will appear as a reserve in the balance sheet. Obviously a business cannot pay a dividend out of this reserve as there is no cash backing it up. The double entry when revaluing assets is to:
 – Debit the asset account.
 – Credit a revaluation reserve account.

Revenue reserves are profits from the activities of the business that have been retained in the business. Revenue reserves consist of unused profits remaining in the appropriation accounts (retained profits) or any amounts that have been transferred to a reserve account from the appropriation account. The double entry for a transaction transferring profits to reserves is:

1. Debit the appropriation account.
2. Credit a reserve account.

The main distinction between capital reserves and revenue reserves is that dividends are not paid out of capital reserves whereas they can be paid out of revenue reserves.

Note 14: Shareholders' funds

This figure represents the amount of funds the shareholders have invested in the company to date. It is the accumulation of issued share capital both preference and ordinary shares and the capital and revenue reserves of the company. It represents the owner's investment in the company.

The Profit and Loss Appropriation Account

The above illustration has introduced many new terms including the profit and loss appropriation account. The key changes relating to the appropriation account require extra attention before progressing to a comprehensive example. Example 14.2 concentrates on the preparation of the appropriation account.

Example 14.2: *The profit and loss appropriation account*

The following details are from the accounts of a hotel company which is financed through a mixture of 200,000 ordinary shares of €1 each and 100,000 – 8 per cent preference shares of €0.50 each. You are required to prepare an appropriation account for two years.

	2004	2003
	€	€
Net profit before tax	150,000	100,000
Transfer to general reserve	25,000	20,000
Transfer to fixed asset replacement reserve	15,000	15,000
Corporation tax	19,000	12,500
Ordinary dividend		
Interim	22,500	15,000
Proposed	15,000	10,000
Retained profit brought forward from last year		100,000

N. Profit
— tax

— preference Dividend
— ordinary dividend

Approach

Profit and Loss Appropriation Account

	2004		2003	
	€	€	€	€
Net profit before tax		150,000		100,000
Corporation tax		(19,000)		(12,500)
Net profit after tax		131,000		87,500
Transfer to reserve				
General reserve	25,000		20,000	
Fixed asset replacement reserve	15,000	(40,000)	15,000	(35,000)
Dividends ~(100,000 × .50 ×8%)				
Preference share dividend	4,000		4,000	
Interim ordinary dividend	22,500		15,000	
Proposed ordinary dividend	15,000	(41,500)	10,000	(29,000)
Retained profit for the year		49,500		23,500
Add retained profit b/f		123,500		100,000
Retained profit c/f		173,000		123,500

Notes

❑ The proposed ordinary dividend of €10,000 in 2003 and €15,000 in 2004 will be shown as a current liability in the balance sheet. For accounting periods beginning on or after 1 January 2005, any dividends proposed after the balance sheet date are shown in a note to the account and will not appear in the appropriation account or balance sheet.

❑ The preference dividend is calculated as follows: 100,000 shares x 0.50 cent x 8 per cent.

A Comprehensive Example

The following example takes into account all the learning points covered in this section so far and applies them to the preparation of the final accounts for a limited company.

Example 14.3: *A comprehensive example*

The following trial balance has been extracted at the close of business on 30 June 2005 for Cool Sportswear Ltd, a chain of retail sports outlets:

	€	€
Sales		267,500
Purchases	173,900	
Opening stock (1 July 2004)	28,500	
Motor expenses	6,000	
Directors' remuneration	22,000	
Rates	10,000	
Wages and salaries	26,000	
Light and heat	6,000	
Insurance	5,000	
Premises at cost	140,000	
Fixtures and fittings at cost	40,000	
Motor vehicles at cost	23,000	
Provision for depreciation (1 July 2004)		
Fixtures and fittings		5,400
Motor vehicles		6,800
Bank	6,300	
Debtors	45,500	
Creditors		12,000
10% debentures (2015) long-term loan.		25,000 2,500
Ordinary share capital (€1 shares)		160,000
Share premium		30,000
General reserve		10,000
Retained profit (1 July 2004) opening balance in P+L appropriation account		22,500
Debenture interest paid	2,000	
Interim ordinary dividend paid	5,000	
	539,200	539,200

Additional information:

1. Closing stock at 30 June 2005 was €52,000.
2. Accrue for debenture interest.
3. You are required to depreciate the following assets on a straight-line basis as follows: fixtures and fittings 10 per cent and motor vehicles 20 per cent.
4. The directors have proposed a final ordinary dividend of 10 cent per share.
5. The directors have decided to transfer €5,000 to reserve.   160,000 × 10c = 16,000
6. An amount of €1,800 is due for light and heat at 30 June 2005.
7. The corporation tax liability for the year amounts to €3,000 and has not been paid by the year-end.

You are required to:

(a) Prepare Cool Sportswear Ltd's trading account, profit and loss account and appropriation account for the year ended 30 June 2005.
(b) Prepare Cool Sportswear Ltd's balance sheet as at 30 June 2005.

Approach

Trading and Profit and Loss Account and Appropriation Account
for the Year Ended 30 June 2005

	€	€
Sales		267,500
Less cost of goods sold		
Opening stock	28,500	
Add purchases	173,900	
Less closing stock	(52,000)	(150,400)
Gross profit		117,100
Less expenses		
Motor expenses	6,000	
Directors' remuneration	22,000	
Rates	10,000	
Wages and salaries	26,000	
Light and heat (6,000 + accrual, 1,800 = 7,800)	7,800	
Insurance	5,000	
Depreciation		
Fixtures and fittings	4,000	
Motor vehicles	4,600	(85,400)
Net profit before interest and tax		31,700
Debenture interest		(2,500)
Net profit before tax		29,200
Corporation tax		(3,000)
Net profit after interest and tax		26,200
Transfer to reserve	5,000	
Dividends		
Interim ordinary dividend	5,000	
Proposed ordinary dividends	16,000	(26,000)
Retained profit for the year		200
Add retained profit b/f		22,500
Retained profit c/f		22,700

Appropriation Account

Balance Sheet as at 30 June 2005

	Cost	Accumulated depreciation	NBV
	€	€	€
Fixed assets			
Premises	140,000	5,400 + 4,000 0	140,000
Fixtures and fittings	40,000	(9,400)	30,600
Motor vehicles	23,000	(11,400)	11,600
	203,000	(20,800)	182,200
Current assets			
Stock		52,000	
Debtors		45,500	
Bank		6,300	
		103,800	
Current liabilities			
Creditors	12,000		
Debenture interest due	500		
Light and heat due (accrual)	1,800		
Proposed dividends	16,000		
Corporation tax	3,000	(33,300)	
Net current assets			70,500
Long-term liabilities			
10% debentures			(25,000)
			227,700
Capital and reserves			
Share capital			
Ordinary share capital			160,000
Reserves			
Share premium			30,000
General reserve			15,000
Retained profit			22,700
			227,700

Notes to the solution

❑ The directors' remuneration appears as an expense in the profit and loss account.
❑ In this example the annual interest rate on the debenture is 10 per cent. Therefore an interest figure of €2,500 (€25,000 at 10%) will appear as an expense in the profit and loss account for the year whether it is paid or not. In

the above case the debenture interest paid (the figure in the trial balance) is €2,000, thus we need to accrue for the balance of €500. The €500 will appear in the balance sheet under current liabilities.

❑ The corporation tax is deducted from profit and since it has not been paid it will also appear in the balance sheet under current liabilities.

❑ The directors have decided to transfer €5,000 to general reserves. Thus €5,000 is deducted from retained profits and added to the general reserve account in the balance sheet. General reserves before the transfer amounted to €10,000 (trial balance figure) and will now appear in the balance sheet at €15,000.

❑ The interim ordinary dividend appears in the appropriation account. Since it has already been paid it will not be a current liability in the balance sheet.

❑ The proposed final dividend is calculated as 10 cent x 160,000 shares x €1 which equals €16,000. This figure is deducted in the appropriation account and shown as a current liability in the balance sheet. For accounting periods beginning on or after 1 January 2005 any dividends proposed after the balance sheet date will be shown only in a note to the accounts and thus will not appear in the appropriation account or as a current liability in the balance sheet.

Published Accounts and Reports

The Companies (Amendment) Act 1986 is the principal act governing the publication of accounts in Ireland and is derived from the EU 4th Directive. All companies in Ireland (both public and private) are required to publish their accounts in accordance with the Companies Acts and all generally accepted accounting principles and standards such as the financial reporting standards that are issued from the accounting bodies. Every company has a legal duty to deliver to the Registrar of Companies a copy of its financial statements. The copies delivered to the Registrar are available for inspection by any member of the public.

The Companies (Amendment) Act 1986 allowed a choice of four different formats for the profit and loss account and two formats for the balance sheet. Also other information is required to be disclosed in notes to the accounts. The objective is to increase the levels of information and comparability.

Small and medium-sized private companies do not have to publish as much information as large companies. For example, small companies do not have to provide a profit and loss account and only need to provide an abridged balance sheet. Medium-sized companies publish an abridged balance sheet as well as a short profit and loss statement starting at gross profit. Small and medium-sized companies are exempt from the full extent of the requirements relating to annual accounts in respect of any financial year if in respect of that year and the financial year immediately preceding that year the company satisfies two of the three following conditions:

Table 14.1: *Exemption requirements*

	Small companies	Medium companies
Balance sheet totals not exceeding	€1.9m	€7.62
Turnover not exceeding	€3.81m	€15.24
Number of employees not exceeding	50	250

Published financial statements

It is beyond the scope of this text to go into detail regarding the format of published accounts. Thus the following example will only give a flavour of the format and presentation of published accounts.

The profit and loss account and balance sheet prepared for publication differ from those that are prepared for internal use by management. The main differences are in the areas of terminology and format.

Terminology in published financial statements

The published accounts use terminology prescribed by law. The regulatory framework, which governs accounting and the way in which accounting statements are presented, has undergone significant change in recent times. There is presently a transition period during which presenters of accounting statements for publication must familiarise themselves with new requirements regarding terminology. There are also different time-frames involved in the implementation of these new requirements depending on whether the accounts are those of a public or private company. Table 14.2 compares some of the main differences in the terminology used and the dates for implementation for both private and public companies:

Table 14.2: *Terminology used in published accounts*

Internal use	Publication by Plc prior to 1/1/2005 by Ltd prior to 1/1/2007	Publication by Plc post 1/1/2005 by Ltd post 1/1/2007
P&L account	P&L account	Income statement
Sales	Turnover	Revenue
Stock (opening and closing)	Stock (opening and closing)	Inventory (opening and closing)
Net profit	Operating profit	Profit from operations
Fixed assets	Fixed assets	Non-current assets
Debtors	Debtors	Receivables
Current liabilities	Creditors: amounts falling due within one year	Current liabilities
Long-term liabilities	Creditors: amounts falling due after more than one year	Non-current liabilities
Working capital	Net current assets	*Not shown*

The format of published financial statements

The information included in published financial statements should conform strictly with the requirements of company law and accounting standards. The financial report of a company should include the profit and loss account, the balance sheet and a cash flow statement. Previous years' figures must be incorporated. The notes to the accounts give explanations and more details on key figures in the accounts. The Companies Acts and financial reporting standards outline the structure the financial statements must take and the notes required.

Case Example: Arnotts

The following published consolidated profit and loss, consolidated balance sheet and a sample of the accompanying notes published by Arnotts give a view of what is required.

Illustration 14.2: *Published accounts of Arnotts*

Arnotts
Group Profit and Loss Account
Year Ended 31 January 2003

	Note	2003 €'000	2002 €'000
Turnover including concession sales		204,192	192,520
Concession sales	2	-56,009	-51,937
Turnover excluding concession sales	2	148,183	140,583
Operating profit	3	21,158	18,020
Share of operating profit of associated undertaking		309	1,294
Profit before interest		21,467	19,314
Net interest payable	4	-1,004	-1,432
Profit before taxation		20,463	17,882
Taxation	5	-3,283	-3,043
Profit for the financial year	6	17,180	14,839
Dividends paid	7	-1,918	-1,678
Dividends proposed	7	-4,671	-4,043
Increase in retained profits		10,591	9,118

Statement of retained profits

		2003	2002
At beginning of year		58,684	51,344
Increase in retained profits		10,591	9,118
Purchase of own shares		-	-1,778
At end of year		69,275	58,684
Earnings per ordinary share	8	96.6c	82.6c
Diluted earnings per ordinary share	8	95.3c	82.0c

Arnotts
Group Balance Sheet
31 January 2003

	Note	2003 €'000	2002 €'000
Fixed assets			
Tangible assets	9	240,042	223,367
Financial assets	10	2,297	2,018
		242,339	225,385
Current assets			
Stocks	11	16,470	16,903
Debtors	12	13,263	13,786
Cash		8,703	7,665
		38,436	38,354
Creditors (amounts falling due within one year)	13	-42,540	-47,727
Net current liabilities		-4,104	-9,373
Total assets less current liabilities		238,235	216,012
Creditors (amounts falling due after more than one year)	14	-9,729	-14,873
Provisions for liabilities and charges	16	-2,259	-2,011
		226,247	199,128
Capital and reserves			
Called-up share capital (Equity and non-equity)	17	23,482	23,448
Share premium account	18	953	871
Revaluation reserve	18	132,311	115,899
Other reserve	18	226	226
P&L account	18	69,275	58,684
Shareholders' funds	19	226,247	199,128

From the published statements you will note that most figures have a reference to a note which gives more detail on the relevant figure in the account. These notes are to be found in the published accounts after the financial statements. There were 33 notes in the Arnotts statements shown above. The following are a sample of such notes:

Note 3: Operating profit

	2003	2002
	€'000	€'000
Turnover	148,183	140,583
Cost of sales	-96,813	-92,216
Gross profit	51,370	48,367
Selling and distribution costs	-28,727	-27,839
Administrative expenses	-5,930	-6,037
Occupancy and other operating expenses	-11,303	-10,546
Other operating income	14,850	14,075
Royalty income from associated undertaking	898	-
Group operating profit	21,158	18,020
Operating profit has been arrived at after charging:		
Depreciation	6,357	6,014
Auditors' remuneration	91	87
Operating lease rentals	1,350	1,225

Note 9: Tangible assets

	Freehold and leasehold land and buildings	Plant, equipment and fittings	Motor vehicles	Total
	€'000	€'000	€'000	€'000
Group				
Cost or valuation				
At 31 January 2002				
Valuation	194,791	-	-	194,791
Cost	3,553	54,231	9	57,793
Additions	2,518	4,102	-	6,620
Surplus on revaluation	14,423	-	-	14,423
At 31 January 2003	215,285	58,333	9	273,627
Accumulated depreciation				
At 31 January 2002	983	28,225	9	29,217
Charge for year	1,006	5,351	-	6,357
Surplus on revaluation	-1,989	-	-	-1,989
At 31 January 2003	-	33,576	9	33,585
Net book amounts				

At 31 January 2002	197,361	26,006	-	223,367
At 31 January 2003				
Valuation	215,285	-	-	215,285
Cost	-	58,333	9	58,342
Accumulated depreciation	-	-33,576	-9	-33,585
	215,285	24,757	-	240,042

The net book value of plant, equipment and fittings (group and company) includes €359,000 (2002: €426,000) in respect of leased assets. The depreciation charge for the year in respect of these assets was €182,000 (2002: €163,000).

Included in the cost of fixed assets (group and company) is interest capitalised of €2,398,000 (2002: €2,398,000).

The freehold and leasehold properties were valued as at 31 January 2003 by Jones Lang LaSalle, Chartered Surveyors, acting as external valuers in accordance with the practice statements published by the Society of Chartered Surveyors in Ireland. Properties occupied by the group were valued on the basis of existing use values and properties held for investment/development were valued on the basis of open market value.

As Arnotts was deemed by the Irish Takeover Panel to be in an offer period from 2 December 2002, a copy of the Jones Lang LaSalle Valuation Certificate is available for inspection, at the offices of William Fry Solicitors, Fitzwilton House, Wilton Place, Dublin 2 (during normal business hours) in accordance with Rule 29.5 of the Irish Takeover Panel Act 1997 Takeover (Amendment) Rules 2002, from 26 March 2003 until the offer period ends.

The estimated useful lives of tangible assets by reference to which depreciation is calculated are as follows:

❑ Buildings   100 years
❑ Plant, equipment and fittings   4, 5, 7, 10 and 20 years
❑ Motor vehicles   4 years

Note 12: Debtors

	2003	2002
	€'000	€'000
Group		
Trade debtors	12,841	13,469
Amounts owed by associated undertaking	33	-
Prepayments and accrued income	389	317
	13,263	13,786

Note 13: Creditors (Amounts falling due within one year)

	2003 €'000	2002 €'000
Group		
Bank loans (unsecured)	5,079	11,745
Bank overdraft (unsecured)	717	729
Trade creditors	17,975	17,886
Other creditors	1,803	1,824
Corporation tax	1,746	3,053
Income tax deducted under PAYE	361	393
Pay-related social insurance	358	367
Value-added tax	2,421	1,650
Accruals	7,232	5,843
Dividends (Note 7)	4,671	4,043
Finance leases	177	194
	42,540	47,727

The full financial report of Arnotts can be viewed on their website: www.arnotts.ie.

FRS 3 Reporting Financial Performance

Financial Reporting Standard 3 was issued to 'aid users in understanding the performance achieved by a reporting entity in a period, and to assist them in forming a basis for their assessment of future results and cash flows'.

This text will limit itself to introducing you to a number of the requirements of FRS 3 which help in achieving the above objectives.

Part of the requirement of FRS 3 is to:

❑   Show the results of continued and discontinued operations.
❑   Provide a statement of total recognised gains and losses.
❑   Provide a statement of reconciliation of movement in shareholders' funds.

Results of continuing and discontinued operations

In comparing company accounts it is important to compare like with like. For a company that has changed its business profile in the current year through various acquisitions or disposals of parts of the business, it would be very difficult to assess the performance of the company as one is not comparing like with like. Also, trying to see what the future would hold for the company would be very difficult. Thus FRS 3 requires the following to be highlighted in the profit and loss account if they are material:

❑ What the results of continuing operations are.
❑ What the results of discontinued operations have been.
❑ What the results of acquired operations are.
❑ The profit or loss on the disposals of discontinued operations, the costs of a fundamental reorganisation or restructuring of the company, profits or losses on the disposals of fixed assets.
❑ The company must split the turnover and operating profit figures into the three categories.

Illustration 14.3: *Results of continued and discontinued operations*

Leisure Hotels Plc
Published Profit and Loss Account for the Year Ended 31 December 2004

	€'000	€'000
Turnover		1,000
Continuing operations	600	
Acquisitions	150	
Discontinued operations	250	
	1,000	
Cost of sales		600
Gross profit		400
Distribution expenses	160	
Administration expenses	90	250
Operating profit		150
Continuing operations	110	
Acquisitions	60	
Discontinued operations	(20)	
	150	
Profit on disposal of discontinued operations		10
Other operating income		30
		190

Statement of total recognised gains and losses

This is a statement introduced to show the extent to which shareholders' funds (share capital and reserves) have increased or decreased from all the various gains and losses recognised in the accounting period. It enables users to consider all recognised gains and losses of a reporting entity in assessing its overall performance. Remember some gains (termed unrealised gains as they are unlikely to be converted into cash in the near future) like the gain on the revaluation of a fixed asset would be credited to a revaluation reserve in the balance sheet rather than credited to the profit and loss account. Also gains or losses on the *translated* value of assets held in foreign countries (outside the euro zone) due to currency fluctuations would be unrealised gains/losses and thus would be credited/debited to unrealised reserves.

Illustration 14.4: *Statement of total recognised gains and losses*

Leisure Hotels Plc
Statement of Total Recognised Gains and Losses

	2004 €'000
Profit on ordinary activities after tax	200
Unrealised surplus on revaluation of properties	12
Unrealised losses on currency translation differences	(8)
Total recognised gains and losses for the year	204

Reconciliation of movement in shareholders' funds

Shareholders' funds are the issued share capital, share premium and reserves of a company. The profit and loss account and the statement of total recognised gains and losses reflect the performance of a reporting entity in a period, but there are other changes that can occur in shareholders' funds that that these two statements do not show, and which can be important in understanding the change in the financial position of an entity. For example, a new share issue would not be reflected in either of the above statements.

The reconciliation of movement in shareholders' funds would look as follows:

Illustration 14.5: *Reconciliation of movements in shareholders' funds*

Leisure Hotels Plc
Reconciliation of Movements in Shareholders' Funds

	2004 €'000
Profit after tax	200
Dividends	(100)
Retained profit	100
Other recognised gains and losses relating to the year (12 - 8)	4
New share capital issued	20
Net addition to shareholders' funds	124
Opening shareholders' funds	300
Closing shareholders' funds	424

FRS 3 is effective for companies in relation to accounting periods ending on or after 22 June 1993. The ASB issued an exposure draft in December 2000 (FRED 22) proposing a new standard to replace FRS 3. However, to date no new standard has been issued.

Summary

Limited liability company status is increasing in popularity as a form of legal organisation in Ireland. This is mainly due to the tax advantages as well as limited liability status. In Ireland the rate of corporation or company tax is 12.5 per cent whereas the profits of sole proprietorships and partnerships are taxed at income tax rates that begin at 20 per cent but quickly move on to 42 per cent. This alone would entice many businesses to incorporate in the future. As limited liability companies are considered separate legal entities from their owners they are governed by the Companies Acts 1963 to present. Along with the Companies Acts, companies must also comply with all SSAPs and FRSs as issued by the ASB, which is the representative body of the main professional accounting bodies in Ireland and the UK. All accounting standards are compulsory and are given full legal backing through company law. In 2005 all listed companies will be obliged to follow IFRSs and this will apply to all private companies by 1 January 2007.

The main information points covered in this chapter are as follows:

❑ Companies are normally financed through a combination of owners' contribution (share capital) and loans.

❑ Companies can be financed by two main types of share capital: preference shares and ordinary shares. Preference shareholders are offered a fixed rate of dividend each year but do not have any voting rights. The ordinary shareholders are the 'real owners' of the company and share fully in the risks and rewards of the company.

❑ Part of a shareholder's reward comes in the form of dividends. Dividends are a share of the profits that the directors decide should be given to the shareholders. The balance of profits are retained in the company.

❑ Loan capital or debt refers to the loans acquired by a company. Loans can be acquired in two ways:
  – Approaching your bank in the normal way.
  – The company issuing its own loans/debentures.

❑ The profit and loss appropriation account is prepared to show how profits or losses are to be divided up or distributed. For a company, the directors must decide on how the profits after tax are to be appropriated. In other words, how much is to be given to shareholders in the form of dividends and how much is to be retained in the business.

❑   Shareholders' fund is the term given to the amount invested in a company by its shareholders. It is made up of share capital and the reserves of the business.

❑   Reserves are profits that have been reinvested in the business and are classified as follows:

–   *Capital reserves*: These are reserves that are not available for distribution in the form of dividend to shareholders.

–   *Revenue reserves*: These are profits from the activities of the business that have been retained in the business. Revenue reserves consist of unused profits remaining in the appropriation accounts (retained profits) or any amounts that have been transferred to a reserve account from the appropriation account.

❑   The Companies (Amendment) Act 1986 is the principal act governing the publication of accounts in Ireland and it derives from the EU 4th Directive.

❑   The profit and loss account and balance sheet prepared for publication differ from those that are prepared for internal use by management. The main differences are in the areas of terminology and format.

❑   FRS 3 was issued to 'aid users in understanding the performance achieved by a reporting entity in a period and to assist them in forming a basis for their assessment of future results and cash flows'. Part of its requirement are for companies to show more information such as:

–   The results of continued and discontinued operations.

–   A statement of total recognised gains and losses.

–   A statement of reconciliation of movement in shareholders' funds.

Review Questions

Question 14.1

Distinguish between each of the following:

(a) Public and private companies.
(b) Shares and debentures.
(c) Ordinary shares and preference shares.
(d) Capital reserves and revenue reserves.
(e) Interim dividend and a final dividend.

Question 14.2

Explain what you understand by the following:

(a) Nominal capital.
(b) Called-up capital.
(c) Paid-up capital.
(d) Authorised capital.
(e) Loan capital.

Question 14.3

As the accountant is unavailable, your help has been requested with the preparation of the year-end company accounts of Ace Tours Ltd. The following data has been provided:

Extracts from the Opening Balance Sheet 1 June 2003

Long-term liabilities	€
10% debentures	500,000

Capital and reserves	
Ordinary share capital 1 million shares €3 each	3,000,000
8% preference share capital	600,000
Share premium	700,000
Fixed asset replacement reserve	150,000
P&L reserve	440,000
General reserve	60,000
	4,950,000

Transactions Paid During the Year

Interim ordinary share dividend paid	€60,000
Debenture interest paid	€35,000

Net operating profit before interest and tax for the year ended 31 May 2004 amounted to €950,000. The following data relates to dividend policy, debt interest payments and adjustments for year ended 31 May 2004:

1. Corporation tax of €80,000 should be provided for.
2. Outstanding debenture interest should be provided for.
3. The preference share dividend should be provided for.
4. A final ordinary share dividend of 65 cent per share has been proposed.
5. An additional transfer of €50,000 to the general reserve is to be processed.

Required

(a) Prepare a profit and loss appropriation account for year ended 31 May 2004.
(b) Show extracts from current liabilities as at 31 May 2004 recognising any outstanding payments from above.
(c) Show the capital and reserves position as at 31 May 2004.

Question 14.4

Zebra RD Ltd is an established company providing both retailing and distribution services. The following trial balance was extracted from the books of Zebra RD Ltd on the 31 August 2004:

	Dr	Cr
	€'000	€'000
Sales		3,700
Returns in *Subtract from sales*	18	
Stock (1/9/2003)	180	
Purchases	1,860	
Carriage in *add to purchases*	22	
Returns out *subtract from purchases.*		26
Rent received		38
Discount received		27
Administration costs *+ accrual*	715	
Sales and distribution costs *- prepayment*	475	
Discount allowed	38	
Carriage out	13	

(1,500,000 – 1,410,000 = 90,000 depreciation)

Premises (cost €1,500,000)	1,410 – current value	
Vehicles (cost €980,000)	700	
Furniture and equipment (cost €450,000)	340	
Bank	30	
Debtors	300	
Creditors		155
12% debentures (due 2015)		225 × 12% = 27,000 – 18
Ordinary shares (300,000 @ €5 per share)		1,500
10% preference shares		350 × 10% = 35,000
General reserve		30
Debenture interest	18	
Interim ordinary dividend paid	15	
Retained profit (1/9/2003)		83
	6,134	6,134

Additional information:

1. A stock count valued stock on the 31 August 2004 at €162,000.
2. Administration fees of €4,000 have yet to be paid and are to be accrued for.
3. Distribution costs of €8,000 have been prepaid at 31 August 2004. subtract
4. Depreciation is to be provided on fixed assets as follows:
    — Premises 2% straight line.
    — Vehicles 10% reducing balance.
    — Furniture and equipment 20% straight line.
5. Any outstanding debenture interest is to be provided for. profit + loss % → 27,000 Balance sheet → 9,000
6. A provision is to be made for preference share dividend. (27,000 – 18,000)
7. A final ordinary share dividend of 30 cent per share is proposed. (300,000 × 30c = 90,000)
8. A transfer should be made to general reserves of €32,000. Balance sheet → 62,000 P+L account → 32,000

Required Total ordinary dividends = interim + final = 16,000 + 90,000 = 105,000

(a) The trading, profit and loss account for the year.
(b) The profit and loss appropriation account for the year.
(c) The balance sheet as at 31 August 2004.

Question 14.5

The following is the trial balance of Gaelic Souvenir Retailers Ltd for the year ended 31 March 2005:

	Dr	Cr
	€	€
Ordinary share capital		250,000
10% debentures		130,000
Buildings as per revaluation estimate	500,000	
Fixtures and fittings at cost	65,000	
Equipment at cost	45,000	
Provision for depreciation fixtures and fittings 1/4/04		35,000
Provision for depreciation equipment 1/4/04		25,000
Stock as at 1/4/04	4,500	
Purchases	78,000	
Sales		242,743
Wages and salaries +3,938	78,000	
Motor expenses	8,250	
Insurance less prepayment.	11,568	
Rates	15,897	
Debenture interest	10,000	
Advertising	9,870	
Light and heat	4,520	
Telephone	4,320	
Carriage inwards	525	
VAT refund due	980	
Debtors	2,500	
Creditors		6,890
General reserve		12,560
Share premium		20,000
Interim ordinary dividend paid	5,000	
General expenses	9,353	
Bad debts	2,560	
Rental income		24,000
Retained profit 1/4/04		12,000
Bank	2,350	
Revaluation reserve		100,000
	858,193	858,193

Additional information:

1. Stock as at 31 March 2005 was valued at €3,780.
2. Accrue for debenture interest.
3. Provide for corporation tax of €2,300.
4. Fixtures and fittings are to be depreciated on a straight-line basis at the annual rate of 10%.

5. Equipment is to be depreciated on the reducing-balance basis at the annual rate of 20%.
6. Provide for a final ordinary dividend of 2%. of ordinary shares
7. Transfer €3,000 to a general reserve account.
8. Insurance prepaid at the year-end amounts to €2,000.
9. PAYE and PRSI due at the year-end amounts to €3,938.
10. A provision for bad debts against a specific debtor is to be made amounting to €500.

Required

(a) Prepare the trading, profit and loss account and the profit and loss appropriation account for the year ended 31 March 2005.
(b) Prepare a balance sheet as at 31 March 2005.

Question 14.6

From the following trial balance you are required to prepare the trading, profit and loss account for the business of Leisure Hotels Ltd for the year ended 30 June 2003 and a balance sheet at that date.

	Dr	Cr
	€	€
Issued 7% preference share capital €1 each		70,000
Issued ordinary share capital €1 each		150,000
6% debentures		250,000
Share premium		50,000
Buildings at cost	550,000	
Furniture at cost	70,000	
Equipment at cost	60,000	
Stock as at 1/7/02	10,000	
Provision for depreciation (1/7/02)		
Furniture		25,000
Equipment		20,000
Directors remuneration	50,000	
Wages and salaries	252,000	
Motor expenses	15,000	
Rates and insurance	12,000	
Sales		590,000

Purchases	158,900	
General expenses	20,000	
Advertising	32,000	
Audit fees	10,000	
Debenture interest paid	2,100	
Debtors	13,000	
Creditors		27,000
Bank		15,000
General reserve		30,000
Interim ordinary dividend paid	5,000	
Retained profits (1/7/02)		33,000
	1,260,000	1,260,000

Additional information:

1. Stock counted and valued at 30 June 2003 amounted to €8,000.
2. Insurance include €3,000 of cover that relates to the year to 30 June 2004.
3. Wages owing at 30 June 2003 amounts to €5,000.
4. A provision for bad debts is to be created at a level of 2% of debtors.
5. It is the policy of the business to depreciate furniture at 10% per annum straight-line method. Equipment is to be depreciated at 20% straight-line method. There is no depreciation on premises.
6. Corporation tax of €3,500 is to be provided for.
7. The directors have proposed the following:
   - Preference dividends and a 5% final ordinary dividend are to be provided for.
   - €5,000 is to be transferred to a general reserve.
8. The authorised share capital of the company is 100,000 preference shares and 250,000 ordinary shares, both having a nominal value of €1.
9. At the year-end the company issued to a private investor 50,000 additional
✱ ordinary shares at a premium of €1.75, the company receiving the money in full. The company used €50,000 from the issue of shares to pay off part of the debenture loan. Neither of these transactions have been accounted for.

   nominal value €1   50,000 × 2·75 = 137,500

Required

(a) Prepare a trading, profit and loss account and profit and loss appropriation account for the year to 30 June 2003.
(b) Prepare a balance sheet at that date.

Question 14.7

The Clothing Company is a retail outlet operating from a premises located in a busy suburb in County Dublin. The store trades in trendy, good-quality clothing. The trial balance below was extracted from the accounts system to assist in the preparation of the annual accounts for 2005.

Trial Balance as at 30 September 2005

	Dr	Cr
	€'000	€'000
Administration costs	230	
Bank	69	
Creditors		138
Debenture interest	7	
Debenture loan (6%)		300
Debtors	305	
Depreciation equipment (1/10/2004)		192
Depreciation shop fittings (1/10/2004)		270
Directors remuneration	68	
Distribution costs	160	
Equipment	235	
Goodwill	350	
Investments	75	
Ordinary share capital		600
Preference share capital		250
Property	770	
Purchases	1,790	
General reserve		90
Retained profit (1/10/2004)		254
Shop fittings	350	
Stock (1/10/2004)	235	
Turnover		2,550
	4,644	4,644

Additional information:

1. Authorised share capital is as follows:
   — 400,000 ordinary shares with a nominal value of €2 each.
   — 150,000 10% preference shares with a nominal value of €2.50 each.
2. Closing stock at 30 September 2005 amounted to €375,000.
3. Depreciation is to be provided on assets as follows:

- Shop fittings 10% reducing balance.
- Equipment 10% straight line.

4. Property was re-valued during the year resulting in an increase in value of €80,000. This has not been accounted for to date.
5. Administration expenses accruals of €30,000 are to be provided for.
6. Distribution expenses accruals of €15,000 are to be provided for.
7. Administration expenses prepayment at 30 September 2005 amount to €22,000.
8. A transfer of €20,000 is to be made to a general reserve.
9. Corporation tax of €40,000 is to be provided for.
10. Debenture interest is to be provided for in full.
11. It is proposed that ordinary shareholders will be paid a dividend of 20 cent per share. Preference dividends should be provided for in full.
12. At the year-end 50,000 ordinary shares were issued at a premium of €1.50, the company receiving the money in full. The company used €100,000 from the issue of shares to pay off part of the debenture loan. Neither of these transactions have been accounted for.

Required

You are required to assist in the preparation of the annual accounts for The Clothing Company by preparing:

(a) The trading, profit and loss and appropriation account for year ended 30 September 2005.
(b) The balance sheet as at 30 September 2005.

CHAPTER 15

Cash Flow Statements

Learning Outcomes

By the end of this chapter you will be able to:

❑ Distinguish between profit and cash.
❑ Outline the categories of cash inflows and outflows in a business.
❑ Be aware of the requirements of FRS 1.
❑ Reconcile operating profit to operating cash flow.
❑ Prepare cash flow statements in accordance with FRS 1.
❑ Show how the increase or decrease in cash for the reporting period links the net funds or net debt at the start and end of the reporting period.
❑ Interpret and understand the information provided by cash flow statements.

Introduction

Cash is the lifeblood of a business. To run out of cash is to die in the same way as heart failure stops the blood supply in a person. The primary measure of performance of a company is the accruals-based profit and loss account. However, as accountancy and accounting concepts come under fire from unethical business practice, reporting cash as an indicator of performance seems to be growing in importance. Thus a new measure of performance 'cash flow per share' is coming of age.

In his book *Accounting for Growth*, Terry Smith stated that 'cash is king', explaining that 'profits can be manufactured by creative accounting but creating cash is impossible'. He goes on to state that 'profits are someone's opinion (true and fair) whereas cash is a fact'. Thus it can be seen that cash is fast becoming an important objective measure of a company's performance, free from unethical financial engineering.

Cash flows in and out of a business in a variety of ways, as Table 15.1 indicates.

Table 15.1: *Typical cash flows*

		CASH FLOWS			
		IN	OUT		
1. Customer payments	→	X	X	→	1. Suppliers' payments
2. Capital grants	→	X	X	→	2. Staff payments
3. Owners buy shares	→	X	X	→	3. Dividends
4. Sale of fixed assets	→	X	X	→	4. Purchase of fixed assets
5. Bank loans	→	X	X	→	5. Repayment of loans
6. Tax refunds	→	X	X	→	6. Tax
7. Interest received	→	X	X	→	7. Interest paid
8. Sale of business	→	X	X	→	8. Business acquisitions
9. Dividends received	→	X	X	→	9. Overheads/expenses

FRS 1 Cash Flow Statements

As mentioned in earlier chapters the accounting bodies periodically issue standards to ensure all companies account for transactions and present their accounting statements in a prescribed format. FRS 1 is an attempt to ensure that all companies report a summary of their cash flows in such a prescribed manner.

The planning, control and reporting of cash flows is a vital aspect of managing a modern business. Traditionally published accounts comprised of a balance sheet and a profit and loss account. In 1975 a third statement was introduced with the publication of SSAP 10 Statement of Source and Application of Funds. This SSAP was replaced by FRS 1 Cash Flow Statements in 1991, which was revised in 1996. FRS 1 (revised) applies to all medium and large companies as defined by the Companies Act 1986 and relates to accounting periods ending on or after 23 March 1997.

FRS 1 defined cash as:

> Cash in hand and deposits repayable on demand with any qualifying financial institution less overdrafts from any qualifying financial institution repayable on demand. Cash includes cash in hand and deposits denominated in foreign currencies. (FRS 1).
>
> Deposits are repayable on demand if they can be withdrawn at any time without penalty and with notice of not more than 24 hours.

The purpose of FRS 1 Cash Flow Statements is threefold:

1. To show the cash inflows and outflows for the financial year and the consequent increase or decrease in cash. The cash flows are reported in various categories to enable the reader to identify key developments.
2. To convert the operating profit or loss into the equivalent amount of cash released or consumed in the day-to-day running of the business. Put simply, profit is not cash and thus the cash flow statement shows the operating net profit reconciled to the operating cash figure.
3. To show how the increase or decrease in cash for the reporting period links the net funds (where cash and bank balances are greater than loans/debt) or net debt (where loans/debt are greater than bank/cash balances) at the start and end of the reporting period.

Cash flow statements – overall approach

FRS 1 (revised) identified eight categories of cash flow. Every conceivable cash movement must be included under one of these categories:

1. Operating activities.
2. Return on investment/servicing of debt.
3. Taxation.
4. Capital expenditure.
5. Acquisitions and disposals.
6. Equity dividends paid.
7. Management of liquid resources.
8. Financing.

The overall cash movement (the difference between cash at the beginning and end of the year) should equal the total of the cash flows from the various categories.

There are two steps required in preparing a cash flow statement:

1. Calculate the overall cash flow. This is calculated by comparing the cash (as per the FRS 1 definition above) at the beginning and end of the accounting period. If it increases over the period, then the company has generated a positive cash flow; if it has decreased, a negative cash flow has been generated.
2. Prepare the cash flow statement as presented in FRS 1. This involves focusing on each of the eight categories of cash as identified in FRS 1, calculating their respective cash flows and the total of the cash flows from all categories should equal the overall movement in cash as calculated in step one.

Illustration 15.1: *Sample of cash flow*

Step One: Calculate Overall Cash Flow

Total cash movement	€'000
Total movement in cash in the reporting period	
Cash at 1 Jan	300
Cash at 31 Dec	470
Cash movement	+170
Cash increased by €170,000 over the year.	

Step Two: Prepare Cash Flow Statement

Categories of cash	€'000
1. Operating activities	500
2. Return on investment/serving of debt	(10)
3. Taxation	(20)
4. Capital expenditure	(200)
5. Acquisitions and disposals	(100)
6. Equity dividends paid	(50)
7. Management of liquid resources	(50)
8. Financing	100
	+170

Explanation

The cash in the company increased by €170,000 over the period. This can be analysed into the various cash categories some of which are cash inflows and others are cash outflows.

The cash flow statement tells us that this business' main source of cash was its operating activities. It also got some financing of €100,000, through either loans or an issue of shares. The main areas in which it spent cash were in investing in new fixed assets, paying taxation and loan interest liabilities, acquiring new businesses and paying dividends to its shareholders.

There is no cash flow category for expenses. This is because they are included in operating activities as will be explained below.

Cash Flow Categories

Let us now look in more detail at each of the eight categories of cash as identified by FRS 1 and how the cash flow from each category is calculated. The most difficult category to understand and calculate is the first one, net cash flow from operating activities.

Category 1: Net cash flow from operating activities

Cash flows from operating activities are the cash effects of transactions relating to the operating or trading activities of the business (the normal trading activities of the business, not capital activities). Operating cash flows will be concerned with:

❑   Cash collected from customers.
❑   Cash paid to trade creditors for purchases.
❑   Cash paid to staff/PAYE/PRSI.
❑   Cash paid for services (overheads).

In calculating the net cash flow from operating activities, two formats are permitted by FRS 1:

1.   The direct method.
2.   The indirect method.

Although FRS 1 does not prescribe which method to use in calculating the operating cash flow figure it requires the indirect method to be shown in a note to the cash flow statement.

1. The direct method
Under this method we gather the information from the cashbook, detailing cash collected from customers and cash paid to suppliers, staff and overheads.

Illustration 15.2: *Calculation of operating cash flow – the direct method*

	€	€
Cash collected from customers		162,100
Less payments to suppliers	88,790	
payments to staff/PAYE/PRSI	26,150	
payments of other operating expenses	15,100	130,040
Net cash generated from operating activities		32,060

The direct method highlights the operating cash figure, which is the cash figure generated from normal activities before interest and other non-trading cash movements.

2. The indirect method

In this format we are adjusting the operating profit figure (net profit before interest and tax) back to an operating cash figure. This is calculated as follows:

1. Adjusting operating profit for items in the profit and loss account that do not appear in the cash book. These items would include the following:
    — Depreciation.
    — Provision for bad debts.
    — Profits or losses on the sale of fixed asset.
    These items are all categorised as 'non-cash'. In other words they do not give rise to a cash transaction/movement and would not appear in the cash/bank account. If these items have reduced the operating profit (if they were expenses), then to adjust for them we need to add them back to operating profit. If they had the effect of increasing profit, then we deduct them from operating profit.

2. Adjust the operating profit for changes in stocks, debtors, prepayments, accruals and creditors. Changes in the above working capital items cause differences between figures in the profit and loss account and figures in the cash/bank account. For example, a business generated sales of €10,000 during the year. If debtors at the beginning of a period were zero and at the year-end were €2,000, then the business only collected cash from its debtors of €8,000. The profit and loss account records sales at €10,000 but the bank/cash account records sales at €8,000. The difference of €2,000 is caused by the increase in debtors during the year. In this case operating profit is €2,000 greater than operating cash. To adjust operating profit back to operating cash, operating profit must be reduced by the increase in debtors. Any changes in stocks, debtors, prepayments, accruals and creditors need to be adjusted for in calculating operating cash flow from operating profit.

The rules for these adjustments are as follows:

If stock, debtors or prepayments increase between the beginning and end of the year, then, in adjusting operating profit back to operating cash, we need to deduct the amount of the increase from operating profit. The reverse applies if they decrease.

   If creditors or accruals increase between the beginning and end of the year, then, in order to adjust operating profit back to operating cash flow, we add the amount of the increase to operating profit. The reverse applies if they decrease.

These adjustments are explained in more detail below.

Illustration 15.3: *Calculation of operating cash flow – indirect method*

	€	€
Net operating profit (before interest and tax)		5,800
Adjust for non-cash items in P&L		
+Depreciation	10,000	
+Increase in provision for bad debts	3,000	
+Loss on sale of fixed assets	2,200	15,200
		21,000
Adjust for movements in working capital		
Increase in stocks (*increases profit so deduct*)	(2,000)	
Increase in prepayments (*deduct*)	(500)	
Decrease in trade debtors	12,100	
Increase in trade creditors	1,210	
Increase in accruals	250	
Net cash flow from operating activities		11,060
		32,060

The operating cash flow is €32,060 whether we use the direct or indirect method. Ultimately the indirect method outlines for us some of the main reasons for differences between the operating profit figure and the operating cash flow figure and must be shown as a note to the cash flow statement.

Movements in working capital and their effects on operating cash explained

Example 15.1: *Debtors, sales and cash received*

The balance sheet of Flower Sales Ltd showed debtors at the start of the financial year at €48,400. During the year the company made sales of €150,000 and at the year-end debtors amounted to €36,300.

Calculate the cash received from debtors/customers.

Approach

To calculate the cash received from debtors, the opening debtors of €48,400 is added to the sales of €150,000 and the closing debtors €36,300 is deducted. This figure amounts to €162,100 (€48,400 + €150,000 – €36,300).

The profit and loss account shows sales at €150,000 while the bank/cash account shows cash received from debtors as €162,100 which represents a difference of €12,100. This is caused by the decrease in debtors of €12,100. Thus changes in debtors will cause differences between the profit and loss sales and the bank/cash sales. To adjust the profit figure back to the cash figure we increase the net operating profit in the indirect method by the amount of the decrease in debtors. (If debtors increased we would deduct the amount of the increase from net profit.)

If debtors/prepayments increase then:

- Cash receipts fall.
- Sales in the profit and loss account is greater than cash sales.
- Operating profit is greater than operating cash.
- To adjust the operating net profit back to operating cash we reduce the net profit by the increase in debtors.

Debtors and prepayments are technically the same thing and are treated in the same fashion. Thus an increase in prepayments will be deducted from operating profit in adjusting back to the operating cash flow position.

Example 15.2: *Creditors, purchases and cash payments for purchases*

The balance sheet of Chat and Chew Cafés Ltd showed trade creditors at the start of the financial year at €10,890. During the year the company made purchases of €90,000 and at the year-end creditors amounted to €12,100.

Calculate the cash payments to trade creditors.

Approach

To calculate the cash payments to trade creditors the opening creditors of €10,890 is added to €90,000 purchases and closing creditors of €12,100 is deducted. This figure amounts to €88,790 (€10,890 + €90,000 − €12,100).

The profit and loss account shows purchases at €90,000 while the bank/cash account shows cash payments to trade creditors as €88,790, a difference of €1,210 which is caused by the increase in creditors of €1,210. Thus changes in creditors will cause differences between the profit and loss purchases and the bank/cash purchases figures. To adjust the profit and loss back to the cash figure, we increase the operating profit in the indirect method by the amount of the increase in trade creditors. (If creditors decreased we would deduct from operating profit.)

Remember an increase in creditors implies that the business is receiving more credit (interest free loans) and thus this is seen as a cash inflow. Obviously a decrease in creditors is seen as a cash outflow.

Creditors and accruals are technically the same thing and are treated in the same fashion. Thus an increase in accruals will be added to net profit in adjusting back to cash.

If creditors/accruals increase then:

- Cash payments to creditors fall.
- Purchases in the profit and loss is greater than cash purchases.
- Expenses in the profit and loss account is greater than cash expenses.
- Operating profit is less than operating cash.
- In adjusting operating profit back to operating cash we must increase net profit by the amount of the increase in creditors.

Example 15.3: *Stocks and cash*

As a separate item on their own, stocks are a non-cash item, as we pay for them through purchases. Stocks do, however, cause a difference between net operating profit and the net operating cash position.

For example, sales for the period are €150,000 with purchases at €90,000. Stocks at the beginning of the year are €10,000 and end of the year €12,000. Let us assume that all purchases and sales are for cash.

Explain the difference in the net cash position and the profit position.

Approach

The net cash position at the end of the period would be €60,000 (sales of €150,000 minus purchases of €90,000). The gross profit would be:

	€	€
Sales		150,000
Less cost of goods sold		
Opening stock	10,000	
Purchases	90,000	
Closing stock	(12,000)	(88,000)
Gross profit		62,000

The difference between the net cash position and the profit is caused by the increase in stock (€10,000 to €12,000), which reduces the cost of goods sold and thus increases gross and net profit. Therefore to adjust the net profit back to the cash flow position the net profit is reduced by the increase in stock.

If stock decreased then profit would be lower than cash and hence the net operating profit figure would be increased in adjusting back to the operating cash position.

If stock increases then:

- Cost of goods sold is less than cash purchases.
- Operating profit is greater than operating cash.
- In adjusting operating net profit back to operating cash we reduce net profit by the amount of the increase in stock.

Category 2: Returns on investments and servicing of debt

The items included under this section are:

❏ Interest received: from loans given to other businesses.
❏ Interest paid: on loans from financial institutions, debentures, interest element on finance lease repayments, dividends paid to non-equity shareholders (preference shareholders).
❏ Dividends received: from investment in subsidiaries, related companies and fixed asset investments.

In general this category would most likely be a cash outflow because for most businesses in the tourism, hospitality and retail sectors the servicing of loans exceeds any interest or dividends received on investments.

Category 3: Taxation

Only corporation tax payments and refunds during the year are reported in this section. It is important to remember that some corporation tax instalments are due for payment after the financial year-end of the company.

Example 15.4: *Cash flow from taxation*

Cruiser Hire Ltd owed corporation tax of €50,000 at the beginning of the year. The corporation tax charge on the current year's profits amount to €120,000. However, the Revenue Commissioners are owed €80,000 in corporation tax at the year-end.

How much corporation tax was paid?

The amount due at the beginning of the year (€50,000) is added to the current year's tax charge of €120,000 and the €80,000 outstanding at the end of year is deducted. The answer is €90,000 (€50,000 + €120,000 - €80,000). This is the figure for corporation tax paid in the cash flow statement.

This category would generally be a cash outflow unless the business received a corporation tax refund from the Revenue Commissioners.

Category 4: Capital expenditure and financial investment

This category of activity includes divesting activities such as cash flow from the sale of tangible, intangible and financial fixed assets, as well as purchases of tangible, intangible and financial fixed assets. Generally a question will require students to calculate the purchases or cash received from the sale of fixed assets.

Example 15.5: *Fixed asset calculations*

A business had assets at cost at the beginning of the year amounting to €10,000. During the year they disposed of assets that originally cost €2,000, receiving €500. The value of assets at cost at the year-end amounted to €13,000.

Calculate the amount of fixed assets purchased during the year.

The business had fixed assets valued at cost at the beginning of the year of €10,000. They disposed of fixed assets that originally cost €2,000, ensuring fixed assets at cost after this transaction equalled €8,000. However, at the year-end the cost of fixed assets in the balance sheet amounted to €13,000. Thus the business purchased fixed assets worth €5,000 (€13,000 - €8000).

Category 5: Acquisitions and disposals

This category includes receipts and payments in respect of disposals or acquisitions of interests in subsidiaries, associated or joint venture companies. The cost of buying a business is reported net of any cash included in the purchase price.

Example 15.6: *Subsidiary acquired*

	€
Cash acquired	50,000
Goodwill	300,000
Other net assets	1,650,000
Consideration	2,000,000

What should the purchase cost of the acquisition be reported at?

The cash cost is reported at €1,950,000. This comes from the consideration of €2,000,000 minus the cash acquired of €50,000.

Category 6: Equity dividends paid

Part of the cash generated by a successful business is paid to the owners as a dividend. This important outflow is reported as a separate item in the cash flow statement.

Example 15.7: *Dividends paid*

Corporate Travel Ltd recorded equity dividends in its balance sheet as a current liability at the beginning of the year of €22,000 and at the end of the year of €35,000. The dividends charged in the profit and loss appropriation account amounted to €50,000.

How much dividend was actually paid during the year?

The dividends of €22,000 at the beginning of the year is added to the €50,000 and the end of year dividends of €35,000 remaining unpaid is deducted. The answer is €37,000 (€22,000 + €50,000 – €35,000).

Category 7: Management of liquid resources

This section deals with receipts and payments in respect of current asset investments, which are considered to be liquid (readily marketable). Under the definitions section in FRS 1, liquid resources are those that can be realised (turned into cash) without disruption to the business of the entity or which can be traded in an active market. Examples include commercial paper and short-term investments readily convertible into cash at their carrying value or close to it. Obviously sale of these liquid resources increases the cash flow whereas investing implies a decrease in cash flow. For example, a business had current asset investment at the beginning of the year amounting to €8,000 and at the year-end amounting to €5,000. The difference is considered a cash inflow as cash was generated by the sale or 'cashing in' of these investments.

Category 8: Financing

This category covers the receipts and payments, which arise from issues or repayments of finance from or to the providers of external finance. Cash inflows from this category would include the issue of shares, debentures/bonds or just simply getting a bank loan. The repayments of the capital elements of loans/debentures would be considered a cash outflow. Any related expenses (stamp duty or broker's fees on the issue of shares/debentures bonds) or commissions regarding the above will be included under this heading.

Reconciliation of Net Cash Flow to Net Debt

The first two objectives or purposes of FRS 1 are achieved through the preparation of the cash flow statement. The third objective of FRS 1 is to show how the increase or decrease in cash for the reporting period links the net funds or net debt at the start and end of the reporting period

Net debt is as per the definitions in FRS 1 'the borrowings of the entity less cash and liquid resources'. If cash and liquid resources exceed debt then the term used becomes net funds. This additional statement was not required under the old FRS 1 but was included in the revised FRS 1 in an effort to provide further information which assists in assessing the liquidity, solvency and financial adaptability of the entity. This additional statement is to be shown in the notes to the accounts. On top of this a further note is required to further analyse the changes in net debt/funds breaking debt into periods of less than one year and greater than one year. Illustration 15.4 shows the format of those notes:

Illustration 15.4: *Reconciliation of net cash flow to movements in net debt*

	€'000
Decrease in cash in the year	(1,244)
Decrease in debt	899
Movement in net debt in the year	(345)
Net debt at beginning of the year	(22,477)
Net debt at end of the year	(22,822)

Analysis of Net Debt

	Cash €'000	Overdraft €'000	Net cash €'000	Debt due < 12 Mts	Debt due > 12 Mts	Total €'000
Bal 1/5/02	9,572	(2,362)	7,210	(749)	(28,938)	(22,477)
Cash flow	(1,670)	426	(1,244)	327	572	(345)
Bal 30/4/03	7,902	(1,936)	5,966	(422)	(28,366)	(22,822)

A Comprehensive Example

The following comprehensive example focuses on all the points covered so far in the preparation of cash flow statements:

Example 15.8: *A worked example*

The following are the summarised accounts of Glennon Health Farms Ltd for the year ended 31 March 2004 with comparatives for the previous year. The company owns and runs a chain of health farms in the Republic of Ireland and mainland Europe.

Trading Profit and Loss Account for the Year Ended

		2004		2003
	€'000	€'000	€'000	€'000
Turnover		4,210		3,695
Cost of goods sold		(1,053)		(924)
Gross profit		3,157		2,771
Administration expenses	1,200		1,012	

Selling and distribution expenses	921	(2,121)	856	(1,868)
Operating profit		1,036		903
Interest		(360)		(230)
Net profit before tax		676		673
Corporation tax		(200)		(180)
Net profit after tax		476		493
Transfer to reserve	250		560	
Dividends – interim	200		200	
Dividends – final ⎦ 400	200	(650)	200	(960)
Retained profits for the year		(174)		(467)
Retained profits b/f		218		685
Retained profits c/f		44		218

Balance Sheet as at 31 March

		2004		2003
	€'000	€'000	€'000	€'000
Fixed assets at NBV		13,120		10,456
Current assets				
Stock	140		120	
Debtors	400		300	
Short-term investments	12		25	
Prepayments and accrued Income	8		10	
Bank	0	560	130	585
Creditors < 12 months				
Trade creditors	480		260	
Taxation	200		180	
Dividends	200		200	
Bank overdraft	110	(990)	10	(650)
Creditors >12 months				
Debentures	4,000		3,500	
Bank loans	600	(4,600)	500	(4,000)
		8,090		**6,391**
Capital and reserves				
Called-up share capital				
Ordinary shares nominal value 0.50 per share		6,000		5,000
Reserves				
Share premium		623		
General reserve		1,423		1,173
Retained profits		44		218
		8,090		**6,391**

Additional information:

1. The authorised share capital of the company is 20,000,000 €0.50 ordinary shares.
2. Included in administration expenses for the year ended 31 March 2004 are the following:
    — Depreciation charged on assets in existence at the year-end amounting to €560,000.
    — Loss on the sale of fixed assets for €80,000. The assets had a net book value of €150,000 when sold.

Required

(a) Show the movement in cash during the accounting period.
(b) Prepare a cash flow statement in accordance with FRS 1 for the year ended 31 March 2004.
(c) Reconcile the movement in net cash flow to net debt over the period.

Approach

(a) Calculate the overall cash flow

	Opening balance	Closing balance	Net cash flow
	€	€	€
Bank	130	0	(130)
Bank overdrafts	10	110	(100)
	120	(110)	(230)

The overall net cash flow is simply calculated by comparing the overall cash and bank balances at the beginning of the year to the cash and bank account balances at the end. If the asset of cash/bank increases then this is a positive cash flow. If it decreases then it is a negative cash flow. In the above example the cash/bank position deteriorated over the period with an overall negative net cash flow of €230,000. The cash flow statement then identifies the main cash inflows and outflows that contributed to the overall negative cash flow of the business.

(b) Prepare the cash flow statement

Cash Flow Statement for the Year Ended 31 March 2004

	€	€
1. Operating activities **Note 1**		1,778
2. Return on investment/servicing of debt *(servicing of finance)*		
Interest paid **Note 2**		(360)
3. Taxation		
Tax paid **Note 3**		(180)
4. Capital expenditure		
Sale of fixed assets **Note 4**	70	
Purchase of fixed assets **Note 5**	(3,374)	(3,304)
5. Acquisitions and disposals		
6. Dividends **Note 6**		(400)
7. Management of liquid resources		
Short-term investments **Note 7**		13
8. Financing **Note 8**		
Issue of debentures	500	
Bank loans	100	
Issue of shares	1,623	2,223
		(230)

(c) Prepare the reconciliation of net debt to net cash flow

	Debt	Cash	Net debt
	€	€	€
Debt and cash at the beginning of the year	(4,000)	120	(3,880)
Debt in cash at year-end	(4,600)	(110)	(4,710)
Movement in debt cash and net debt	(600)	(230)	(830)

Reconciliation

	€
Movement in cash	(230)
Movement in debt	(600)
	(830)
Net debt at beginning of the year	(3,880)
Net debt at year-end	(4,710)

Note 1: Operating activities

The net cash flow from operating activities can be calculated in two ways and FRS 1 requires the indirect method to be shown. This is where we start with the operating net profit (net profit before interest and tax) and adjust it back to the operating net cash flow. This is simply done by making the following adjustments:

- Adjusting for non-cash items in the profit and loss account such as depreciation or profits or losses on the sale of fixed assets. In this case depreciation and the loss on the sale of fixed assets are added back. The reason for this is that they are both expenses and have been deducted from gross profit in the profit and loss account. To adjust for them we must add them back.
- Adjusting for movements in working capital, specifically debtors, stocks, creditors, prepayments and accruals. As mentioned earlier if debtors, stocks or prepayments increase from the beginning of the year to the end, then we must deduct these increases from operating profit in order to work back to operating cash. If creditors or accruals increase then in adjusting operating profit back to operating cash, we must increase operating profit with the amount of these increases.

Reconciliation of Operating Profit to Operating Cash Flow

	€	€
Net profit before interest and tax (operating profit)		1,036
Adjust for non-cash items		
Depreciation	560	
Loss on sale of fixed assets	80	640
		1,676
Adjust for increases/decreases in working capital		
Stock	(20)	
Debtors	(100)	
Creditors	220	
Prepayments	2	102
		1,778

Note 2: Interest paid

The interest figure is a cash outflow and is obtained from the interest charged in the profit and loss account for 2004.

Note 3: Tax paid

The taxation paid figure is calculated as follows. In the balance sheet for 2003 the company owed the Revenue Commissioners €180,000. This represents amounts of tax owed for previous years. This year, 2004, the tax charged on profits amounted to €200,000. Thus the business owed the Revenue Commissioners €380,000. However, by the year-end, the balance sheet shows tax owing at only €200,000. That implies the business paid the Revenue Commissioners €180,000 during the year.

Note 4: Sale of fixed assets

Sales of fixed assets figure can be calculated from note two in the accounts. The assets sold had a net book value of €150,000 and the business made a loss on sale of €80,000. Thus they must have only received cash of €70,000 for the assets.

Note 5: Purchase of fixed assets

The calculation of this figure is quite complex. The net book value of assets at the beginning of the year amounts to €10,456,000 and during the year some assets with a net book value of €150,000 were sold, thus bringing the balance of assets at book value down to €10,306,000. These assets were depreciated by €560,000, which would have decreased the net book value of the assets to €9,746,000. However, at the year-end, the net book value of fixed assets stood at €13,120,000. Thus the business purchased new assets to the tune of (€13,120 - €9,746) €3,374,000.

Note 6: Dividends

Dividends paid are calculated in the same manner as tax. At the beginning of the year the balance sheet showed that the company owed the shareholders dividends of €200,000. During the year the company promised to pay out of current year's profits a dividend of €400,000, thus owing the shareholders €600,000. At the year-end the dividends owed in the balance sheet amounted to €200,000. Thus the company must have paid out dividends to shareholders of €400,000 during the year ended 31 March 2004.

Note 7: Management of liquid resources

This is calculated by comparing the current asset investments from one year to the next. In the balance sheet, current asset investments decreased from €25,000 to €12,000, which represents a decrease of €13,000. This is considered a cash inflow, as the business is liquidating some of its short-term investments.

Note 8: Financing

This is calculated by simply comparing the share capital, share premium, debentures and bank loans (not overdrafts) figures at the beginning and end of the year. An increase in any of these implies that the business is receiving finance and this is a cash inflow. In this example debentures increased by €500,000 (€4,000,000 – €3,500,000), bank loans increased by €100,000 (€600,000 – €500,000) and 2,000,000 50 cent shares were issued at a premium of €623,000, bringing the total amount received by the company from issuing shares to €1,623,000

Interpreting Cash Flow Statements

When analysing cash flow statements the following key factors should be quickly assessed before preparing ratios:

1. Is the overall cash movement positive or negative and is the cash movement significant?
2. Is the company heavily in overdraft?
3. What is the net debt/funds situation and is it getting better or worse?
4. Compare the operating net profit to operating cash flow. Is the company generating sufficient cash from its operating activities? If the company is not generating sufficient cash from its operating activities, is this due to large increases in stocks and debtors, which can signal poor control over working capital?
5. Identify the main cash inflows to the business. The biggest cash inflow for a business should be its operating activities but other major ones would be issues of shares/debentures.
6. Identify the major cash outflows of a business. These in general would be in the whole area of capital expenditure (investing in new fixed assets or investments). Try to assess how this capital expenditure was financed. Was it through a new issue of shares, debentures or from the cash flows generated from operating activities?
7. Try to come to an overall conclusion about the cash position of the business in terms of the business' ability to generate cash and how it spends it. Also link this to the profitability performance of the business.

Did You Know?

The tourism and retail sectors are generally classified as cash sectors. Add to that the fact that depreciation on fixed assets is deducted in the calculation of profit and not deducted in the calculation of operating cash, then the norm would be that operating cash flow would be greater than operating net profit. For example, in the accounts for Jury's Doyle Hotels operating cash flow exceeds operating profits by as much as 49 per cent in the year 2000 and 33 per cent in 2003. However, it only exceeded operating profit by 5.7 per cent in 2002.

In analysing Glennon Health Farms Ltd the following points should be made:

1. The overall cash flow is negative. Cash fell by €230,000 and the business went from having a positive cash position of €120,000 at the beginning of the year to being in overdraft by €110,000 at the end of the year.
2. The net debt situation has also deteriorated from €3,880,000 to €4,710,000 in the year. This amounts to an increase in net debt of 21 per cent.
3. The main sources of cash for the business were:
    — Net cash flow from operating activities. Glennon Health Farms Ltd generated a cash flow from operating activities of €1,778,500. This was 72 per cent greater than operating profit mainly due to the company's high depreciation charges as well as reducing stocks, debtors and increasing credit with suppliers.
    — Financing. The company acquired much finance during the period, mainly through the issue of shares and debentures. It also increased its bank borrowing and overdrafts. Much of this finance was used to acquire new fixed assets, which increased by 25 per cent.
    — The company sold some of its old fixed assets and it also cashed in some current asset investments.
4. The main uses of cash during the year were:
    — The purchase of fixed assets as mentioned above.
    — Servicing the debt, which obviously increased as the company issued debentures and acquired new loans.
    — Dividends. The company paid out dividends totalling €400,000.
    — Corporation tax liabilities were paid up to date.

Overall the company generated much cash from its operating activities and together with the extra financing managed to increase fixed assets and expand. This resulted in higher sales and ultimately higher profits for the year. However, it should monitor its short-term obligations to ensure cash is available when required.

Case Example: Arnotts

This case example presents the cash flow statement of Arnotts Group Plc for year ended 31 January 2003 with comparatives for the previous year.

	2003	2002
	€'000	€'000
Cash flow from operating activities	30,420	23,719
Returns on investments and servicing of finance		
Interest received	64	124
Interest paid	(1,042)	(1,442)
Interest element of finance lease rental payments	(23)	(23)
Premium paid on redemption of debenture stock	—	(3)
Preference dividends paid	(6)	(6)
Net cash outflow from returns on investments and servicing of finance	(1,007)	(1,350)
Taxation		
Corporation tax paid	(4,315)	(3,129)
Capital expenditure and financial investment		
Purchase of tangible fixed assets	(6,253)	(9,136)
Repayment of loan by associated undertaking	—	64
Net cash outflow from capital expenditure and financial investment	(6,253)	(9,072)
Equity dividends paid	(5,955)	(5,107)
Cash inflow before financing	12,890	5,061
Financing	(11,840)	(8,961)
Increase/(decrease) in cash in the year	1,050	(3,900)

Source: Arnotts Annual Report 2003

Summary Analysis of Arnotts Cash Flow Statement

For the year ended 31 January 2003 the company generated a positive net cash flow of €1,050,000. This compares favourably to the previous year where the company generated a negative €3,900,000 million cash flow. The main sources of cash for the business to 31 March 2003 were:

❑ Operating activities. The normal trading activities of the business generated €30.42 million in cash, up 28 per cent on 2002. This was the main source of cash for the business amounting to 99.8 per cent of cash generated in 2003.

❑   Through its investments the company generated a positive cash flow of €64,000
    – although not as high as previous year.

The main uses of cash were:

❑   Capital expenditure on tangible fixed assets amounted to €6.2 million.
❑   Equity dividends paid amounted to €5.9 million – an increase on the previous
    year.
❑   Taxation amounted to €4.3 million.
❑   Interest of €1 million – a reduction from previous year.
❑   The company reduced its debt significantly.

Overall the group's cash flow performance improved over 2002 with cash generated
from operating activities financing the increased investment in fixed assets of over €6
million and reducing net debt from €19.9 million to €7 million. This source of
finance also ensured that payments to the Revenue Commissioners, equity
shareholders and servicing debt were made.

Summary

A cash flow statement is an extremely important and useful addition to the final
accounts (trading, profit and loss account and balance sheet) of a business. It links the
information provided in the profit and loss account with the information provided
in the balance sheet. As cash is the life blood of a business, a statement giving
information on cash movements within a business is essential. The cash flow
statement under FRS 1 (revised) is such a statement.

   The following are the main information points covered in this chapter:

❑   Cash is fast becoming an important objective measure of a company's
    performance, free from unethical financial engineering.
❑   FRS 1 is an attempt to ensure that all companies report a summary of their cash
    flows in a prescribed manner.
❑   FRS 1 defined cash as 'Cash in hand and deposits repayable on demand with any
    qualifying financial institution less overdrafts from any qualifying financial
    institution repayable on demand. Cash includes cash in hand and deposits
    denominated in foreign currencies'.
❑   The purpose of FRS 1 Cash Flow Statements is as follows:
    — To show the cash inflows and outflows for the financial year and the
      consequent increase or decrease in cash.

- — To convert the operating profit or loss into the equivalent amount of cash released or consumed in the day-to-day running of the business.
- — To show how the increase or decrease in cash for the reporting period links the net funds or net debt at the start and end of the reporting period.
- ❑ There are two steps required in preparing a cash flow statement:
  1. Calculate the overall cash flow. This is calculated by comparing the cash (as per the FRS 1 definition above) at the beginning and end of the accounting period.
  2. Prepare the cash flow statement as presented in FRS 1. This involves focusing on each of the eight categories of cash as identified in FRS 1, calculating their respective cash flows and the total of the cash flows from all categories should equal the overall movement in cash as calculated in step one.
- ❑ FRS 1 identified eight categories of cash flow, namely operating activities, return on investment/servicing of debt, taxation, capital expenditure, acquisitions and disposals, dividends, management of liquid resources and financing.
- ❑ Cash flows from operating activities are the cash effects of transactions relating to the operating or trading activities of the business. In calculating this figure two formats are permitted by FRS 1, called the direct and indirect methods. FRS 1 requires the indirect method to be shown in a note to the cash flow statement.
- ❑ The indirect method involves adjusting the operating profit back to operating cash. This requires two adjustments:
  1. Adjusting operating profits for items in the profit and loss account that do not involve the movement of cash.
  2. Adjusting operating profit for movements in stocks, debtors, prepayments, creditors and accruals.
- ❑ Net debt is as per the definitions in FRS 1 'the borrowings of the entity less cash and liquid resources'. If cash and liquid resources exceed debt then the term used becomes net funds.
- ❑ Cash flow statements are a valuable source of information for the users of accounts and thus the ability to interpret cash flow statements is essential.

Review Questions

Question 15.1

Indicate whether each of the following statements are true or false:

	True	False
An increase in debtors increases the cash position of the business	☐	☐
A decrease in stock increases the cash position of the business	☐	☐
Depreciation reduces the cash position of the business	☐	☐
Net profit is the difference between cash received and cash paid	☐	☐
Operating net cash flow is the operating profit less any payments for fixed assets	☐	☐
An increase in creditors increases the cash position of the business	☐	☐
If accruals goes up then cash goes down	☐	☐

Question 15.2

Distinguish between the following:

(a) Net debt and net funds.
(b) Operating net profit and operating net cash flow.
(c) The direct and indirect method of calculating operating net cash flow.
(d) Operating net cash flow and the overall net cash flow.

Question 15.3

Briefly outline what you understand by the following terms:

(a) Liquid resources.
(b) Operating cash flow.
(c) Non–cash items.
(d) Operating activities.

Question 15.4

(a) Outline the main categories of cash inflows and outflows for a business.
(b) Outline the objectives of preparing cash flow statements.

Question 15.5

The following are the summarised accounts of City Tourism Ltd, a company which has specialised in the hotel, tourism and leisure sector for a number of years:

Trading, Profit and Loss Account for the Year Ended

	31/12/2003		31/12/2002	
	€'000	€'000	€'000	€'000
Turnover		9,200		7,500
Cost of sales		(3,190)		(2,146)
Gross profit		6,010		5,354
Administration expenses	2,024		1,500	
Selling and distribution expenses	2,970	(4,994)	2,146	(3,646)
Operating profit		1,016		1,708
Interest		(416)		(370)
Net profit before tax		600		1,338
Corporation tax		(460)		(470)
Net profit after tax		140		868
Transfer to reserve	1,000		500	
Dividends interim	250		250	
Dividends final	250	(1,500)	250	1,000
Retained profits for year		(1,360)		(132)
Retained profits b/f		762		894
Retained profits c/f		(598)		762

Balance Sheet as at

	31/12/2003		1/12/2002	
	€'000	€'000	€'000	€'000
Fixed assets at cost		25,583		23,540
Accumulated depreciation		10,190		9,540
Net book value		15,393		14,000
Current assets				
Stock	227		250	
Debtors	56		50	
Short-term investments	25		12	
Prepayments and accrued income	12		10	
Bank	0	320	120	442

Current liabilities – creditors < 12 months

Trade creditors	290		350	
Accruals and deferred income	15		12	
Taxation	460		470	
Dividends	250		250	
Bank loans and borrowings	100	(1,115)	0	(1,082)

Long-term liabilities – creditors >12 months

Debentures	4,200		4,081	
Bank loans	1,000	(5,200)	1,200	(5,281)
		9,398		**8,079**

Capital and reserves

Called-up share capital

Ordinary shares nominal value 0.50 cent per share	8,272	6,593

Reserves

General reserve	1,724	724
Retained profits	(598)	762
	9,398	**8,079**

Additional information:

Included in administration expenses for the year ended 31 December 2003 is a profit on the sale of fixed assets of €50,000. The assets, which cost €450,000, had a net book value of €300,000 on the date of sale.

Required

(a) Prepare a cash flow statement in accordance with FRS 1 for the year ended 31 December 2003.
(b) Reconcile the movement in net cash flow to net debt over the period.
(c) Comment on the financial performance of City Tourism Ltd as revealed to you by the cash flow statement.

Question 15.6

The following are the summarised accounts of the International Tourism Company Ltd for the year ended 31 March 2004 with comparatives for the previous year. The company specialises in European destination holidays and owns a portfolio of holiday apartments and hotels throughout Europe.

Trading, Profit and Loss Account for the Year Ended

	31/03/2004		31/03/2003	
	€'000	€'000	€'000	€'000
Turnover		11,250		8,970
Cost of goods sold		(3,670)		(2,650)
Gross profit		7,580		6,320
Administration expenses	2,275		2,019	
Selling and distribution expenses	2,670	(4,945)	1,987	(4,006)
Operating profit		2,635		2,314
Interest		(600)		(518)
Net profit before tax		2,035		1,796
Corporation tax		(750)		(490)
Net profit after tax		1,285		1,306
Transfer to reserve	500		360	
Dividends – interim	300		300	
Dividends – final	600	(1,400)	300	(960)
Retained profits for year		(115)		346
Retained profits b/f		802		456
Retained profits c/f		687		802

Balance Sheet

	31/03/2004		31/03/2003	
	€'000	€'000	€'000	€'000
Fixed assets at NBV		22,968		18,705
Current assets				
Stock	300		325	
Debtors	190		215	
Short-term investments	50		75	
Prepayments and accrued income	12		10	
Bank	10	562	220	845
Current liabilities – creditors < 12 months				
Trade creditors	460		480	
Accruals and deferred income	15		20	
Taxation	750		490	
Dividends	600		300	
Bank loans and borrowings	110	(1,935)	10	(1,300)

Long-term liabilities – creditors >12 months

Debentures	6,500		5,500	
Bank loans	1,000	(7,500)	980	(6,480)
		14,095		**11,770**

Capital and reserves

Called-up share capital

Ordinary shares nominal value 0.50 per share	12,200	10,608
Reserves		
Share premium	348	
General reserve	860	360
Retained profits	687	802
	14,095	**11,770**

Additional information:

1. The authorised share capital of the company is 50,000,000 €0.50 ordinary shares.
2. Included in administration expenses for the year ended 31 March 2004 are the following:
    – Depreciation charged on assets in existence at the year-end amounting to €780,000.
    – Loss on the sale of fixed assets of €185,000. The assets had a net book value on the date of sale of €320,000.

Required

(a) Prepare a cash flow statement in accordance with FRS 1 for the year ended 31 March 2004.
(b) Comment on the cash flow performance of the International Tourism Company Ltd for the year ended 31 March 2004.

Question 15.7

The following are the summarised accounts of Dungan Hotel and Leisure Ltd for the year ended 31 October 2003 with comparatives for the previous year. The company has a portfolio of hotels all with city centre locations.

Trading, Profit and Loss Account for the Year Ended

	31/10/2003			31/10/2002
	€'000	€'000	€'000	€'000
Turnover		13,851		10,090
Cost of goods sold		(4,590)		(3,210)
Gross profit		9,261		6,880
Administration expenses	3,047		2,412	
Selling and distribution expenses	2,560	(5,607)	2,111	(4,523)
Operating profit		3,654		2,357
Interest		(560)		(650)
Net profit before tax		3,094		1,707
Corporation tax		(850)		(490)
Net profit after tax		2,244		1,217
Transfer to reserve	1,000		560	
Dividends interim	500		400	
Dividends final	600	(2,100)	300	(1,260)
Retained profits for the year		144		(43)
Retained profits b/f		642		685
Retained profits c/f		786		642

Balance Sheet as at

	31/10/2003			31/10/2002
	€'000	€'000	€'000	€'000
Fixed assets at cost		32,668		29,995
Accumulated depreciation		10,700		10,000
NBV		21,968		19,995
Current assets				
Stock	227		225	
Debtors	165		185	
Short-term investments	50		75	
Prepayments and accrued income	12		10	
Bank	0	454	220	715
Current liabilities				
Trade creditors	480		560	
Accruals and deferred income	15		20	
Taxation	850		490	

Dividends	600		300	
Bank loans and borrowings	<u>110</u>	(2,055)	<u>10</u>	(1,380)
Long-term liabilities				
Debentures	5,347		6,500	
Bank loans	<u>1,000</u>	(6,347)	<u>1,020</u>	(7,520)
		14,020		**11,810**

Capital and reserves

Called-up share capital

Ordinary shares nominal value 0.50 per share	11,500		10,608
Reserves			
Share premium	174		0
General reserve	1,560		560
Retained profits	786		642
	14,020		**11,810**

Additional information:

1. The authorised share capital of the company is 50,000,000 €0.50 ordinary shares.
2. Included in administration expenses for the year ended 31 October 2003 are the following:
    — Depreciation charged on assets in existence at the year-end amounting to €890,000.
    — Loss on sale of fixed assets of €120,000. The assets had a net book value of €320,000 on the date of sale.

Required

(a) Prepare a cash flow statement in accordance with FRS 1 for the year ended 31 October 2003.
(b) Reconcile the movement in net cash flow to net debt over the period.
(c) Comment on the financial performance of the group as revealed to you by the cash flow statement.

CHAPTER 16

The Interpretation of Financial Statements

Learning Outcomes

By the end of this chapter you will be able to:

❑ Appreciate the use of ratio analysis as a tool in assessing organisational financial performance.
❑ Discuss the advantages and disadvantages of financial statements and ratio analysis.
❑ Identify the key areas of relevance to the main users of financial statements.
❑ Identify and prepare key ratios from financial statements under the headings of profitability, liquidity, management's use of assets (efficiency), capital structure and investment.
❑ Compute and interpret key operating ratios.
❑ Compare financial statements over time.
❑ Write reports interpreting the ratios calculated and analysing the financial performance of a commercial organisation.
❑ Appreciate how financial statements and key ratios can be used to manipulate a company's financial performance.

Introduction

The final accounts are all that is available to external users (investors, lenders, creditors, suppliers, Revenue Commissioners and the general public) when evaluating the performance of an organisation. A profit and loss account and balance sheet indicate the profit (or loss) made by an organisation during an accounting period and provide a summary of the assets and liabilities at a given date. On their own they do not provide the user with very much information about how that organisation has performed. A net profit of €100,000 might at first sight appear to be adequate but how does the profit measure in relation to sales? How much capital was required to generate such a profit and what percentage return on capital does that profit represent to an investor or potential investors?

It is possible to gain a better understanding of how an organisation has performed by examining the figures contained in the accounts using ratio analysis. Ratios are relationships between figures expressed as a ratio or more commonly as a percentage. Interpretation of accounts can be defined as the explanation, and translation into clear and simple form, of the data presented by the profit and loss account and balance sheet of a business.

Performance Measurement through Ratio Analysis

The performance of an organisation will be assessed by users with different requirements. The needs of investors will be different to the needs of short-term creditors. Ratio analysis is usually carried out under the following headings as the performance of an organisation is appraised:

❏ **Profitability**: Is the business profitable, both as to return on capital invested and as to the proportion of sales revenue remaining as profit? Has the company the potential to remain profitable and even increase profitability in the future?

❏ **Efficiency**: Is the business managed efficiently with particular reference to control over asset levels? For example, are management efficient in dealing with the following:
  – Ensuring assets generate sufficient turnover/sales?
  – Ensuring assets are efficiently used to minimise costs but not at the expense of quality?
  – Collecting debts due from customers?
  – Minimising stock holding and stock holding costs?
  – Ensuring money/cash is available when needed to repay creditors, loans and financial capital expenditure?

❏ **Liquidity**: Is the business on a sound financial footing, able to pay its creditors and fulfil other obligations as they fall due?

❏ **Capital structure**: What are the organisation's long-term financing arrangements? How dependant is the organisation on borrowed funds (financial risk)?

❏ **Return to investors**: Investors' returns come in the form of a dividend (share of current profits) and a capital gain (an increase in the value of the business).

Any return whether of a capital or dividend nature must be sufficient to reward the investor for the risk attached to that investment. Ultimately the main objective of a company is to increase the wealth of its shareholders. This wealth is not just measured in terms of present performance, but also in terms of future potential.

Why Use Ratio Analysis?

As stated above, the final accounts provide limited information about an organisation. Applying a set of measures from which the performance of an organisation can be evaluated will give a useful framework from which a more informative view can be established. The use of ratios in this regard can be quite helpful.

1. It is easier to compare an organisation's performance with that of previous years. Ratios provide a framework which ensures a more informative comparative analysis than simply comparing profit.
2. Ratio analysis can help spot trends towards better or poorer performance from which areas of concern can be identified.
3. As target performance measures can be set, ratio analysis can help in finding significant deviations from agreed standards or targets.
4. Looking at an organisation in isolation can be unwise. Ratio analysis allows comparisons by applying the same measures to similar organisations operating in the same sector or industry. This allows an organisation to benchmark its performance.

Limitations

Ratio analysis does have certain limitations, which must be taken into account when using them. The limitations of ratio analysis also reflect the limitations of financial statements.

1. Accounting statements present a limited picture only of a business. The information included in the accounts does not cover all aspects of a business. For example, human assets and inherent goodwill are excluded from the accounts.
2. Changes in a company's accounting policies and estimates can significantly distort any inter-firm comparisons and trend analysis.
3. Ratios are based upon past performance and hence historical data. Although they can indicate future trends there is no guarantee these forecasts will be correct.
4. Ratios can be misleading if used in isolation. It is important to use comparisons with past performance or a similar company in the same business sector. Any

comparison must take into account changing economic conditions and the risk factors of the particular business and sector.

5. Inflation and its effects can be ignored.
6. Key financial indicators do not highlight whether a company is over-dependant on one customer, one product line or one supplier. Other factors that increase the commercial/business risk associated with a company may also be missed.
7. Ratios are based on the figures in the financial accounts, which contain estimates with regard to items such as provisions, revaluation's, contingencies etc. Should any of these estimates be significantly incorrect the ratios will be misleading.

Ratio Formulae and Calculations

Measuring the performance of an organisation through ratio analysis is relatively simple. Example 16.1 shows a sample of final accounts from which ratios under the key headings of performance measurement are calculated.

Example 16.1: *Ratio analysis of final accounts*

Profit Statements for Year Ended 31/12/05	€	€	Balance Sheet as at 31/12/05	€	€	€
Sales		9,885	*Fixed assets*			8,595
Less cost of sales						
Opening stock	500		*Current assets*			
Net purchases	6,800		Stock	850		
Closing stock	(850)	(6,450)	Debtors	780		
Gross profit		**3,435**	Bank	120	1,750	
Less expenses		(1,200)				
Net operating profit (PBIT)		**2,235**	*Current liabilities*			
Interest payable		(162)	Creditors	585		
Net profit before tax		2,073	Bank/short-term loans	500	(1,085)	665
Taxation		(413)				
Profit after interest and tax		**1,660**	*Long-term liabilities*			
Dividends preference		(100)	Debentures			(1,800)
Dividends ordinary		(800)				7,460
Retained profit for the year		760				
Retained profit b/f		1,200	**Capital and reserves**			
Retained profit c/f		1,960	Ordinary shares (8,000 @ 50 cent)			4,000
			Preference shares			1,000
Market price of shares	*1.21*		Retained profit			1,960
8 million ordinary shares issued			Reserves			500
						7,460

You are required to calculate the key ratios using the final accounts above.

Approach

The performance of the company can be assessed by calculating ratios under the headings of profitability, efficiency/asset utilisation, liquidity, capital structure and investment.

Ratio Calculations

PROFITABILITY			
Gross profit margin	Gross profit x 100 / Sales	€3,435 x 100 / €9,885	34.7%
Net profit margin	Net profit (PBIT) x 100 / Sales	€2,235 x 100 / €9,885	22.6%
Expenses to sales	Expenses x 100 / sales	€1,200 x 100 / €9,885	12.1%
Return on capital employed (ROCE)	Net profit (PBIT) x 100 / Capital employed	€2,235 x 100 / €9,260	24.1%
Return on owners' equity (ROOE) before tax	Net profit before tax x 100 / Shareholders' funds	€2,073 x 100 / €7,460	27.8%
Return on owners' equity (ROOE) after tax	Net profit after interest & tax x 100 / Shareholders' funds	€1,660 x 100 / €7,460	22.3%
EFFICIENCY			
Fixed asset turnover	Sales / Fixed assets	€9,885 / €8,595	1.15:1
Total asset turnover	Sales / Total assets	€9,885 / €9,260	1.067:1
Stock turnover	Cost of sales / Average stock	€6,450 / €675	9.6 times
Stock days	Average stock x 365 / Cost of sales	€675 x 365 / €6,450	38.2 days

Debtors days	$\dfrac{\text{Trade debtors} \times 365}{\text{Credit sales}}$	$\dfrac{€780 \times 365}{€9,885}$	28.8 days
Creditors days	$\dfrac{\text{Trade creditors} \times 365}{\text{Credit purchases}}$	$\dfrac{€585 \times 365}{€6,800}$	31.4 days
LIQUIDITY			
Current ratio	$\dfrac{\text{Current assets}}{\text{Current liabilities}}$	$\dfrac{€1,750}{€1,085}$	1.61:1
Quick-acid-test ratio	$\dfrac{\text{Current assets - stock}}{\text{Current liabilities}}$	$\dfrac{€900}{€1,085}$	0.83:1
CAPITAL STRUCTURE			
Gearing	$\dfrac{\text{Fixed interest debt}}{\text{Shareholders' funds}}$	$\dfrac{€2,800}{€7,460}$	0.38 : 1
Interest cover	$\dfrac{\text{Net profit (PBIT)}}{\text{Interest}}$	$\dfrac{€2,235}{€162}$	13.8 times
INVESTMENT			
Earnings per share	$\dfrac{\text{Net profit after Interest, tax \& pref. dividend}}{\text{Number of shares}}$	$\dfrac{€1,560}{8,000}$	€0.195
Price earnings ratio (P/E)	$\dfrac{\text{Market price of share}}{\text{EPS}}$	$\dfrac{€1.21}{€0.195}$	6.2 times
Dividend cover	$\dfrac{\text{Profit available to pay dividend}}{\text{Dividends paid and proposed}}$	$\dfrac{€1,560}{€800}$	1.95 times
Dividend yield	$\dfrac{\text{Dividend per share} \times 100}{\text{Market price per share}}$	$\dfrac{€0.10 \times 100}{€1.21}$	8.3%

Each of the ratios outlined in Example 16.1 will now be explained in detail. This will be achieved by using data from the annual reports of a number of Irish listed companies within the hospitality and tourism sectors. The following companies were chosen:

Jury's Doyle Group	*Hotel and leisure*
Gresham Group	*Hotel and leisure*
Ryanair	*Low-cost airline*
Aer Lingus	*State airline*
ICG	*Shipping company*

A case study of Arnotts will provide a retail context.

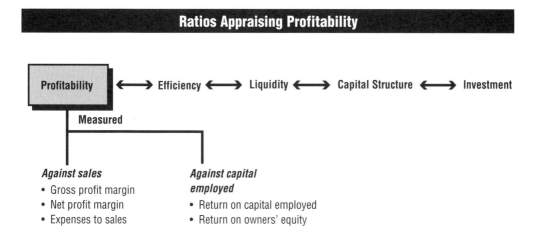

Profit is the excess of revenues less expenses and is the ultimate measure of the success of a business. However, the profit figure on its own can only say so much about an organisation. What is more informative to users of accounts is to compare profit to the level of sales and investment required to achieve these profits.

As can be seen from the diagram above, profitability is normally measured in two ways:

1. Against sales.
2. Against capital employed.

Gross profit margin

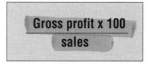

The gross profit margin indicates the margin of profit between sales and cost of sales. A gross profit percentage of 60 per cent tells us that for every €100 of sales, a gross profit of €60 is earned and the cost of goods sold will amount to €40.

The gross profit percentage can fluctuate and management should be aware of the main reasons for the fluctuation. A fluctuating gross profit percentage can be caused by:

Reduction	Increase
❏ Reduction in selling price. ❏ Increase in the cost price of stock purchases. ❏ Changes in the product sales mix with the business selling a higher proportion of goods with a lower gross profit margin. ❏ Theft stock/waste.	❏ Increase in selling price. ❏ Reduction in cost price of stock purchases. ❏ Changes in the product sales mix with the business selling a higher proportion of goods with a higher gross profit margin.

An increase in sales volume will lead to an increase in gross profit but *not* to an increase in gross profit percentage.

Illustration 16.1: *Gross profit margin (hotel sector)*

	2001 (%)	2002 (%)	2003 (%)
Jury's Doyle	36.25	35.7	32.65
Gresham	54.04	49.23	48.5

The trends for both companies show a falling gross profit percentage. This means that both companies are generating less gross profit per euro sales. The reasons for this could be any of those described above. However, most analysts felt that both companies reduced their selling prices and took on lower margin business (tour groups) to sustain their occupancy rates. The context for all this was the 'foot and mouth' crises in Ireland in 2001 and the aftermath of the September 11 terrorist attacks, as well as a depressed local and global economy, which had the effect of severely curtailing business and tourist travel. To maintain occupancy levels hotels reduced prices. Generally a hotel's customer base can be simply categorised into business, tourist and tour operators, of which the tour operator provides the least profit for the hotel company.

The gross profit margins are significantly different for both companies, indicating, for example, that in 2003 Jury's Doyle achieve a significantly lower gross profit per euro sales than Gresham. This, however, is misleading. The Companies Act 1986 identifies three categories of expenses:

1. Cost of goods sold.
2. Sales expenses.
3. Administration expenses.

The act does not give definitions of each category and thus we can reasonably conclude that Jury's includes a significant proportion of labour costs in its cost of goods sold computation while Gresham clearly does not. The net profit margins are, however, quite similar (see below).

It is important to remember that many companies in the tourism/leisure sector provide services rather than sell a tangible product and thus will not calculate a gross profit and gross profit margin. Examples include sectors such as airlines, accommodation providers and tour operators.

Operating profit margin

> **Operating profit (PBIT) x 100**
> **Sales**

The net operating profit percentage expresses an organisation's net profit as a percentage of sales. The percentage tells us how much a company's sales revenue remains behind as profit after all operating expenses have been deducted. Operating profits is the net profit before interest and tax. A fluctuating operating profit margin can be caused by:

Reduction	Increase
❑ Reduction in gross profit margin.	❑ Increase in gross profit margin (see above).
❑ Increase in expenses to sales %.	❑ Decrease in expenses to sales %.

Illustration 16.2: *Net operating profit margin (hotel sector)*

	2001 (%)	2002 (%)	2003 (%)
Jury's Doyle	29.57	27.57	23.5
Gresham	24.07	-0.17	8.7

For hotels the percentage varies but Gresham hotels and Jury's consistently achieved net operating margins in the low 20 per cent range. In the booming Celtic tiger economy they achieved net operating margins of greater than 30 per cent. This was because hotel cost structures have a high proportion of fixed costs which do not increase proportionate to sales increases. Thus when sales are booming, profit margins will increase significantly. Obviously as sales decrease so too will profit margins. This characteristic would also apply to many leisure businesses as well as the travel sector.

The optimal gross and operating profit percentage will vary from industry to industry. What is of particular importance is that an organisation reviews trends in its gross and operating profit percentages over time and investigates any significant changes.

Did you Know

According to the Restaurants Association of Ireland (RAI) the average gross profit margin achieved by restaurants in Ireland was 64.4 per cent with net margins at 3.5 per cent. The association's 'Do you know' card outlines the following average expense percentages:

	% of sales net of VAT
Food and drink	35.6
Wages and salaries	35.6
Overheads	25.3
Total expenses	96.5

Source: *Irish Independent,* 9 June 2005

Expenses to sales

$$\frac{\text{Expenses} \times 100}{\text{Sales}}$$

The expenses to sales ratio tells us how much each item of expense is as a percentage of sales. It examines the amount of sales that is required to cover the running costs or expenses of the business. It is simply expenses divided by sales expressed as a percentage.

A significant decrease in the net profit percentage, which is not accompanied by a similar change in the gross profit margin, indicates that an organisation needs to improve control of its expenses. Questions to be addressed include any area of expense where significant increases have occurred. Wages can be an area for particular concern and a review of the level of overtime payments and the grade and numbers of staff employed could be considered. The ratio can be further analysed by calculating each category of expense to sales, for example labour costs to sales percentage or advertising to sales percentage.

Illustration 16.3: *Expenses to sales percentage Jury's Doyle and Gresham Hotels*

	2001 (%)	2002 (%)	2003 (%)
Jury's Doyle	6.68	7.83	9.1
Gresham	29.97	50	40

The expenses to sales percentage for both companies increased significantly. To give management a greater insight into why the percentage increased they would need to identify which items of expense increased significantly and why. Management should assess the reason for the increase and question the value received from the increased expenditure in the area.

It is also important to remember that the expenses to sales percentage can increase due to a reduction in sales and this was the main reason why the ratio increased so significantly for both companies between 2001 and 2003. Hotel companies' operating costs would be mainly characterised as fixed costs and thus would not fall as sales fall. Hence the expense to sales percentage increases.

Both Gresham and Jury's hotels' operating profit percentages decreased between 2001 and 2002 due to a combination of a reduction in the gross profit percentage and an increase in the expenses to sales percentage. In Gresham hotels' case the increase in expenses is very significant. The reduction in the gross profit percentage could be due to greater competition and its effects on the selling price. Obviously both businesses are accepting lower margin business to ensure occupancy rates are held. This is in contrast to the then Celtic tiger period where both companies experienced high occupancy rates and increased their gross profit and operating profit margins by swapping their lower margin tour group business for the higher yield tourist trade and business sector.

Sector comparison and commentary

The three profitability ratios measured over sales can be compared for the companies chosen. The following illustration shows the operating profit margins and expense to sales ratios.

Illustration 16.4: *Profitability ratios (measured against sales) 2003*

	Gross profit margin (%)	Net profit margin (%)	Expenses to sales (%)
Jury's	32.65	23.50	9.15
Gresham	48.50	8.70	39.80
Ryanair		36.00	68.70
Aer Lingus	26.65	8.35	18.3
ICG	23.20	7.92	15.28

In comparing Ryanair and Aer Lingus's operating margins the differences reflect how Ryanair have perfected their low-cost model and this is reflected in very high operating margins. For a national carrier, Aer Lingus is unique in terms of achieving a profit and, as the company develops its own low-cost model and continues to rationalise, operating margins should improve.

'We work on the basis that we net 8% of the price of every pint'

Source: *Sunday Times*, 28 November 2004

Oliver Hughes is the owner of the Porterhouse chain of niche pubs in Dublin and London. He also commented that the net margins in London are far higher than in Dublin at 20% or 2.5 times the Dublin margins. The main reasons are that staff costs and insurance are significantly higher in Dublin than in London.

Return on capital employed (ROCE)

$$\frac{\text{Net profit (PBIT) x 100}}{\text{Capital employed}}$$

This ratio measures the net profit before interest and tax (operating return) a business is achieving for the total amount of capital employed in the business (both equity and debt). Capital employed is defined as: Share Capital + Reserves + Loan Capital. Effectively it is the total capital required to finance the assets of the business. Net profit before interest and tax is the operating profit of the business that is attributable to the total capital employed (debt and equity) in the business. Return on capital employed is the return on the business before any payments are made to providers of capital (loan interest and dividends) and the revenue commissioners (corporation tax).

The ROCE is an important measure of profitability for a number of reasons:

❑ The ultimate measure of a business' profitability and sustainability is whether it can consistently achieve high returns on its capital employed. If that is achieved then the business is, in effect, creating real shareholder wealth, which is the ultimate objective of a business.

❑ It can serve as a guide to the company and to potential investors in assessing possible acquisitions. If the ROCE is not attractive, investment should be avoided. Similarly a persistently low ROCE in any part of the business suggests it could be a candidate for disposal if it is not an integral part of the business.

The calculation of capital employed can be quite complex and different interpretations of the profit and capital employed occur. Some companies include short-term loans and overdrafts as part of the capital employed and some do not. Others deduct cash balances from the overdrafts before including them in capital employed. Some include government grants. Ultimately one should state clearly the basis on which the ratio is calculated to ensure the same basis is used when making inter-firm comparisons.

**Return on owners' equity (ROOE)
before tax**

Net profit before tax x 100
Shareholders' funds

Or

**Return on owners' equity (ROOE)
after tax**

Net profit after interest & tax x 100
Shareholders' funds

The ROOE assesses the return before tax for the ordinary (equity) shareholders alone. Thus we exclude loan capital/debt finance from the denominator and for the numerator we deduct loan interest charges from net profit before interest and tax. This is to ensure we only take account of the profit before tax available to equity shareholders. This ratio should also be calculated using profit after tax, as this is the overall return/profit that belongs to shareholders.

Both ratios (ROCE and ROOE) indicate how efficiently an organisation uses the resources invested in it, expressing its profit as a percentage of the capital employed to achieve that profit. It is important for investors to compare their return on capital to other returns within that particular industry. How high should the return be? This really is a matter of opinion for the investor and depends on a number of factors such as the current economic situation, the alternative investment opportunities available to the investor and the current expected returns from the sectors concerned. The following table should only be used only as a rule of thumb.

% Return	Comment
<5	Poor
5–10	Fair
10–15	Good
>15	Excellent

Illustration 16.5: *ROCE/ROOE (hotel sector)*

	2001 (%)	2002 (%)	2003 (%)
Jury's Doyle			
ROCE	9.02	6.89	6.11
ROOE (before tax)	12.6	7.2	6.6
Gresham			
ROCE	6.33	-	2.4
ROOE	7.57	-	1.43

From Illustration 16.5 one can see the returns are decreasing for both companies. Gresham actually made an operating loss in 2002. In evaluating these returns it is important to take into account external factors that could affect the returns of some sectors. For example, the above returns for both Gresham and Jury's are very low. However, the hotel sector was severely hit by both the foot and mouth epidemic and the aftermath of the terrorist attacks in 2001. The years 2002 and 2003 were characterised by a depressed global economy and a strengthening euro. Gresham hotels are, however, showing an improvement from their disastrous year in 2002.

The profitability ratios measured over capital employed can now be compared for the chosen companies.

Illustration 16.6: *Profitability ratios (profit against capital employed) 2003*

	ROCE (%)	ROOE (%) (before tax)	ROCE (%) (after tax)
Jury's	6.11	6.60	5.44
Gresham	2.40	1.43	1.57
Ryanair	12.60	20.20	18.28
Aer Lingus	8.17	15.16	13.2
ICG	7.95	9.07	8.92

In commenting on the returns for Ryanair and Aer Lingus it must be pointed out that these returns would be significantly higher except for the policy of both companies to hold very high cash reserves in current assets. In both companies the cash reserves nearly equate with the investment in tangible fixed assets and thus have a significant effect on the ROCE and ROOE.

Comparisons of returns should be made with companies within the same sectors and of similar size. Of the two ratios the ROCE is more popular as it gives an overall indication of the profitability of the whole business. One should, however, prepare both ratios in evaluating the financial performance of a business.

Bus operator on route to growth

Aircoach was launched in 1999 with initial capital of €3 million and quickly built its reputation by challenging the standards of its competitors. Luxury coaches, pleasant drivers and a €12 return fare from south Dublin to the airport has ensured high levels of customer satisfaction. Aircoach is now making more than €1 million a year profits on its €7.2 million turnover. The service now runs 24 hours a day.

The business had to cope with its fair share of difficulties over its first five years:

1. A docklands service introduced in late 2000 proved a loss maker and was axed after twelve months.
2. The company lost more than €500,000 at a vulnerable stage in the company's development, caused by the effects of September 11 and the immediate drop in air travel.
3. In march 2001 insurance costs increased by 250% to €520,000.

In response it parked seven buses and took twenty persons off their payroll. They were awarded the shuttle bus contract from Air Rianta and in addition they established a €5 a day car park close to the airport.

Aircoach also launched an inter-provincial service called CityConnect, which runs services to Cork, Portlaoise and Belfast. The next driver of growth for the company is the prospect of deregulation in the bus market both nationally and in Dublin.

Source: *Sunday Times*, 24 October 2004

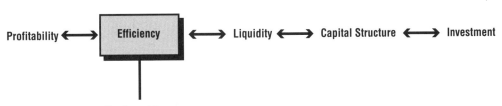

Ratios Appraising Management Efficiency

Profitability ⟷ Efficiency ⟷ Liquidity ⟷ Capital Structure ⟷ Investment

- Fixed asset turnover
- Total asset turnover
- Stock turnover/stock days
- Debtors days
- Creditors days

Several ratios are used to indicate how efficiently an organisation is utilising its assets. Assets generate sales and profits; the more efficiently assets are used, the greater the level of sales and profits for a business. It is also important that a business has an appropriate level of investment in assets for the level of business it can generate. For example, a 500 bed-roomed hotel in the middle of nowhere may not be able to sustain the occupancy levels required for such investment and hence not enough sales would be generated to cover costs and the required return on such assets. The following are the main ratios used to evaluate management efficiency in utilising the assets of the business.

Fixed asset turnover

$$\frac{\text{Sales}}{\text{Fixed assets}}$$

The fixed asset turnover compares sales with the fixed assets that generated the sales, and measures the utilisation a firm is obtaining from its investment in fixed assets. It indicates how much each €1 invested in fixed assets generates in sales. In general, a higher ratio of sales to fixed assets indicates that fixed assets are being utilised more efficiently.

Total asset turnover

$$\frac{\text{Sales}}{\text{Total assets}}$$

The total asset turnover is calculated in the same way as the fixed asset turnover except the total asset figure is used. Total assets are: Fixed Assets + Current Assets – Current Liabilities. As per the fixed asset ratio, it tells us the amount of sales generated per €1 invested in total assets of the company. Remember, the total assets of the business (Fixed Assets + Current Assets – Current Liabilities) should always equal to the capital employed (Share Capital + Reserves + Loans) of the business. Thus the ratio is telling us the amount of sales generated per euro invested in the business.

This is an important part of the ROCE ratio. The overall return on a business is made up of two essential components: the operating margin (operating profit/sales) and the total asset turnover (sales/total assets).

$$\text{ROCE} \quad = \quad \frac{\text{OPERATING PROFIT}}{\text{CAPITAL EMPLOYED}} \quad = \quad \frac{\text{SALES}}{\text{FA+CA-CL}} \quad \text{x} \quad \frac{\text{NPBIT}}{\text{SALES}}$$

N.B. Operating profit represents the net profit before interest and tax

An ROCE of 20 per cent could be due to the fact that the company makes a net profit margin of 10 per cent and for every €1 invested in the company it generates €2 sales. Thus the company makes a return of 20 per cent per €1 invested in the company. (ROCE = 10% x 2 = 20%.)

Illustration 16.7: *Asset turnover ratios (hotel sector)*

	2001	2002	2003
Jury's Doyle			
Fixed asset turnover	0.25	0.24	0.233
Total asset turnover	0.31	0.25	0.26
Gresham			
Fixed asset turnover	0.26	0.26	0.27
Total asset turnover	0.26	0.25	0.275

Overall the asset turnover ratios tell us the amount of sales generated per euro invested in the business. Obviously, the higher the ratio the better. Both companies have very similar ratios. In the Celtic tiger era these ratios were as high as 0.42. However, mainly due to external factors the ratios have fallen significantly. Also there is very little difference between the fixed asset and total asset turnover ratios for both companies confirming the fact that there is very little investment in current assets for hotel companies and that this investment is financed completely through current liabilities.

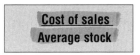

Stock turnover $\dfrac{\text{Cost of sales}}{\text{Average stock}}$ **Stock days** $\dfrac{\text{Average stock} \times 365}{\text{Cost of sales}}$

There are two measures relating to stock: stock turnover and stock days. Stock turnover measures the number of times stock is sold in a period whereas stock days is the number of days it takes to sell stock. One ratio is simply the inverse of the other and is just a different way of expressing the same thing. For example, if it takes a company on average thirty days to sell its stock (stock days) then its stock turnover rate is twelve times per annum.

A fluctuating stock turnover ratio indicates the following:

Decrease in stock turnover	Increase in stock turnover
❏ A fall in sales demand.	❏ An increase in sales demand.
❏ A policy to increase stock levels.	❏ A policy to lower stock levels.

It is important to be mindful that as well as tying up an organisation's resources, holding unnecessarily high levels of stock is expensive in terms of storage, insurance and security costs. Also the longer an organisation holds its stock the greater the risk that the stock will perish or become obsolete. Thus companies should have a policy that minimises stock holding costs but at the same time ensuring no stock outs (running out of stock) occur.

It is important to use the stock figure that is representative of the average stock held during the year. If stock is seasonally high or low at the balance sheet date then the ratio may be distorted. Thus it is important to use average stock levels when computing the ratio. Average stock is calculated as opening stock plus closing stock and divided by two. If it is impossible to calculate the average stock, the closing stock figure can be used.

Consider this

Hotels, airlines, tour bus companies all deal in stocks that are classified as fixed assets. A hotel's largest stock is its stock of bedrooms which it rents out. This stock is classified as a fixed asset. The same goes for airlines and tour bus companies that sell seats. This stock is treated as a fixed asset. This is in marked contrast to the retail sector that supplies stocks that are classified as current assets. This is because once the item is sold it does not belong to the company, whereas for hotels, airlines and tour bus companies they rent out the rooms or seats.

Debtors days

$$\frac{\text{Trade debtors} \times 365}{\text{Credit sales}}$$

The debtors collection period indicates the average number of days between a credit sale taking place and an organisation receiving payment from a customer. The shorter the collection period the better, since liquidity will improve and the risk of bad debts will be reduced. Credit control is essential in organisations that allow credit to customers, especially where a high proportion of credit sales exist. If debtors take too long to pay, an organisation will struggle to meet its own credit payments as they fall due. The ratio refers to trade debtors (customers) not loan debtors and if the credit sales figure is not available then one should use the sales figure.

Decrease in debtors days	Increase in days
❑ Liquidity improves.	❑ Liquidity may worsen.
❑ Risk of bad debts reduces.	❑ Risk of bad debts increases.
	❑ Better control over debtors is required.

Creditors days

Trade creditors x 365
Credit purchases

The creditors turnover (creditors days) shows the average number of days that a business takes to pay its suppliers for goods purchased on credit. Although some organisations see trade credit as an interest free form of funding (with no collateral involved) it does in fact have a cost. Delays in paying suppliers will result in an organisation foregoing discounts for prompt payment. Trade creditors are used for this ratio, not loan creditors or preferential creditors, i.e. VAT and PAYE/PRSI due. Should the credit purchases figure not be available then one should use the purchases or cost of goods sold figure. It is important to keep in mind that in order to maintain suppliers' goodwill, a company will try to pay its bills reasonably promptly.

Decrease in creditors days	Increase in days
❑ Paying suppliers quicker and availing of discounts.	❑ Taking longer to pay suppliers.
❑ Goodwill of suppliers maintained.	❑ Risk of loosing goodwill of suppliers.
❑ Losing a form of interest free credit.	❑ Are there liquidity issues?

Sector comparison and commentary

The key efficiency ratios can now be compared for the chosen companies.

Illustration 16.8: *Efficiency ratios 2003*

	Jury's	Gresham	Ryanair	Aer Lingus	ICG
Fixed asset turnover	0.233	0.27	0.54	1.5	0.91
Total asset turnover	0.26	0.275	0.35	.98	1
Stock turnover	74 times	23 times			334 times
Debtors collections	25 days	26 days	7.5 days	27 days	62 days
Creditors payment	30 days	44 days	54 days	18 days	44 days

For both hotel groups and ICG the fixed asset and total asset turnover ratio should be quite similar. This is due to the low investment in current assets and the fact that this investment is mainly financed by current liabilities, as we will see from the low liquidity ratios for these companies. In fact, in all three companies the total asset turnover ratio is slightly higher due to the excess of current liabilities to current assets. The situation is different for Ryanair due to their policy of holding high levels of cash reserves.

The stock turnover is quite high in the hotel companies as well as ICG. This is, however, due to the low levels of stock in all three companies, especially when compared to the retail sector.

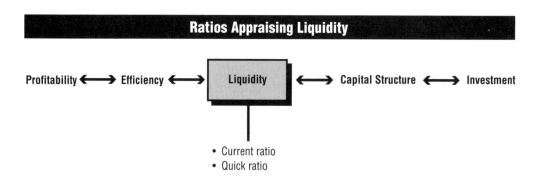

Liquidity refers to the ability of a company to meet its liabilities as they fall due. It is not uncommon for a business which (on paper) is making a profit to experience severe liquidity problems. There are two key ratios to calculate when appraising liquidity: the current ratio and the quick–acid-test ratio.

Current ratio

$$\frac{\text{Current assets}}{\text{Current liabilities}}$$

The current ratio measures a business' ability to pay its debts over a six to twelve month period. There is no standard or recommended current ratio (except the standard text-book conservative rule of thumb of 2:1 mainly recommended for wholesale businesses), since it will vary depending upon the sector in which the organisation operates. The following table outlines the current ratio norms for various business sectors:

Illustration 16.9: *Expected sector liquidity ratios*

Industry Type	Current Ratio
Manufacturing	2.5–4.5:1
Wholesalers	2:1
Retail/supermarkets	0.8:1
Hotels, restaurants, fast foods	0.4:1

Generally, manufacturing and wholesalers will have higher current ratios due to the high levels of stocks and debtors that are the norm for these sectors. The hospitality sector tends to operate with lower current ratios due to the low levels of stock and debtors that apply in the sector. In such organisations cash, not credit, is the currency and hence low current ratios are the norm.

Quick-acid-test ratio

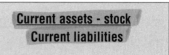

$$\frac{\text{Current assets - stock}}{\text{Current liabilities}}$$

This ratio measures a business' ability to pay its debts immediately, i.e. within a few weeks. It thus ignores stock and concentrates upon those assets which can be converted into cash quickly. In the event of severe liquidity difficulties an organisation can encourage debtors to pay more quickly, while short-term investments can be sold and converted into cash. However, stock takes longer to convert and thus is excluded from the ratio. Once again the minimum safe ratio will vary from sector to sector. As hotels, restaurants and fast food outlets can operate with low stock levels, there is often no significant difference between the quick and current ratios of these business types. Football clubs are another organisation that operates with low current and quick ratios for exactly the same reason. Tottenham Hotspur's current ratio is normally around 0.17:1.

A current or acid-test ratio that is significantly different to that of other organisations of similar size and nature might indicate a number of problems and should be investigated further.

1. Ratios significantly lower than those of other organisations within the same sector can indicate the organisation is too dependent upon short-term borrowings (creditors, bank overdrafts, short-term loans) for the funding of its day-to-day operations.
2. Significantly high current and acid-test ratios indicate that cash flow is not a problem; however, they might suggest that an organisation is not using its resources as efficiently as it could be, resulting in lower than expected rates of return, displeasing current and potential shareholders. Therefore a high ratio can indicate consistently high cash and bank balances, which may need to be invested elsewhere to earn a higher return.
3. A high ratio can indicate poor credit control and prompt management to review its credit control policy and minimise the threat of bad debts. This would not be a problem for cash-based businesses
4. A high current ratio can indicate excessively high stock levels which may prompt management to improve their system of stock control, or may help to identify slow moving or obsolete items which require revaluation (lower of cost and net realisable value (NRV)).

A business should maintain its working capital elements at the lowest possible level. This implies that stock levels should be kept at a minimum in order to reduce costs and the risk of deterioration. Debtors should be collected promptly, mindful of not losing customer goodwill, and cash should not be allowed to lie idle in a current account. If a company's liquidity ratios are too high, resources, which should be invested in income-producing fixed assets, are invested in non-productive stock and debtors and high cash balances. It is the equivalent of an individual investing their savings in a current account that earns no interest compared to a long–term deposit account that earns a fixed rate of interest.

Sector comparison and commentary

The liquidity ratios will vary widely across the different sectors and Illustration 16.9 should be born in mind when looking at the ratios for the companies.

Illustration 16.10: *Liquidity ratios*

	Jury's	Gresham	Ryanair	Aer Lingus	ICG
Current ratio	0.21:1	1.81:1	2.95:1	1.77:1	0.67:1
Acid test	0.19:1	1.71:1	2.89:1	1.76:1	0.66:1

The above shows Jury's ratios slightly lower than the norm for the sector. As the hotel business is predominantly a cash business with low levels of stock and debtors these ratios would not be too disturbing. However, Gresham ratios are very high due in the main to the fact that the company sold a number of hotels and had paid off a lot of its liabilities. In particular it reduced its bank overdraft and paid off its short-term leasing liabilities before the year-end. Thus the ratio, while accurate, is not the norm for the sector.

Ryanair's ratios are also quite high and this is due to a company having €120.9 million held on deposit to hedge its exposure to adverse movements in currency and interest rates for existing and planned debt. Many airlines operate on much lower current ratios, such as Southwest Airlines at 0.67:1.

Ultimately all the above ratios indicate that each company is quite liquid and has no difficulties in paying their debts as they fall due.

How Ratios Relate

The Du Pont ratio pyramid

At this stage we can introduce you to the family tree of ratios, commencing with the ROCE and then dividing into its two main branches:

1. Profitability and cost/sales ratios.
2. Asset turnover ratios (including liquidity ratios).

The following pyramid, showing the relationship between the various ratios, was first developed by the Du Pont organisation in America. The Du Pont system is shown below in summarised from.

Diagram 16.1: *Du Pont ratio pyramid*

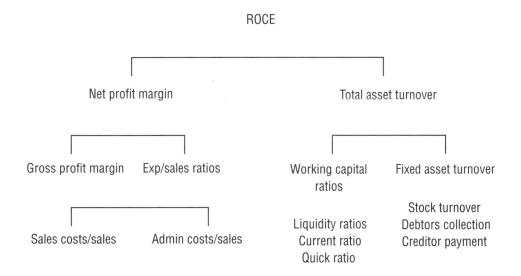

As can be seen from above, the ROCE is made up of two ratios: the net profit margin and the total asset turnover ratio.

The following table compares the ROCE of Jury's Doyle Hotel Group Plc for 2003 and 2002 broken into its two component parts.

Illustration 16.11: *Efficiency ratios*

	ROCE		Operating profit margin	X	Total asset turnover
Jury's Doyle – 2003	6.11%	=	23.5%	X	0.26
Jury's Doyle – 2002	6.89%	=	27.57%	X	0.25

From the table one can see that Jury's Doyle ROCE fell in 2003. When analysing the ROCE into its two component parts, the asset turnover ratio is slightly down, telling us that the business generated slightly less sales per euro invested in the business. However, the main reason for this fall was the reduction in the operating margin of 4 per cent. Further analysis needs to be done to see whether this was due to increases in expenses/sales percentages or a reduction in the gross profit percentage. From Illustration 16.1 the gross profit fell by 3 per cent (35.7 per cent to 32.65 per cent) whereas the expenses to sales percentage increased by 1 per cent. Management now need to focus on the exact reason why the gross profit margin fell and expenses to sales increased. In the light of the weak global economy that affected business over the period it is not surprising that Jury's Doyle reduced prices to stimulate demand and this adversely affected their gross and net profit margins.

The following table shows the break-down of ROCE into its two component parts for the five companies under review.

Illustration 16.12: *Breakdown of ROCE*

	ROCE (%)	=	Operating profit margin (%)	X	Total asset turnover
Jury's Doyle	6.10	=	23.5	X	0.26
Gresham	2.4	=	8.7	X	0.275
Ryanair	12.6	=	36	X	0.35
Aer Lingus	8.17	=	8.35	X	0.98
ICG	7.95	=	7.92	X	1.0

Key Operating Ratios – Hospitality Industry

Every business sector will have its own specific or unique performance measurements. The hospitality sector is no different, with a number of key ratios/measurements that are important to the industry and important in comparing performance within the industry. The following are the key operating ratios specific to the hospitality industry:

Name	Calculation	Meaning/Use/Interpretation
Occupancy ratios 1	$\dfrac{\text{Rooms occupied} \times 100}{\text{Rooms available}}$	Where a hotel has 100 rooms of which 65 are occupied then the occupancy ratio is 65%. The ratio is important when comparing year to year or hotel to hotel. However, its main weakness is that it does not take into account price per room which has a direct effect on the occupancy levels of a hotel.
2	$\dfrac{\text{Number of guests} \times 100}{\text{Guest capacity}}$	This occupancy ratio compares guest capacity with the number of guests staying in the hotel. It is seen as more accurate than 1 above, as it takes into account the possibility that some double rooms could be sold as singles.
3	$\dfrac{\text{Actual room revenue} \times 100}{\text{Potential room revenue}}$	This is known as rooms sales potential and takes into account the lowering of prices to boost occupancy. Thus a hotel with a high occupancy level could have a low rooms sales potential due to the lowering of prices to boost occupancy.
Average room rate	$\dfrac{\text{Room revenue}}{\text{Rooms occupied}}$	It measures the relationship between room sales and the number of rooms occupied. It gives an average room sales rate.
Average rate per guest	$\dfrac{\text{Room revenue}}{\text{Number of guests}}$	This gives the average rate per guest staying in the hotel and again is essential in interpreting any occupancy ratios as the rate may fall to boost room sales.
Average spend	$\dfrac{\text{Sales}}{\text{Number of covers}}$	This is a useful ratio for restaurants as it calculates the average spend per cover/customer. This can be done separately for lunch and dinner (à la carte) menus. It is an important ratio in terms of budgeting and forecasting.
Sales mix	$\dfrac{\text{Rooms revenue} \times 100}{\text{Total hotel revenue}}$ $\dfrac{\text{Food revenue} \times 100}{\text{Total hotel revenue}}$ $\dfrac{\text{Bar revenue} \times 100}{\text{Total hotel revenue}}$	This tells us the percentage of total sales that is made up from rooms revenue or restaurant or bar revenues.
Sale per room	$\dfrac{\text{Total hotel revenue}}{\text{Room sales}}$	These ratios are generally used to spot trends in hotel or restaurant revenue. It makes up part of the performance statistics for the business and can be quite useful in forecasting sales.
Sales per seat	$\dfrac{\text{Total restaurant revenue}}{\text{Number of seats}}$	
Sales per employee	$\dfrac{\text{Total sales}}{\text{Number of employees}}$	
Labour costs as a % of sales	$\dfrac{\text{Labour costs} \times 100}{\text{Sales}}$	This indicates the extent revenue is being absorbed by staff costs. As labour costs are mostly fixed, this ratio will fall as the business experiences increases in sales and will increase as sales falls.

Ratios Appraising Capital Structure

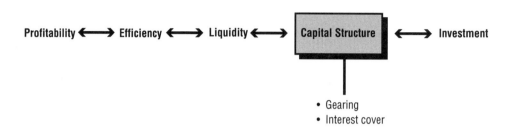

Profitability ⟷ Efficiency ⟷ Liquidity ⟷ **Capital Structure** ⟷ Investment

• Gearing
• Interest cover

Each business must decide how it is to finance its fixed assets and working capital requirements. In general this is down to a choice (after grant aid) between debt, equity or a mixture of both. Debt is where finance is arranged through third parties who are not owners of the business. Equity relates to the owner's contribution or investment in the business. Capital structure measures the funding mix of a business. At this stage it is important to be aware of the characteristics of both debt and equity funding. The following points should be understood.

❑ Each source of finance has a cost to it. Interest is the cost of debt and dividends are part of the cost of equity.

❑ Debt as a source of finance is cheaper than equity for a business due to the fact that interest is tax deductible (reducing the tax charge on profits) whereas dividends are not. Loan interest is paid for the term of the loan whereas dividends are paid forever. Also, as equity shareholders take a greater risk than providers of debt capital then, in theory at least, they require a greater return for taking that risk. It is important to remember that profit is a payment for risk taking.

❑ Debt is a riskier source of finance for the business because when a company experiences difficult trading conditions and cash flow is a problem, debt interest still has to be paid. On the other hand, dividends can be deferred or cancelled. Also, at some stage, debt will need to be repaid whereas equity does not.

Financing through debt	Financing through equity
❑ Interest must be paid on the debt.	❑ Dividends will be paid to shareholders.
❑ Interest is tax deductible.	❑ Dividends are not tax deductible.
❑ Debt generally cheaper.	❑ Equity requires higher returns to
❑ Debt is risky because interest *must* be paid.	compensate for risk.
❑ Loan must be repaid.	❑ Dividends are at discretion of
	management and may be deferred.
	❑ Equity does not require repayment

Investors, potential investors and other lenders will be particularly interested in an organisation's long-term funding arrangements. The higher the ratio of debt to equity, the more dependent the organisation is upon borrowed funds and the greater the risk that it will be unable to meet interest payments on these funds as they fall due. This is what is known as financial risk (as distinct from commercial risk) and is measured through the gearing ratio.

Gearing ratio – debts:equity

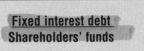

The term fixed interest debt includes preference share capital, debentures/loan capital and any leasing liabilities. Bank overdrafts and short-term loans may be included on the assumption that the bank overdrafts are effectively a permanent source of finance and that short-term loans may be renewed or replaced when they mature. If short-term loans and bank overdrafts are included as part of debt, then any existing cash balances should be deducted from debt to get the net debt. Capital and reserves is normally taken as equity share capital and reserves.

For example, if fixed interest debt is €200,000 and equity capital is €300,000, then the gearing ratio is 200/300 = .67:1 or 67 per cent. If one measures gearing as a proportion of total capital (Debt + Equity), then the ratio is 200/500 = 40 per cent. This text will concentrate on the debt to equity ratio and the following table acts as a guide to interpreting this ratio.

Low gearing = where debt is less than capital & reserves	**< 100%**
Neutral gearing = debt equals capital & reserves	**= 100%**
High gearing = debt is greater than capital & reserves	**> 100%**

Illustration 16.13: *Gearing ratios*

	2001 (%)	2002 (%)	2003 (%)
Jury's Doyle	81	50	42
Gresham	42	59	27

The above ratios show that both companies would be considered low geared (mainly financed by equity). Also the trend shows that the gearing levels of both companies are falling. In 2003 Gresham hotels sold a number of its hotels and used the proceeds to reduce its debt levels. It is important to remember that debt is a cheaper source of finance and as such will increase the returns for the business and equity shareholders. However, if the gearing ratios are too high then the company increases its financial risk (the risk that it may be unable to meet the commitments of the debt finance). This has repercussions on the company's ability to acquire further debt finance at a reasonable cost. Both companies are low geared and, it would seem, could benefit from extra debt finance in the future.

Another ratio that helps assess the appropriate level of debt for a business is the interest cover ratio.

Interest cover

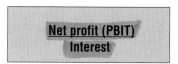

Net profit (PBIT)
Interest

Interest cover indicates how many times interest payments on debt are covered by profit before interest and tax. The higher the interest cover, the less likely that interest payments will not be met and hence the lower the level of financial risk associated with the organisation. If the interest cover is low the greater the chance that a decline in profits will result in either:

❑ Interest payments not being met.
❑ Profits available for distribution to shareholders being very small resulting in small or zero dividend payments.

Financial institutions generally require a minimum level of cover of 3:1. If lenders were not happy with the capital structure ratios calculated (in other words they are too high), an organisation would find it difficult to raise additional, long-term finance or would have to pay a premium (risk premium) for such funds in the form of higher interest rates.

Sector comparison and commentary

The following table outlines the gearing and interest cover for four companies.

Illustration 16.14: *Risk ratios 2003*

	Jury's	Gresham	Ryanair	ICG
Gearing-debt : equity	42%	27%	60%	59%
Interest cover (net)	4.3 times	1.7 times	n/a	3.76 times

The table tells us that all the companies are low geared but the interest cover for Gresham is quite low at 1.7 times. In other words the business can pay its interest out of profits 1.7 times. This is quite low compared to Jury's Doyle at 4.3 times. In 2003 Gresham reduced its gearing and interest costs significantly but profit was recovering from an operating loss in 2002 and was quite low. Thus its interest cover is low but improving. This shows the levels of financial risk attached to a business that is highly geared in an economic recession, where sales and profits fall to levels that ensure the business finds it difficult to comply with its debt obligations.

Ryanair's interest earned (high levels of cash on deposit) is greater than its interest charged and thus the ratio is not applicable here.

Consider this

The hotel sector and, to a lesser extent, the retail sector can be characterised as having high value properties in their balance sheet. Once a company decides to value its properties at current value these assets must be re-valued over time. The effect of a revaluation is to increase property asset values and to show this profit as an unrealised reserve in the balance sheet. Thus assets and shareholders' funds increase as a result of a revaluation. According to FRS 15 a full property valuation is required at least every five years which must involve an external qualified valuer. Should a significant revaluation occur this can significantly reduce the following key ratios:

❑   ROCE and ROOE.
❑   Fixed asset turnover and total asset turnover.
❑   Debt to equity ratio.

It is important in interpreting ratios that revaluations of property assets do not distort the trend analysis and thus it is important to be aware of the effects of revaluations

---

Case Example: Arnotts

This case example focuses on the financial performance of Arnotts, which trades within the retail sector. The analysis focuses on the period 2002–2003. The financial statements are presented and key performance indicators calculated. Finally a report is prepared summarising the analysis of their financial performance under the headings of profitability, use of assets, liquidity and capital structure.

The published accounts of Arnotts

Arnotts
Group Profit and Loss Account
Year ended 31 January 2003

	Note	2003	2002
		€'000	€'000
Turnover including			
concession sales		204,192	192,520
Concession sales	2	-56,009	-51,937
Turnover excluding			
concession sales	2	148,183	140,583
Operating profit	3	21,158	18,020
Share of operating profit			
of associated undertaking		309	1,294
Profit before interest		21,467	19,314
Net interest payable	4	-1,004	-1,432
Profit before taxation		20,463	17,882
Taxation	5	-3,283	-3,043
Profit for the financial year	6	17,180	14,839
Dividends paid	7	-1,918	-1,678
Dividends proposed	7	-4,671	-4,043
Increase in retained profits		10,591	9,118
Statement of retained profits			
At beginning of year		58,684	51,344
Increase in retained profits		10,591	9,118
Purchase of own shares		-	-1,778
At end of year		69,275	58,684
Earnings per ordinary share	8	96.6c	82.6c
Diluted earnings per			
ordinary share	8	95.3c	82.0c

Arnotts
Group Balance Sheet
31 January 2003

	Note	2003	2002
		€'000	€'000
Fixed assets			
Tangible assets	9	240,042	223,367
Financial assets	10	2,297	2,018
		242,339	225,385
Current assets			
Stocks	11	16,470	16,903
Debtors	12	13,263	13,786
Cash		8,703	7,665
		38,436	38,354
Creditors (amounts falling			
due within one year)	13	-42,540	-47,727
Net current liabilities		-4,104	-9,373
Total assets less current			
liabilities		238,235	216,012
Creditors (amounts falling			
due after more than			
one year)	14	-9,729	-14,873
Provisions for liabilities			
and charges	16	-2,259	-2,011
		226,247	199,128
Capital and reserves			
Called-up share capital			
(equity and non-equity)	17	23,482	23,448
Share premium account	18	953	871
Revaluation reserve	18	132,311	115,899
Other reserve	18	226	226
P & L account	18	69,275	58,684
Shareholders' funds	19	226,247	199,128

Data needed from the notes to the accounts.

		2003	2002
		€'000	€'000
Turnover	from Note 3	148,183	140,583
Cost of sales	from Note 3	96,813	92,216
Gross profit	from Note 3	51,370	48,367
Expenses	from Note 3	45,963	44,422
Other operating income	from Note 3	15,748	14,075
Trade debtors	from Note 12	12,841	13,469
Trade creditors	from Note 13	17,975	17,886
Creditors > 1 year include bank loans and overdrafts		5,796	12,474
Closing stock in 2001 amounted to €14,107,000			

If the published accounts of the Arnotts for 2003 and 2002 are examined an overall picture of company performance can be established.

Ratio Analysis of Arnotts

		2003		2002	
Gross profit margin	Gross profit x 100 / Sales	5,1370 x 100 / 148,183	34.7%	48,367 x 100 / 140,583	34.4%
Net profit margin	Net profit (PBIT) x 100 / Sales	21,158 x 100 / 148,183	14.3%	18,020 x 100 / 140,583	12.8%
Expenses to sales	Expenses x 100 / Sales	45,960 x 100 / 148,183	31.0%	44,422 x 100 / 140,583	31.6%
Return on capital employed (ROCE)	Net profit (PBIT) x 100 / Capital employed	21,158 x 100 / 238,235	8.88%	18,020 x 100 / 216,012	8.34%
Return on owners' equity (ROOE) before tax	Net profit before tax x 100 / Shareholders' funds	20,463 x 100 / 226,247	9.04%	17,882 x 100 / 199,128	8.98%
Fixed asset turnover	Sales / Fixed assets	148,183 / 240,042	0.617 times	140,583 / 225,385	0.629 times
Total asset turnover	Sales / Net asset	148,183 / 238,235	0.622 times	140,583 / 223,367	0.65 times
Stock turnover	Cost of sales / Average stock	96,813 / 16,687	5.80 times	92,216 / 15,505	5.95 times
Stock days	Average stock x 365 / Cost of sales	16,687 x 365 / 96,813	62.9 days	15,505 x 365 / 92,216	61.4 days
Debtors days	Trade debtors x 365 / Credit sales	12,841 x 365 / 148,183	31.6 days	13,469 x 365 / 140,583	35 days
Creditors days	Trade creditors x 365 / Credit purchases *	17,795 x 365 / 96,380	67.4 days	17,886 x 365 / 95,012	68.7 days

Current ratio	Current assets	38,436	0.9 : 1	38,354	0.8 : 1
	Current liabilities	42,540		47,727	
Quick-acid-test ratio	Current assets - stock	21,966	0.52 : 1	21,451	0.45 : 1
	Current liabilities	42,540		47,727	
Gearing	Fixed interest debt	9,729 x 100	4.3%	14,602 x 100	7.3%
	Shareholders' funds	226,247		199,128	
Interest cover	Net profit (PBIT)	21,467	21.4 times	19,314	13.5 times
	Interest	1,004		1,432	

* Purchases = COS + Closing Stock - Opening Stock, 2003 = 96813 + 16470 - 16903 = 96380. 2002 = 92216 + 16903 - 14107 = 95012
Credit Sales and credit purchases were not disclosed in the reports, so total sales and total purchases were used in the ratios for debtors and creditors days.

Summary of Increases/Decreases in Key Items Over 2002 Level

	%
Turnover excluding concession sales	5.4
Cost of sales	5.0
Gross profit	6.2
Expenses	3.5
Other operating income	9.97
Operating profit	17.4
Net interest payable	-29.9
Tangible assets	7.5
Stocks	-2.6
Debtors	-3.8
Cash	13.5
Creditors (amounts falling due within one year)	-10.9
Creditors (amounts falling due after more than one year)	-34.6
Capital employed	10.3

Summary of Key Ratios

		2003	2002
Profitability	Gross profit margin	34.7%	34.4%
	Net profit margin	14.3%	12.8%
	Expenses to sales	31.0%	31.6%
	ROCE *return on capital investment*	8.88%	8.34%
	ROOE	9.04%	8.98%
Efficiency	Fixed asset turnover	0.617 times	0.629 times
	Total asset turnover	0.622 times	0.65 times
	Stock turnover	5.80 times	5.95 times
	Stock days	62.9 days	61.4 days
	Debtors days	31.6 days	35 days
	Creditors days	67.4 days	68.7 days
Liquidity	Current ratio	0.9:1	0.8:1
	Quick ratio	0.52:1	0.45:1
Capital structure	Gearing	4.3%	7.3%
	Interest cover	21.4 times	13.5 times

Report on the financial performance of Arnotts for year ended 31 January 2003

Introduction

Arnotts operates in the retailing sector via a number of department stores with key stores being Arnotts in Henry Street and Boyers in North Earl Street both in Dublin city centre. The financial statements presented relate to financial years ending 31 January 2003 and 2002. At that time the economy was experiencing a downturn compared to the economic highs of the Celtic tiger period of 1999 and 2000 and there were many concerns expressed by leading economists of house price bubbles and a looming recession. Both could have a significant effect on the retail trade.

The chairman's statement, however, focused on the positives, commenting: 'the results for the year maintain the group's strong growth record. EPS has increased at a compound rate of 20.3 per cent over the past five years. Over the same period, turnover has grown at a compound rate of 15.4 per cent, net dividend at 17.5 per cent and net asset value per ordinary share at 16.6 per cent'.

The performance of Arnotts will now be analysed within the above context under the key headings of profitability, efficiency/use of assets, liquidity and capital structure.

Profitability

In the calculations above, turnover is taken to be 'turnover excluding concession sales', as concession sales relates to outlets such as River Island that rent space within the Arnotts department stores.

In 2003 Arnotts achieved a 5.4 per cent increase in turnover and an increase in operating profit of 17.4 per cent. This signals a good improvement in performance from 2002. There was a healthy increase in the ROCE from 8.34 per cent to 8.88 per cent. The ROOE increased from 8.98 per cent to 9.04 per cent.

ROCE is made up of two components: operating profit margin and asset turnover. The operating profit margin improved significantly and was responsible for the improvement in the ROCE because the asset turnover declined from 0.65 in 2002 to 0.622 in 2003.

Turnover increased over the period by 5.4 per cent and gross profit margin showed a slight improvement moving from 34.4 per cent to 34.7 per cent. The operating profit margin, however, rose from 12.8 per cent to 14.3 per cent. The expenses to sales ratio decreased slightly from 31.6 per cent to 31 per cent but the main reason for the improved operating margin was other operating income, which rose by 5.5 per cent and in addition Arnotts received a royalty income, which did not exist in 2002. The operating profit margin of 14.3 per cent compares favourably with international peers, such as Marks & Spencer (10.4 per cent) and Debenhams (9.7 per cent). However, management will be disappointed in the negative movement in the total asset turnover ratio.

While overall the return on capital ratios is improving, it should get into double figures to compensate equity investors for the risk they are taking. It must be pointed out, however, that Arnotts revalued their property assets over the period resulting in the revaluation reserve increasing by €16,412,000. The effect of a revaluation is to dilute the ROCE and ROOE ratios. If the revaluation had not occurred then the ROCE and the ROOE for 2003 would be 9.5 per cent and 9.75 per cent respectively.

Efficiency/Use of assets

Management use assets to generate sales and profits. The performance indicators under this heading measure how efficient management are in generating turnover and profits from the assets at their disposal.

The fixed asset turnover measures the amount of sales generated per euro invested in fixed assets. Although reasonably consistent with 2002, it is somewhat low at 62 cent for every €1 of fixed assets. Property was revalued during the year resulting in increases in property values on the balance sheet of 10 per cent on 2002. This would have a diluting effect on the fixed and total asset turnover ratios. If the revaluation was adjusted for, the total asset turnover ratios would be 0.67 for 2003 thus recording an increase.

	Arnotts	**Marks & Spencer**	**Debenhams**
Fixed asset turnover	0.62	2.33	0.54

The fixed asset turnover of Debenhams is lower at .54 while Marks & Spencer is significantly more efficient. The total asset turnover decreased from 0.65 to 0.622 a decrease of 9.57 per cent. Management must focus on this performance indicator and ensure it does not develop into a trend.

Stock days, debtors and creditors are broadly similar to 2002 levels. Stock days at 62.9 days is higher than that of comparable retail outlets but this is could be due to the nature of the stock items held by Arnotts. Debenhams holds stock on average 52.5 days while Marks & Spencer holds stock on average 26 days. It should be remembered that Marks & Spencer deals in food items so a lower stock holding period would be required on perishable items resulting in a lower overall holding period. One should also take into account, that the ratios are based upon stock position at the end of year which may not be representative of the entire period. Arnotts' year-end is 31 January, when spring/summer ranges have been launched.

The management of debtors and creditors shows slight improvements. Delaying the payment of creditors can be a useful method of financing a business in the short-term but it comes with a cost, as early payment discounts are lost as well as the possible loss of goodwill on behalf of suppliers if delayed payment is pushed too far.

Liquidity
The group has ample cash available, with cash in excess of €8.7 million. There are no major movements in current assets. Current liabilities show a reduction of over 10 per cent on 2002 levels, which was mainly achieved by reducing unsecured bank loans by over 57 per cent.

Both liquidity ratios show an improvement on 2002 levels, generally brought about by the reduction in current liabilities. The current ratio, which examines an organisation's ability to pay short-term debt over a six to twelve month period, has improved from 0.8:1 to 0.9:1. The norm for the retail sector is about 0.8:1. The quick ratio which examines an organisation's ability to cover short-term liability without the need to liquidate stock also improved from 0.45:1 to 0.52:1. The norm for the retail sector is about 0.6:1 for the quick ratio.

The retail sector generally survives on lower than normal ratios due to the cash nature of operations. What is important is to look at the sector that the organisation operates in and assess the norms for that sector. The figures below relate to a similar time-frame.

	Arnotts	**Marks & Spencer**	**Debenhams**
Current ratio	.9:1	.98:1	.75:1
Quick ratio	.52:1	.7:1	.2:1

Arnotts' ratios are in line with the retail sector norms for liquidity. The trend is also improving, with the company developing stronger liquidity ratios. The nature of retailing involves high operating cash flows and this should ensure there is money available to pay creditors as they fall due.

Capital structure

Capital structure measures how the business is financed. Ultimately the higher a business is financed through debt the greater its financial risk. However, debt is considered a cheaper and more tax efficient form of finance to equity.

Arnotts is low geared with low levels of fixed interest debt. Long-term debt was reduced during the year by 34.6 per cent. This has reduced the gearing ratio from 7.3 per cent to 4.3 per cent. Arnotts is mainly funded by equity rather than debt. The reduction in debt has resulted in a significant improvement in interest cover, with cover moving from 13.5 times to 21.4 times. There are no concerns with Arnotts' ability to cover interest payments on debt. Again it must be pointed out that, because of the revaluation in property assets, the gearing ratio will be diluted. If the revaluation was adjusted for, gearing for Arnotts in 2003 would be 4.6 per cent.

Conclusion

Taking into account the economic environment and its effect on the retail sector, Arnotts has performed reasonably well for the year ending 31 January 2003. Turnover and profits are up and this is reflected in an improved return on capital. The liquidity indicators have held up strongly and the company has further reduced its debt over the year resulting in significantly higher interest cover ratios. The company can be considered very low geared with minimal financial risk. However, the overall returns on capital are slightly disappointing despite the increased turnover and profit for the period.

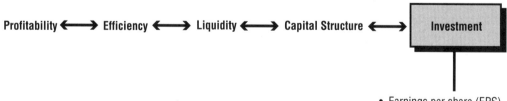

Investment Ratios – Stock Market Indicators

Profitability ⟷ Efficiency ⟷ Liquidity ⟷ Capital Structure ⟷ Investment

- Earnings per share (EPS)
- Price earnings ratio (P/E)
- Dividend cover
- Dividend yield

Investment ratios are used when appraising listed companies in relation to stock market performance. It gives an indication of past performance and the market's impression of the future financial performance and dividend policy of a company. In buying the shares of a particular company the investor is effectively spending now in order to procure even greater future cash flows, whether of a dividend or a capital nature. Thus an investor is not just interested in the future earnings efficiency of a company but also the value of the share price in the future. For this reason several ratios are used by investors to appraise the performance of companies in terms of share price and share yields. These include:

1. The return on capital employed/owners' equity (ROCE/ROOE) (see profitability section).
2. The stock exchange ratios, the most important of which are:
   a) Earnings per share (EPS).
   b) Price earnings ratio (P/E).
   c) Dividend yield ratio.
   d) Dividend cover.

Earnings per share (EPS)

$$\frac{\text{Net profit after interest, tax, preference dividend}}{\text{Number of shares}}$$

EPS is concerned with the profits available to ordinary shareholders from which a dividend can be paid. EPS tells the investor how much profit has been earned during an accounting period that is available to the ordinary shareholder per share.

If a company's issued share capital is 100,000 shares and the profit available for distribution is €40,000, then the EPS is 40 cent. It is a much better measure of a company's performance than just comparing profit figures, as profit figures on their own can be boosted by purchasing profit-making companies and paid for by issuing shares.

As well as making comparisons with other organisations, shareholders and other users of accounts will be interested in seeing a steady growth in EPS from one period to the next.

Illustration 16.15: *Earnings per share 2003*

	Jury's	Gresham	Ryanair	ICG	Arnotts
Earnings per share	60.4 cent	2.69 cent	31.71 cent	71.6 cent	96.6 cent

Price earnings ratio (P/E)

$$\frac{\text{Market price of share}}{\text{Earnings per share (EPS)}}$$

This ratio is a measure of a company's share price as a multiple of its earnings per share. It compares the present earnings of a business to its market price. If the market price of a share is €2.00 and the current EPS is 15 cent, then the P/E ratio is 13.3. What this means is that if €2.00 is paid for these shares, then 13.3 years of current earnings are being bought. Because the market value of a share reflects the expectations of investors concerning the future profits of a company, the ratio is effectively measuring the market's anticipation of future earnings compared to the present earnings of the company. The P/E ratio reflects the market's valuation of a company expressed as a multiple of past/present profits (remember the main reason for acquiring shares is to participate in future profits). Therefore the P/E ratio is an indicator of the confidence the stock market has in the company and its future profitability. A low P/E suggests low confidence in the immediate future of the company, which suggests static profit levels or the fact that the company is operating in a riskier sector for investors. A high P/E suggests high confidence in the company, its management team and future profits and dividends. Thus the market expects increased future profits and this expectancy is already reflected in the share price. The P/E ratio depends mainly on four things:

1. The overall level of the stock market (for example bull or bear).
2. The industry in which the company operates.
3. The company's record.
4. The market's view on the company's prospects.

The following table should only be used as a rule of thumb:

P/E ratio	Commentary
<8	The market feels that these companies have poor future prospects and/or are trading in unfashionable business sectors. Its lack of confidence is reflected in a low share price and thus a low P/E.
8–12	The market feels that these companies have reasonable prospects but are unsure regarding if and when these companies will shine. Again much depends on the sector the companies operate in.
12–20	The market feels these companies have very good prospects and that these prospects are beginning to be reflected in the share price as demand for the share increases. Companies with P/Es of 15 are considered good, safe, blue chip investments.
>20	These are the boom stocks or high flyers. Their potential is generally reflected already in their share price and the demand for the share is on the increase. These type of companies tend to be young high flyers who retain all their profits for future growth. They would also be operating in fashionable sectors.

The P/E ratio of a company depends not only on the company itself, but also on the industry in which it operates and on the level of the stock market, which tends to rise more than the increases in profits when the business cycle swings up and to fall more than profits in a downturn.

P/Es of the Financial Times 500 Index

19 May 1972 peak of Bull market	19.88
13 December 1974 bottom of Bear market	3.71
16 July 1987 peak of Bull market	21.03

Source: Holmes and Sugdon Interpreting Company Reports and Accounts

In the late 1990s one of the more fashionable sectors for share dealings was the high-tech sector involving internet companies. These companies had P/E ratings of over 100. This was purely based on speculation (not past performance, as these companies had very little history) about future profits and the way business would be conducted in the future. They were considered high risk. One of the world's most famous stock market players, Warren Buffet, refused to invest in the 'dot com frenzy', as he simply didn't know where these companies would be in ten years time. He was proved to be right, as they fell in popularity in early 2000 and many investors lost considerable fortunes.

Illustration 16.16: *EPS and P/E ratios 2003*

	Jury's	Ryanair	ICG
Earnings per share	60.4 cent	31.71 cent	71.6 cent
Share price as at year-end 03	€9.80	€ 6.45	€10.50
P/E	16.23	20.34	14.66

The above table shows the EPS, share price and P/E ratio in 2003 for Jury's Doyle, Ryanair and ICG, all companies presently quoted on the Irish stock exchange. The P/E ratio for all four companies is quite high, showing that the market believes the companies, in the light of its current earnings per share, have a good future. Ryanair's P/E is in the 'high flyer' category and it has many of the characteristics of such high flyers. It is a relatively young company, expanding rapidly, with 100 per cent of profits reinvested to finance such expansion. It does not declare dividends and is a leader in its business sector category – low-cost airlines. The high P/E for Jury's Doyle also reflects the markets opinion of its 'low-cost' Inn's model, which over the last number of years has driven the growth in the company. Overall, the P/Es are positive, which also reflects a more optimistic mindset in the equities market as Irish travel and tourism businesses recover from the effects of the September 11 terrorism attacks and the 'foot and mouth' crisis.

Dividend cover

$$\frac{\text{Profit available to pay dividend}}{\text{Dividends paid and proposed}}$$

This ratio indicates the proportion of available profits, which is distributed to shareholders, and the amount which is retained by the organisation. If a company's profits available for distribution amount to €25,000 and the gross dividend payable to ordinary shareholders is €10,000, the dividend cover is 2.5:1, indicating that for every €2.50 made in profit, €1.00 is distributed to shareholders with the balance retained in the business. A company with a high dividend cover is one which retains a high proportion of profit for reinvestment in the company. A company with a low dividend cover is one which apportions high dividends out of profits. However, there exists a risk that the company will not be able to maintain the current profit and dividend levels, as there is little reinvestment in the future.

Care must be taken to ensure that investors are satisfied with the dividend declared whilst enough profit is retained to fund the future growth of the organisation.

Dividend policy and the P/E ratio are very much related. Blue chip companies like to pay a reasonable dividend and to increase it each year to counteract the effects of inflation. This means that major companies usually pay out between 30 per cent and 40 per cent of profits and retain the balance to reinvest in future growth.

Some companies pay tiny dividends and plough back most of their profits to finance growth. These companies (generally young growth companies, for example Ryanair Plc) will enjoy a glamour rating but this rating is vulnerable to any set back in profits, as there is little dividend yield to support the price.

Dividend yield

$$\frac{\text{Dividend per share x 100}}{\text{Market price per share}}$$

The return on any equity investment is made up of a dividend element and the capital appreciation of the share value/price. Dividend yield calculates the return on the investment in the form of dividends – excluding capital appreciation of the share. Research shows that over the last 100 years dividend yields accounted for 50 per cent of the total return from US equities. In contrast, during the 1995–2000 period they accounted for only 20 per cent of the total return on equities in the US. The reason for this was booming share prices, which ensured that investors were more concerned with the capital appreciation element of equity returns, rather than the dividend yield element. Now in the post 2000 period and a bear market atmosphere, dividend yields have risen again but this is more to do with falling share prices than increased dividend levels.

The dividend yield expresses the shareholders' dividend as a percentage of the market value of the share. If a company declares an ordinary dividend of 25 cent per share and the market price per share is €3.75, the dividend yield will be 6.67 per cent (0.25 ÷ 3.75 x 100).

It is important to note that dividend yield can be calculated in two ways:

1. Gross dividend yield ⸺⸺⸺⸺⸺⸺ Dividend per share ÷ share price
2. Net dividend yield ⸺⸺⸺⸺⸺⸺ Dividend per share x (1–20%) ÷ share price

The difference in the net yield is after the deduction of income tax at the standard rate of 20 per cent, deducted at source. On a dividend of 25 cent as above, the shareholder will only receive 20 cent (25 cent x (1–20 per cent) as income tax is deducted by the company at source. It is important to compare like with like and not to compare the gross yield of one company with the net yield of another. In general the gross yield is more popular and if a company's dividend yield is quoted net, then one must gross up the dividend element to calculate the gross yield. This is simply done as follows: 20 cent x 100 ÷ 80 = 25 cent. Whether this satisfies a shareholder depends on the yield that could be earned elsewhere.

The yield is influenced by the dividend policy of an organisation. A company which has traditionally paid high dividends will be popular with some shareholders (dividend conscious ones) but the share price will not rise too high due to lack of investment in the future. From an investors' point of view the dividend yield indicates the cash return that an investor earns from holding shares in a particular company, and the higher the yield the better. A low yield might persuade investors to dispose of shares and invest the proceeds elsewhere. Generally investors looking for income will go for companies with high dividend yields. Some investors may settle for lower yields in the expectation of growth in the years ahead and thus an appreciation in the capital value of the shares. In a low inflation environment, gross yield on shares can often be better than the more conventional methods of saving, such as deposit accounts.

The following table shows the average dividend yield for the major world markets over the last twenty years.

	Dividend yield (%)
UK	2.7
Ireland	1.8
Eurobloc (ex UK)	2.4
USA	1.5
Japan	0.9
Asia pacific (ex Japan)	3.1

Source: *The Irish Times* Business Supplement

Illustration 16.17: *Investor ratios – Jury's Doyle 2003 and 2002*

	2003	2002
Return on capital employed (ROCE)	6.10%	6.88%
Return on owners' equity (ROOE) before tax	6.60%	7.2%
Return on owners' equity (ROOE) after tax	5.44%	5.6%
Earnings per share (EPS)	60.4 cent	66 cent
Price earnings ratio (P/E)	16.2	10.91
Dividend per share	23.7 cent	21.9 cent
Dividend cover	2.55	3.01
Dividend yield	2.4%	3.04%
Share price as at year-end	€9.80	€7.20

Overall the returns for Jury's Doyle fell slightly in 2003 and EPS fell 8.5 per cent. The company continued to give a dividend to its shareholders and dividend per share increased by 8.2 per cent. The dividend yield fell by 21 per cent, but this was due to the increase in the share price, which went from €7.20 at the end of 2002 to €9.80 in 2003 – an increase of 36 per cent. The P/E rating increased to 16.2 mainly due to the increased share price. Despite the low returns and a falling EPS, in 2003 the market is positive about the future of the company and this is reflected in increased demand for the shares and thus an increased share price. The main reasons for this positive outlook are:

1. The improved trading conditions in the second half of 2003, leading to greater confidence regarding 2004 and a general global recovery.
2. The good operating performance from the Jury's Inns portfolio along with the opening of two new Inns in 2003. Presently the occupancy rates and operating margins on this low-cost Inns concept far exceed the occupancy rates and margins of the group's other four and five star hotels.
3. The announcements of increased expansion in the Jury's Inns brand with more Inns to come on board in 2004 and 2005.

Consider this

The biggest acquisition in the history of the Irish hotel industry took place in May 1999 between the Doyle Group (a family run, private group of companies) and Jury's (a public company). This was an expensive acquisition for Jury's shareholders, with the final deal putting the value on Doyle's 11 hotels at £248 million (approx £50 million over the current estimated value of Doyles). This worked out at £118,000 per bedroom. This price valued Doyles on a P/E of £22.54 (£248 million/present earnings of £11 million PA). Although the market was more bullish than bear, it was felt by more than one financial analyst that a more equitable P/E would be 18.

Setting a Context for Financial Statement Analysis

The following factors, which provide a context from which to analyse financial performance, should be considered.

The age of the business: Any young business is quite vulnerable to the many internal and external factors or shocks that can occur. Many young businesses are highly financed by debt and will be vulnerable to interest rate and exchange rate movements as they try to develop a brand name and reputation. Providers of finance are known to add a premium to the loan interest charge for young companies, as they would view them as high risk. It is reasonable to assume that a new business compared to an established business will always carry a greater level of business risk.

The size of the business: The larger the business, the less vulnerable it may be to external factors. Providers of finance ensure cheaper finance for a sound large company that has been in existence for a number of years, as they would perceive the business risk to be lower. Also larger businesses may have diversified their investments and this again protects them or reduces their business risk.

Xtra-vision Diversifies

Sales at Xtra-vision, Ireland's biggest DVD and video rental chain, rose by 25% last year to €89 million as the company diversified into providing snacks, mobile phones, computer games and computer electronics. A small number of stores also sell DVD players, televisions, camcorders and home cinema systems. Pre-tax profits rose by 17% to €7.5 million, ensuring a net profit before tax margin on sales of 8.4%. Xtra-vision, one of the high flyers of the 1980s with more than 300 stores, now operates from 147 stores.

Source: *Sunday Times*, 12 December 2004

The economic and political environment: The economy both local and global, inflation, exchange rates and interest rates all affect a business. Should the euro strengthen against the dollar or sterling then tourism will be affected as it becomes more expensive for tourists to travel. If an economy has spiralling inflation, then the products and services produced will have a high cost base and thus will not be competitive in relation to other countries. From a tourism and business perspective this can lead to reduced tourist numbers and reduced foreign direct investment. Any country experiencing political upheaval and uncertainty will always find it difficult to entice business and tourism investment. In interpreting any financial statements, one must take into account the prevailing economic and political circumstances. The effects of the September 11 terrorist attacks have to be taken into account when comparing a company's performance over the period 1999 to 2003. The effects of inflation must be taken into account when looking at a company's performance over a few years. For countries experiencing high inflation, any profit made could be wiped out in real terms.

Industry trends: Technology innovation and the trends towards deregulation are just two examples of industry trends. In the hospitality industry, technological innovations such as central reservation systems (CRS) mean that business can suffer unless one keeps up with advancements. In interpreting any financial statements, one must be aware of the trends and pressures within the specific industry. For example, the increased phenomenon of disintermediation (booking holidays direct and leaving out the middle-man) presents new challenges to travel agents and tour operators. The increased popularity and success of low-cost airlines and the success of the low-cost Jury's Inns model all point to changes within the hospitality, travel and tourism sectors.

The trend towards deregulation has occurred in the travel sector with air travel and taxi deregulation. The bus market could be the next for deregulation, where bus operators could compete for city and nationwide bus routes.

'The Travel Agents Feel the Chill'

Aer Lingus and Ryanair have done it. Now Budget Travel has decided from January 2005 to slash the commission its pays to travel agents selling its holidays from 10% to 5%. Budget has said that the decision is partly in light of the impact Ryanair and Aer Lingus are having on its sales as both airlines offer direct flights to many sun destinations previously the preserve of chartered carriers. One worry for travel agents could be that other tour operators such as Panorama and Falcon might also decide to cut commissions.

Stein Travel had a healthy trade in flight-only packages to Alicante and Malaga. However, their accounts for the twelve months ended 31 October 2003 showed a fall in turnover of almost 20% to €47.1 million from €57.1 million in 2002. The company went from a pre-tax profit of €3.4 million in 2002 to a pre-tax loss of €1.8 million in 2003. The effect of Aer Lingus offering direct flights to these destinations was partly to blame.

The core package market has also been hit by the number of people who have bought second homes abroad and in turn offer them to friends and family for holidays.

Source: *Sunday Tribune*, 24 October 2004

'Don't just blame the internet'

Profits at JWT, the biggest Irish owned tour operator and travel agent, more than halved in 2003, as increasing numbers of holidays makers booked their flights and accommodation direct from airlines and hotels via the internet. The firm suffered a 14% slump in sales with accounts for the year to the 31 December 2003 showing pre-tax profits falling to €136,596 from €283,814 in 2002. However, it is not only the internet that's to blame. Travel agents have also felt the heat as Aer Lingus and Ryanair have slashed the commissions they pay to agents on ticket sales.

Source: *Sunday Times*, 24 October 2004

Key Factors to Assess

Summary of initial key factors to assess when analysing financial statements

When scanning a set of financial statements the following key factors should be quickly assessed before preparing financial ratios. This may only take a few minutes but is vital in gaining a feel for the financial performance and position of the business.

When comparing one company over a number of years the following initial checks should be made:

❑ Have sales increased or decreased and by what percentage? In calculating a percentage increase in sales between two years, find the difference and divide it by the base (earlier) year multiplying by 100 to get the percentage.

❑ Has operating profit increased or decreased and by what percentage?

❑ Has loan interest increased or decreased and by what percentage? Check the long-term loans in the balance sheet to see if they have increased or decreased.

❑ Compare profit after tax to see if it has increased or decreased.

❑ Calculate percentage increase/decrease in fixed assets. If assets have been increased, has this been financed through increased loans or issued share capital?

❑ Check to see if the business has cash or an overdraft and if this is increasing or decreasing.

❑ Check current assets and liabilities for any major increases. For example, a doubling in stocks, debtors or creditors.

❑ Check the percentage increase/decrease in long-term loans.

When comparing two separate businesses the following checks should be made:

❑ Check both businesses are in the same industry/sector.

❑ Compare the size of each business. This is normally done by comparing the total asset levels in the balance sheet (fixed assets + current assets - current liabilities).

❑ Compare sales and profit levels.

❑ Compare financing. For example, is one company highly geared and the other low geared?

❑ Compare cash balances/overdraft levels.

Summary

This chapter focused on the main tool of financial statement analysis, namely ratio analysis and the key ratios that need to be calculated when interpreting financial statements.

The following are the main points covered in this chapter:

❑ Interpretation of accounts can be defined as the explanation, and translation into clear and simple form, of the data presented by the financial statements of a business.

❑ Ratios are relationships between figures expressed as a ratio – or more commonly as a percentage.

❑ Ratio analysis is usually carried out under the following headings as the performance of an organisation is appraised:
  – **Profitability**: Is the business profitable, both in terms of return on capital invested and the proportion of sales revenue remaining as profit? The key

ratios under this heading are ROCE, ROOE, operating profit margin, gross profit margin and expenses to sales ratios.

- **Efficiency/asset utilisation**: Are the assets generating sufficient turnover and profits for the business? Is the business over or under capitalised? The key ratios under this heading are the fixed asset turnover, total asset turnover, stock turnover, debtors collection and creditor payment period.
- **Liquidity**: Is the business on a sound financial footing and able to pay its creditors and other obligations as they fall due? The key ratios under this heading are the current and the quick (acid-test) ratios.
- **Capital structure**: What are the organisation's long-term financing arrangements and how dependant is the organisation on borrowed funds (financial risk)? The key ratios under this heading are the debt to equity ratio and the interest cover ratio.
- **Return to investors**: Investors' returns come in the form of a dividend (share of current profits) and a capital gain (an increase in the value of the business). Any return, whether of a capital or dividend nature, must be sufficient to reward the investor for the risk attached to that investment. The key ratios under this heading are ROCE, ROOE, earnings per share, price earning ratio, dividend yield and dividend cover.

❑ The Du Pont pyramid shows the relationship between each ratio and the overall goal of providing a return on capital.

❑ When analysing and comparing financial statements of businesses, one should always keep in mind the age and size of the business, the economic and political environment for the period under review and the general trends for the sector, as these provide a context from which to analyse the financial statements.

❑ Ratio analysis does have certain limitations, which must be taken into account when using them. The limitations of ratio analysis also reflect the limitations of financial statements.

Review Questions

Question 16.1

Briefly outline the limitations of ratio analysis.

Question 16.2

Outline the effect each of the following decisions would have on the return on capital employed ratio:

(a) Increasing sales price.
(b) Paying off a long-term loan with cash in hand.
(c) Reducing fixed costs in the profit and loss account.
(d) Arranging an overdraft facility.

Question 16.3

Outline the factors one needs to take account of in order to put any financial analysis in context.

Question 16.4

Outline the factors that cause fluctuations to the gross profit margin.

Question 16.5

The following are the summarised accounts of Yocomana Hotels Ltd. The company has been in operation in the hotel sector for a number of years with a portfolio of three and four star hotels.

Summary Profit and Loss Accounts

	31/07/2003		31/07/2002	
	€'000	€'000	€'000	€'000
Turnover		14,890		12,594
Cost of goods sold		5,190		4,420
Gross profit		9,700		8,174
Administration expenses	3,276		2,916	
Selling and distribution expenses	2,670	5,946	2,350	5,266
Operating profit		3,754		2,908
Interest		560		650
Net profit before tax		3,194		2,258
Corporation tax		590		520
Net profit after tax		2,604		1,738
Transfer to reserve	1,000		500	
Interim dividend	500		500	
Final dividend	1,000	2,500	750	1,750
Retained profit for the year		104		-12
Retained profits b/f		673		685
Retained profits c/f		777		673

Summary Balance Sheets

	2003		2002	
	€'000	€'000	€'000	€'000
Fixed assets at NBV		22,393		20,902
Current assets				
Stock	227		350	
Debtors	56		85	
Short-term investments	25		60	
Prepayments and accrued income	12		10	
Bank	0	320	220	725
Current liabilities				
Trade creditors	290		420	

Accruals and deferred income	15		20	
Taxation	460		520	
Dividends	1,000		750	
Bank loans and borrowings	<u>110</u>	1,875	<u>10</u>	1,720
Long-term liabilities				
Debentures	5,347		6,500	
Bank loans	<u>1,000</u>	<u>6,347</u>	<u>1,020</u>	<u>7,520</u>
		14,491		**12,387**
Capital and reserves				
Called-up share capital				
Ordinary shares nominal value 0.50				
per share		11,500		11,000
Reserves				
Share premium		500		
General reserve		1,714		714
Retained profits		<u>777</u>		<u>673</u>
		14,491		**12,387**

You are required to analyse the financial performance of Yocomana Hotels Ltd using whatever techniques and tools you require under the headings of profitability, liquidity, managements use of assets and financial risk.

Question 16.6

The following is the five-year trading record of Lowry's Hotel and Leisure Group for the financial years 2000 to 2004. The company's year-end is 30 November.

Summary Profit and Loss Account

	2004 €'000	2003 €'000	2002 €'000	2001 €'000	2000 €'000
Turnover	57,715	49,329	41,340	33,600	16,200
Operating profit	14,100	10,420	7,470	5,127	3,968
Interest payable	300	912	1,400	1,400	1,650
Net profit before tax	13,800	9,508	6,070	3,727	2,318
Corporation tax	2,800	1,735	520	450	300
Net profit after tax	11,000	7,773	5,550	3,277	2,018
Earnings per share	24.9	18.5	15.6	10.8	7

Summary Balance Sheet

	2004 €'000	2003 €'000	2002 €'000	2001 €'000	2000 €'000
Assets employed					
Fixed assets	162,130	132,200	122,000	104,200	92,500
Current assets	13,135	12,780	3,035	2,706	3,078
Current liabilities	20,670	16,800	15,459	10,274	12,800
	154,595	128,180	109,576	96,632	82,778
Financed by					
Called-up share capital	11,086	11,053	8,672	8,568	6,600
Share premium	28,910	28,577	14,800	14,384	8,460
Revaluation reserve	39,900	39,900	39,900	39,500	39,500
Retained profits	26,789	19,012	14,300	11,450	9,870
Shareholders' funds	106,685	98,542	77,672	73,902	64,430
Long-term debt and provisions					
Deferred tax	400	790	550	600	700
Loans	47,510	28,848	31,354	22,130	17,648
	154,595	128,180	109,576	96,632	82,778

The company has maintained stock levels at €500,000 each year.

Required

Evaluate the liquidity position, capital structure and profitability performance of Lowry's Hotel and Leisure Group for the years above.

Question 16.7

The following are the summarised accounts of the Dunne Hotel group and Gibson hotels for the year ended 31 December 2004. Both companies are resident in Ireland with a portfolio mix of three and four star hotels.

Profit and Loss Accounts

	Dunne Group		Gibson Hotels	
		2004		2004
	€'000	€'000	€'000	€'000
Turnover		17,589		15,222
Cost of goods sold		6,012		5,360
Gross profit		11,577		9,862
Administration expenses	3,598		3,125	
Selling and distribution expenses	3,012	6,610	2,598	5,723
Operating profit		4,967		4,139
Interest		923		356
Net profit before tax		4,044		3,783
Corporation tax		1,023		811
Net profit after tax		3,021		2,972
Transfer to reserve	1,000		1,000	
Interim dividend	500		500	
Final dividend	1,000	2,500	750	2,250
Retained profits for the year		521		722
Retained profit b/f		2,468		1,085
Retained profits c/f		2,989		1,807

Balance Sheets

	Dunne Group		Gibson Hotels	
		2004		**2004**
	€'000	€'000	€'000	€'000
Fixed assets at NBV		30,017		21,250
Current assets				
Stock	227		270	
Debtors	60		56	
Short-term investments	25		60	
Prepayments and accrued income	8		10	
Bank	0	320	312	
				708
Current liabilities				
Trade creditors	290		300	
Accruals and deferred income	15		20	
Taxation	1,023		811	
Dividends	1,000		750	
Bank loans and borrowings	145	2,473	0	1,881
Long-term liabilities				
Debentures	11,037		6,500	
Bank loans	1,088	12,125	1,020	7,520
		15,739		**12,557**
Capital and reserves				
Called-up share capital				
Ordinary shares nominal value 0.50 per share		10,750		8,750
Reserves				
Share premium				
General reserve		2,000		2,000
Retained profits		2,989		1,807
		15,739		**12,557**

You are required to analyse and compare the operating performance of both hotel groups using whatever techniques and tools you require under the headings of profitability, liquidity, efficiency and capital structure.

Question 16.8

Using the financial statements reproduced below from the annual report of D&A Department Stores Ltd analyse the performance of the organisation and comment on the results of your calculations.

Profit and Loss Account for Year Ended 31 December

	2004	2003
	€'000	€'000
Turnover	844	803
Cost of sales	(724)	(688)
Gross profit	**120**	**115**
Distribution costs	(17)	(15)
Administrative expenses	(21)	(22)
Operating profit	**82**	**78**
Net interest payable and similar charges	(3)	(4)
Profit on ordinary activities before taxation	**79**	**74**
Taxation	(22)	(21)
Profit for the financial year	**57**	**53**
Dividends	(25)	(22)
Retained profit for year	**32**	**31**

Balance Sheet at 31 December

	2004	2003
	€'000	€'000
Fixed assets	**470**	**438**
Current assets	–	–
Stocks	102	106
Trade debtors	10	8
Other debtors	19	15
Cash at bank and in hand	15	7
	146	136
Current liabilities		
Funding debt – bank overdraft	(49)	(39)
Trade creditors	(35)	(30)
Other creditors	(109)	(113)
	(193)	**(182)**
Long-term liabilities		
Funding debt	(61)	(62)
	362	**330**

Capital and reserves

Called-up share capital	19	19
Other reserves	23	23
P&L account	320	288
	362	**330**

Question 16.9

The table below shows the key ratios for four large retail outlets.

	Store 1	Store 2	Store 3	Store 4
Gross profit margin	35%	7%	7.5%	34%
Operating profit margin	15%	3%	5%	11%
Expenses to sales	20%	4%	2.5%	23%
ROCE	9%	10%	16%	8%
Fixed asset turnover	0.6 times	3.5 times	4 times	0.6 times
Stock days	63 days	17 days	15 days	62 days
Debtors days	32 days	9 days	5 days	35 days
Creditors days	67 days	40 days	46 days	69 days
Current ratio	0.9:1	0.8:1	0.4:1	0.8:1
Quick ratio	0.5:1	0.6:1	0.2:1	0.4:1
Gearing	4.3%	23%	32%	12%
Interest cover	21.4 times	13 times	9.5 times	3 times

Required

Comment on the performance of the stores.

Question 16.10

The following are the summarised accounts of Elite Holidays Group Plc for the years ended 31 October 2003 and 31 October 2004. The group is listed on the ISEQ index and presently is quoted at €1.56.

Profit and Loss Accounts

	31/10/2004		31/10/2003	
	€'000	€'000	€'000	€'000
Turnover		9,100		10,825
Cost of goods sold		2,639		2,706
Gross profit		6,461		8,119
Administration expenses	2,002		2,165	
Selling and distribution expenses	2,275	4,277	2,706	4,871
Operating profit		2,184		3,248
Interest		529		492
Net profit before tax		1,655		2,756
Corporation tax		298		496
Net profit after tax		1,357		2,260
Transfer to reserve	1,000		500	
Interim dividend	170		282	
Final dividend	170	1,339	282	1,065
Retained profits for the year		18		1,195
Retained profits b/f		2,089		894
Retained profits c/f		2,107		2,089

Balance Sheets

	2004		2003	
	€'000	€'000	€'000	€'000
Fixed assets at NBV		14,102		12,687
Investments at cost		123		722
Current assets				
Stock	275		300	
Debtors	60		75	
Short-term investments	25		12	
Prepayments and accrued income	11		10	
Bank	0		120	
		371		517

Current liabilities				
Trade creditors	320		301	
Accruals and deferred income	15		12	
Taxation	460		496	
Dividends	170		282	
Bank loans and borrowings	200		0	
		1,165		1,091
Long-term liabilities				
Debentures	5,600		6,122	
Bank loans	1,000	6,600	900	7,022
		6,831		**5,813**
Capital and reserves				
Called-up share capital				
Ordinary shares nominal value				
0.50 per share		3,000		3,000
Reserves				
General reserve		1,724		724
Fixed asset replacement reserve				
Retained profits		2,107		2,089
		6,831		**5,813**
Market price per share as at 31 Oct.		1.7		2

Required

(a) Calculate twelve key accounting ratios for Elite Holidays Group Plc for the years ended 31 October 2003 and 31 October 2004.

(b) From the information available to you, including the ratios calculated in part (a) of the question, write a report to the directors of Elite Holidays Group Plc analysing performance for the year ended 31 October 2004 under the headings of profitability, liquidity, efficiency, capital structure and investor analysis.

Question 16.11

NEXT Plc is a major clothing retailer trading in high quality clothing. The success of NEXT is in part down to knowing their customer and what they like to buy. Using the extracts from the published accounts of NEXT Plc, comment on the performance of the organisation for both 2004 and 2003.

Consolidated Profit and Loss Account

For the financial year ended 31 January	2004	2003
	£m	£m
	(Unaudited)	
Turnover	2,516.0	2,202.6
Profit before interest	370.6	301.5
Net interest payable	(17.3)	(0.3)
Profit on ordinary activities before taxation	353.3	301.2
Taxation on profit on ordinary activities	(108.1)	(90.7)
Profit on ordinary activities after taxation	245.2	210.5
Dividends	(89.3)	(86.0)
Profit for the year transferred to reserves	155.9	124.5
Earnings per share	92.1p	68.7p
Diluted earnings per share	91.2p	68.1p

Consolidated Balance Sheet as at 31 January

	2004	2003
	£m	£m
	(Unaudited)	
Fixed assets		
Goodwill	36.2	31.0
Tangible assets	355.7	323.1
Investments	1.0	0.5
Investment in own shares	65.9	47.0
	458.8	401.6
Current assets		
Property development stocks	5.9	9.1
Stocks	263.5	234.9
Debtors	378.5	318.1
Cash at bank and in hand	62.3	32.6
	710.2	594.7
Current liabilities		
Creditors: amounts falling due within one year	576.6	664.9

Net current assets/(liabilities)	133.6	(70.2)
Long-term liabilities	371.40	56.30
	221.0	275.1
Capital and reserves		
Called-up share capital	26.5	28.7
Share premium account	0.6	—
Revaluation reserve	14.0	14.8
Capital redemption reserve	3.4	1.2
Other reserves	(1,448.9)	(1,448.9)
P&L account	1,625.4	1,679.3
	221.0	275.1

From the Notes

For the financial year ended 31 January	2004	2003
	£m	£m
	(Unaudited)	
Turnover	2,516.0	2,202.6
Cost of sales	(1,762.5)	(1,548.1)
Gross profit	753.5	654.5
Distribution	(158.9)	(145.0)
Administration	(226.0)	(210.7)
Group operating profit	368.6	298.8
Share of profit in association undertaking	2.0	2.7
Profit before interest	370.6	301.5
Trade debtors	303.0	248.3
Trade creditors	131.9	108.0

Notes
- ❏ Closing stock in 2002 amounted to £165.6 million.
- ❏ NEXT began to buy back own shares in March 2000 and, since then, 109 million shares, representing 29% of the shares in issue at that date, have been cancelled.

CHAPTER 17

Departmental Accounts

Learning Outcomes

By the end of this chapter you will be able to:

❑ Appreciate the use of departmental accounts as a management information tool.
❑ Outline the objectives of departmental accounting.
❑ List the main methods of departmental accounting.
❑ Prepare departmental accounts using each of the three listed methods.
❑ Describe and use the main methods of apportioning costs.

Introduction

The final accounts of a business are a very important part of the overall management information system used to plan, control and support decision making. The larger an organisation grows the more important control mechanisms become as part of the overall business structure. Most large hospitality and retail organisations divide their businesses into departments, which produce their own profit and loss statements. This system of departmental accounts can provide valuable information to management. For example, which is more informative – the accounts showing the organisation making an overall profit of €100,000 or a breakdown of profit showing the contribution of each department to the overall profit? Obviously the latter, as more information is given. It is important to remember an overall profit of €100,000 could hide a department making a net loss of €20,000. This is very much a part of responsibility accounting where the department manager is responsible for levels of revenues, costs and profit associated with their department. If any department is showing reduced profit levels – or making a loss – then management can identify that department and focus on remedying the situation.

Illustration 17.1: *Profit statement*

Entertainment Plaza
Profit and Loss Account for Year Ended 31/12/2005

	Total
	€
Sales	500,000
Expenses	(400,000)
Net profit	100,000

Looking at the summary profit statement shown in Illustration 17.1 it appears that the organisation is performing successfully with a profit return of 20 per cent. If the figures are further analysed and broken down into departments, a different picture can emerge.

Illustration 17.2: *Departmental profit statement*

Entertainment Plaza
Department Profit Statement for Year Ended 31/12/2005

	Restaurant	Cinema	Bar	Total
	€	€	€	€
Sales	100,000	250,000	150,000	500,000
Expenses	(120,000)	(200,000)	(80,000)	(400,000)
Profit/loss	(20,000)	50,000	70,000	100,000

The overall profit figure on its own would hide the fact that the restaurant is making a loss and if management were not aware of the restaurant's position, they would be unable to rectify the situation. Ultimately a well-designed system of departmental accounting will promote responsibility accounting and an awareness of the costs, and the contribution, that each department brings to the overall profit of the business.

Methods of Departmental Accounting

There are three main methods by which departmental accounts can be prepared:

1. Gross profit method.
2. Departmental profit method.
3. Net profit method.

We will use one scenario to illustrate all three methods.

Gross profit method

The gross profit method breaks down sales, purchases and stock items into the various departments with the aim of controlling the gross profit of each department. It is the simplest of all the three methods. Each department reports its gross profit which, when added together, gives the total gross profit for the organisation. From this, all the other expenses of the business are deducted to give a total net operating profit.

Illustration 17.3: *Gross profit method*

	Household	Lighting	Soft Furnishings	Total Company
	€	€	€	€
Sales revenue	320,000	390,000	220,000	930,000
Less cost of sales	(128,000)	(117,000)	(110,000)	(355,000)
Gross profit	192,000	273,000	110,000	575,000
Less expenses				
Wages				280,000
Administration				120,000
General expenses				50,000
Total expenses				(450,000)
Net profit				125,000

The advantages of the gross profit method are its simplicity and the fact that sales purchases and stock levels are all within the control of the department head. However, its disadvantages are that no attempt is made to associate other expenses with the department, such as wages, salaries, light and heat etc., and hence there may be a lack of control over these expenses. Also a department may achieve a high gross profit but if its overheads are high it contributes little to the net profit of the business.

Departmental profit method

The departmental profit method deducts all the expenses attributable to, and controlled by, a department from departmental sales. The aim is to ascertain and control the revenues, costs and thus profits of each department. The expenses that are not directly attributable to a specific department – such as rent, rates and advertising

– are charged against the total departmental profit to give a total operating profit for the organisation.

Illustration 17.4: *Departmental profit method*

	Household	Lighting	Soft Furnishings	Total Company
	€	€	€	€
Sales revenue	320,000	390,000	220,000	930,000
Less cost of sales	(128,000)	(117,000)	(110,000)	(355,000)
Gross profit	192,000	273,000	110,000	575,000
Less departmental expenses				
Wages	(84,000)	(112,000)	(84,000)	(280,000)
Departmental profit	108,000	161,000	26,000	295,000
Administration				120,000
General expenses				50,000
Total expenses				(170,000)
Net profit				125,000

The advantages of this method are:

❑ More information is given to management regarding the performance of their departments.
❑ As only controllable costs are included in the calculation of departmental profitability, this provides a form of responsibility accounting, as each department manager knows what revenues and costs they are responsible for.
❑ As this is a fairer approach to assessing management performance, it can help to motivate department heads.

The disadvantage of this approach is that it requires an elaborate accounting system to provide the information and many smaller businesses would not have access to such accounting systems.

Net profit method

Under this method all the expenses of the business are charged to each revenue-producing department whether they are directly related and controlled by that department or not. Thus the departmental profit and loss account would include two categories of expense:

1. Those directly related to the department, for example purchases and wages of personnel working in the department.

2. Those not direct related to any department but which are incurred as part of the costs of the overall organisation, such as advertising, rates, rent, depreciation, administration expenses, head office expenses and general manager's salary. These costs must be apportioned to each department on some fair and reasonable basis. For example, rent and rates could be apportioned on the basis of floor space occupied by each department and the general manager's salary could be apportioned on the basis of the sales turnover of each department.

Illustration 17.5: *Net profit method*

	Household	Lighting	Soft Furnishings	Total Company
	€	€	€	€
Sales revenue	320,000	390,000	220,000	930,000
Less cost of sales	(128,000)	(117,000)	(110,000)	(355,000)
Gross profit	192,000	273,000	110,000	575,000
Less expenses				
Wages	84,000	112,000	84,000	280,000
Administration	40,000	40,000	40,000	*120,000*
General expenses	17,000	21,000	12,000	*50,000*
Total expenses	(141,000)	(173,000)	(136,000)	(450,000)
Net profit	51,000	100,000	(26,000)	125,000

(The basis for cost apportionment will be discussed later.)

The advantages of the net profit method are:

❑ Profit reflects the benefit a department receives from shared expenses such as rent and advertising.
❑ It focuses each department on net profit rather than gross profit.

The disadvantages of the net profit method are:

❑ The method of apportionment can be an arbitrary, subjective process.
❑ Depending on the method of apportionment, a formerly profitable department may now show a loss. This could lead to the department being closed down.
❑ It may adversely affect managers' motivation, as their performance assessment is influenced by events and costs that are beyond their control.

Departmental accounts as a management information tool in hotels

Research conducted by Smullen and O'Donoghue (2005) in relation to the use and influence of certain financial decision support models within the hospitality sector showed the following in relation to the use of departmental accounts as part of the overall management information systems in hotels:

1. Of hotels surveyed, 90 per cent used departmental accounts as a decision support tool.
2. In preparing departmental accounts, 80 per cent used the departmental profit method.
3. The information provided by departmental accounts supported decisions within the following areas:
   - Management performance evaluation.
   - Staffing.
   - Resource allocation and further investment.

The research was conducted in early 2005 and was based on hotels with a 3-star standard or higher and with 30 or more bedrooms.

Cost Apportionment

Cost apportionment represents the assignment of a cost to a number of departments or cost centres. This is where the cost or expense item is not directly related to any one department but services a number of departments. Thus the accountant must use a subjective method of apportioning the cost to the various departments/products. The basis of apportioning costs to various departments is a matter of opinion and there is no single best objective method to use. Usually costs would be assigned to departments based on the principle of the 'greatest benefit'. In other words, the department that gets the greatest benefit from the cost would be assigned most of the actual cost. However, in some cases, working this out is time consuming and costly and thus many businesses will use a more simple but arbitrary method. The following bases of apportionment are most common:

Cost type	→	Basis of apportionment
Equipment insurance and depreciation.	→	Book value of equipment.
Advertising.	→	Departmental sales revenue.
Rent and rates.	→	Floor space.
Insurance of building.	→	Floor space.
Light and heat, repairs.	→	Floor space.
Building depreciation.	→	Floor space.
Machine maintenance.	→	Machine running hous.
Administration costs.	→	Number of employees.
Canteen subsidies.	→	Number of employees.
Personnel costs.	→	Number of employees.

Example 17.1: *Apportioning costs*

The following costs were incurred by Southside Stores Ltd for the month of January 2005:

	€
Depreciation of buildings	10,000
Repairs and maintenance to buildings	3,250
Depreciation of equipment	5,400
Insurance of equipment	2,600
Heating and lighting	3,560
Canteen costs	4,000
Administration costs	3,000
	31,810

Southside Stores is a clothing retail business with three key departments as outlined below:

	Men's Dept.	Women's Dept.	Children's Dept.
Floor area (square metres)	1,000	2,000	500
Number of employees	50	80	20
Book value of equipment	€500,000	€300,000	€50,000

You are required to share out the costs among the three departments.

Approach

The costs are apportioned to each department using the most appropriate basis to each department and the results are presented as follows.

Department Cost Apportionment

Cost Item	Basis of Apportionment	Total Cost	Men's Dept	Women's Dept	Children's Dept
		€	€	€	€
Depreciation of building	Floor area	10,000	2,857	5,714	1,429
Repairs to buildings	Floor area	3,250	929	1,857	464
Depreciation of equipment	Book value of equipment	5,400	3,176	1,906	318
Insurance of equipment	Book value of equipment	2,600	1,529	918	153
Light and heat	Floor area	3,560	1,017	2,034	509
Canteen costs	No. of employees	4,000	1,333	2,133	534
Administration	No. of employees	3,000	1,000	1,600	400
Total		**31,810**	**11,841**	**16,162**	**3,807**

Apportioning costs can be subjective but if the net profit method is in operation, it is essential to have some means of dividing out shared costs.

A Comprehensive Example

The example below brings together all the learning points discussed above and applies them to a hospitality setting.

Example 17.2: *Comprehensive example of departmental accounts*

The following information relates to NiteLife Ltd, a company that operates an establishment consisting of three departments: restaurant, banqueting and bar. The company uses a system of departmental accounts. The following details are available for the year ended 31 December 2004.

		€
Sales	Restaurant	750,000
	Banqueting	450,000
	Bar	300,000
Purchases of food and beverages	Restaurant	300,000
	Banqueting	150,000
	Bar	112,500
Stock food and beverages as at 1/1/04		
	Restaurant	6,000
	Banqueting	4,000
	Bar	3,000
Wages and salaries	Restaurant	217,500
	Banqueting	112,500
	Bar	22,500
Repairs	Restaurant	31,500
	Banqueting	19,500
	Bar	6,000
Electricity and power		60,000
Rent and rates		150,000
Depreciation		105,000
Postage and telephone		27,500
Advertising		60,000
Laundry and cleaning		9,000
Administration		90,000

Note: All expenses are apportioned to each department on the basis of turnover except the following:

1. Electricity and power	Restaurant	60%
	Banqueting	35%
	Bar	5%

2. Rent, rates and depreciation are apportioned on the basis of floor space occupied as follows

	Restaurant	6,000 square metres
	Banqueting	3,000 square metres
	Bar	1,000 square metres

3. Stock food and beverages as at 31 December 2004

	€
Restaurant	8,000
Banqueting	3,500
Bar	2,000

Prepare a departmental trading, profit and loss account for the year ended 31 December 2004 based on the following methods:
1. Gross profit method.
2. Departmental profit method.
3. Net profit method.

Gross profit approach

The following are the departmental accounts for Nite Life Ltd based on the gross profit method.

Nite Life Ltd Departmental Accounts for the Year Ended 31 December 2004

	Restaurant	Banqueting	Bar	Total
	€	€	€	€
Sales	750,000	450,000	300,000	1,500,000
Less cost of sales				
Opening stock	6,000	4,000	3,000	13,000
Purchases	300,000	150,000	112,500	562,500
Closing stock	(8,000)	(3,500)	(2,000)	(13,500)
Cost of sales	(298,000)	(150,500)	(113,500)	(562,000)
Gross profit	452,000	299,500	186,500	938,000
Less expenses				
Wages and salaries				352,500
Repairs				57,000
Electricity and power				60,000
Rent and rates				150,000
Depreciation				105,000
Postage and telephone				27,500
Advertising				60,000
Laundry and cleaning				9,000
Administration				90,000
Total expenses				911,000
Net profit				27,000

Departmental profit approach

The following are the departmental accounts for NiteLife Ltd based on the departmental profit method:

NiteLife Ltd Departmental Accounts for the Year Ended 31 December 2004

	Restaurant	Banqueting	Bar	Total
	€	€	€	€
Sales	750,000	450,000	300,000	1,500,000
Less cost of sales				
Opening stock	6,000	4,000	3,000	13,000
Purchases	300,000	150,000	112,500	562,500
Closing stock	(8,000)	(3,500)	(2,000)	(13,500)
Cost of sales	(298,000)	(150,500)	(113,500)	(562,000)
Gross profit	452,000	299,500	186,500	938,000
Less department expenses				
Wages and salaries	217,500	112,500	22,500	352,500
Repairs	31,500	19,500	6,000	57,000
Departmental expenses	(249,000)	(132,000)	(28,500)	(409,500)
Department profit	203,000	167,500	158,000	528,500
Less expenses				
Electricity and power				60,000
Rent and rates				150,000
Depreciation				105,000
Postage and telephone				27,500
Advertising				60,000
Laundry and cleaning				9,000
Administration				90,000
Total expenses				501,500
Net profit				27,000

Net profit approach

The following are the departmental accounts for NiteLife Ltd based on the net profit method.

NiteLife Ltd Departmental Accounts for the Year Ended 31 December 2004

	Restaurant		Banqueting		Bar		Total
	€		€		€		€
Sales	750,000		450,000		300,000		1,500,000
Less cost of sales							
Opening stock	6,000		4,000		3,000		13,000
Purchases	300,000		150,000		112,500		562,500
Closing stock	(8,000)		(3,500)		(2,000)		(13,500)
Cost of sales	(298,000)		(150,500)		(113,500)		(562,000)
Gross profit	452,000		299,500		186,500		938,000
Less department expenses							
Wages and salaries		217,500		112,500		22,500	352,500
Repairs		31,500		19,500		6,000	57,000
Electricity and power	60%	36,000	35%	21,000	5%	3,000	60,000
Rent and rates	60%	90,000	30%	45,000	10%	15,000	150,000
Depreciation	60%	63,000	30%	31,500	10%	10,500	105,000
Postage and telephone	50%	13,750	30%	8,250	20%	5,500	27,500
Advertising	50%	30,000	30%	18,000	20%	12,000	60,000
Laundry and cleaning	50%	4,500	30%	2,700	20%	1,800	9,000
Administration	50%	45,000	30%	27,000	20%	18,000	90,000
Total expenses		531,250		285,450		94,300	911,000
Net profit/(loss)		(79,250)		14,050		92,200	27,000

Note: Under this method the restaurant is showing a loss of €79,250. This could lead general management to consider closing the restaurant. However, many of the apportioned expenses could be termed fixed costs which implies that they would not decrease significantly even if the restaurant were to close, as they are associated with the business as a whole rather than just the restaurant. For example, would advertising decrease by 50 per cent because the restaurant closes? In all probability, advertising expenses would not decrease significantly. In the departmental profit method we see that the restaurant has provided a contribution of €203,000 to cover the fixed costs of the business. This figure is more indicative of the worth and contribution the restaurant provides to the business. The point is that the net profit method can provide misleading information that could influence management decision making.

Uniform System of Accounts for the Lodging Industry (USALI)

The uniform system of accounts is a system of presenting the financial statements of accommodation providers that is quite popular in the USA and to a lesser extent in the UK.

The Uniform System of Accounts for Hotels was first produced in 1926 by the Hotel Association of New York City. After many revisions and updates the Hotel Association of New York City and the American Hotel and Motel Association joined forces in 1996 and produced a single updated and authoritative Uniform System of Accounts for the Lodging Industry (USALI). The system is now in its ninth revised edition.

The system can be adapted for use by large and small lodging operations and is designed to be used at property level rather than at the corporate level of a hotel. The association recognises that lodging organisations prepare income statements (profit and loss account) for both external and internal uses. The format of the income statement (for internal use) is based on responsibility accounting whereby the focus in on departmental results. The departmental income statement is divided into three major sections:

1. Operating department

This is where the focus is on each revenue-producing department. Examples of departments include room sales, food sales, beverage sales, telephone sales, leisure centre, golf club, tennis, garage and parking, rental income from lease of retail space etc. For each department generating revenue, direct expenses are deducted in calculating the income or loss for each department. Direct expenses consist of three major categories:

- ❑ Cost of sales.
- ❑ Payroll relating to employees in each department.
- ❑ Other expenses that are directly related to each department such as laundry, linen and dry cleaning for the rooms department.

The total income or loss of each department is added to get the total operating income for the hotel.

2. Undistributed operating expenses

This section deals with deducting from the total operating income, undistributed operating expenses of which there are nine major categories such as administration, marketing, human resources, security, information systems, property maintenance, transportation, franchise fees and utility costs. These are all expense items that are related to service departments and cannot be objectively associated with any one revenue-producing department. Deducting the total undistributed operating expenses from the total operating department income results in a figure called income after undistributed operating expenses. Operating management are considered fully responsible for all revenues and expenses reported to this point in the income statement.

3. Management fees and fixed charges

The expenses listed in this section relate directly to decisions made by the board of directors of the hotel property and are their responsibility. The expenses include management fees, which are made up of the cost of using an independent management company to operate the hotel. Their fees often consist of a basic fee based on a percentage of sales and an incentive fee based on income (profit). Fixed charges include rent, property tax, insurance, depreciation, amortisation and loan interest. Management fees and fixed charges, once deducted from profit after undistributed operating expenses, give us the income before tax figures.

Below is an illustration of the USALI departmental income statement.

Departmental Statement of Income
Current Period

	Schedule	Net Revenues	Cost of Sales	Payroll and Related Expenses	Other Expenses	Income (loss)
Operating departments	Schedule					
Rooms	1	$	$	$	$	$
Food and beverage	2					
Telephone	3					
Garage and parking	4					
Guest laundry	5					
Golf course	6					
Golf pro shop	7					
Tennis racquet club	8					
Tennis pro shop	9					
Health club	10					
Swimming pool – cabanas and baths	11					
Other operating departments						
Rental and other income	12					
Total operating Departmental income						

Undistributed operating expenses

Administration and general	13				
Data processing	14				
Human resources	15				
Transportation	16				
Marketing	17				
Guest entertainment	18				
Energy costs	19				
Property operation and maintenance	20				
Total undistributed Operating expenses		——	——		——
Income before management fees and fixed charges	$	$	$	$	
Management fees	21			$	
Rent, taxes and insurance	21				
Interest expenses	21				
Depreciation and amortisation	21			——	——
Income before Income taxes					
Income taxes	21				
Net income					$——

Reference: Hotel Association of New York City, Inc.

Summary

The main purpose of departmental accounts is to show the contribution each department makes to overall profit. The larger the establishment, the more important it is for each department to account for its performance and to show its contribution to the overall profitability of the organisation.

The following are the main information points covered in this chapter:

❑ Most large hospitality tourism and retail organisations are divided into departments, which produce their own profit and loss statements. These are called departmental accounts. A well-designed system of departmental accounting will promote responsibility accounting and an awareness of the costs and the contribution that each department brings to the overall profit of the business.

❏ There are three main methods by which departmental accounts can be prepared:
  – Gross profit method.
  – Departmental profit method.
  – Net profit method.

❏ The gross profit method is quite simple, concentrating on sales purchases and stocks of each department. The main weakness is that it ignores other expenses that are directly related to a particular department, such as wages of department personnel.

❏ The departmental method is considered the fairest, as it only includes the direct costs associated and controlled by the department. This allows departmental managers to be appraised by their general manager based on the revenues and costs they can control.

❏ The net profit method is considered to be the most subjective, as it requires management to choose between various methods of apportioning costs and some methods may not apportion costs on an equitable basis.

❏ Departmental accounts when prepared and used properly are an important element of any management information system that informs decision making.

❏ The Uniform System of Accounts for the Lodging Industry shows how a sector can come together to present their financial information whether for internal or external use in a manner and format that promotes uniformity and comparability and produces better information for managers.

Review Questions

Question 17.1

(a) Briefly outline the advantages of preparing departmental accounts for a hotel.
(b) Briefly describe the following methods of preparing departmental accounts, outlining the advantages and disadvantages of each.
  – Gross profit method.
  – Departmental profit method.
  – Net profit method.

Question 17.2

(a) Discuss why it is necessary to apportion costs.
(b) What method of apportionment would you use in respect of the following:
  – Depreciation of equipment.
  – General manager's salary.
  – Head office administration costs.
  – Depreciation of premises.
  – Rent and rates.
  – Advertising.
  – Accounting.

Question 17.3

The following information applies to Supreme Hotels Ltd for the year ended 31 December 2003. The company operates a system of departmental accounting where the business is separated into three departments: accommodation, restaurant and bar.

		€
Sales	Accommodation	500,000
	Restaurant	250,000
	Bar	200,000
Purchases	Restaurant	120,000
	Bar	90,000
Stock as at 1/1/03	Restaurant	4,000
	Bar	3,000
Wages & salaries	Accommodation	117,500
	Restaurant	80,120
	Bar	32,500

Repairs and replacements	Accommodation	29,500
	Restaurant	14,500
	Bar	6,000
Electricity and power		45,000
Rent and rates		122,000
Depreciation		60,000
Postage and telephone		17,500
Advertising		45,000
Laundry & cleaning		9,000
Administration		70,000

Additional information:

1. Expenses which cannot be apportioned to particular departments are apportioned as follows:

Electricity and power	Accommodation	60%
	Restaurant	35%
	Bar	5%

   Rent, rates and depreciation are apportioned on the basis of floor space occupied as follows:

	Accommodation	6,000 square foot
	Restaurant	3,000 square foot
	Bar	1,000 square foot

   All other expenses are apportioned on the basis of turnover.
2. Stock as at 31 December 2003

	Restaurant	€3,500
	Bar	€2,000

Required

(a) Prepare a trading, profit and loss account for the year ended 31 December 2003 based on the net profit method.

(b) Outline the main disadvantages associated with the net profit method of departmental accounting.

Question 17.4

The following information relates to Marneys Department Stores Ltd for the year ended 31 December 2003. Marneys use a departmental accounts systems which reports monthly accounts for its three departments – electrical, furniture and leisure goods.

	Electrical	Furniture	Leisure
	€'000	€'000	€'000
Stock as at 1/1/03	100	120	80
Sales	2,100	3,000	1,200
Purchases	1,050	1,200	700
Wages and payroll	200	150	130
Repairs and maintenance	50	40	20
Stock as at 31/12/03	80	105	65

Other expenses not directly associated any department	€'000
Rent	800
Light and heat	150
Insurance	200
Administration and accounting	80
Personnel	200
Head office costs	120
General expenses	50
Depreciation	10
Canteen costs	20

It is company policy to apportion expenses that cannot be attributed to any particular department as follows:

– Floor area – rent, light and heat and insurance
– Turnover – general expenses, head office costs and depreciation
– Number of employees – administration and accounting, canteen and personnel

The floor area and number of employees are as follows:

	Electrical	Furniture	Leisure
Floor area (square metres)	5,000	6,000	4,000
Number of employees	20	15	5

Required

(a) Prepare departmental accounts for each department based on the departmental profit method.
(b) Prepare departmental accounts for each department based on the net profit method.
(c) Discuss the appropriateness of some methods of apportionment chosen by the company and outline how this can distort the information provided by departmental accounts.

A Sole Trader Organisation
Company Annual Accounts

Trading, Profit and Loss Account for Period Ended dd/mm/yy

Sales		x	
Less returns in		(x)	x
Less cost of goods sold			
Opening stock		x	
Purchases	x		
Add carriage in	x		
Less returns out	(x)	x	
Closing stock		(x)	
Cost of goods sold			(x)
Gross profit			**x or (x)**
Add gains			
Rent received		x	
Discount received		x	
Commission received		x	x
Less expenses			
Rent		x	
Wages		x	
Salaries		x	
Telephone		x	
Postage		x	
Stationery		x	
Insurance		x	
Carriage out		x	
Discount allowed		x	
Motor expenses		x	
General expenses		x	(x)
Net profit or loss			**x or (x)**

Balance Sheet as at dd/mm/yy

	Cost	Accumulated depreciation	NBV
Fixed assets			
Premises	x	(x)	x
Fixtures and fittings	x	(x)	x
Plant and equipment	x	(x)	x
Vehicles	x	(x)	x
	x	(x)	x
Current assets			
Stock	x	x	
Debtors	x	x	
Less provision bad debts	(x)		
Less provision discount	(x)		
Bank		x	
Cash		x	
Prepayments		x	
Current liabilities			
Creditors	x		
Accruals	x		
Short-term loan	x		
Net current assets (working capital)		(x)	x
Long-term liabilities			
Long-term loan			(x)
			x
Financed by			
Capital			x
Profit & loss account			x
Less drawings			(x)
			x

Profit and Loss Account for Period Ended dd/mm/yy

Turnover	x
Cost of sales	(x)
Gross profit or loss	**x or (x)**
Expenses	
Details	x
	x
	x
	(x)
Net operating profit/loss	**x or (x)**
Other operating income	x
	x or (x)
Interest payable and similar charges	(x)
Net profit before tax	**x or (x)**
Corporation tax	(x)
Net profit after tax	**x or (x)**
Transfer to reserves	(x)
Dividends	
Preference share dividend	(x)
Ordinary share dividend	(x)
Retained profit for the year	**x or (x)**
Retained profit b/f	x or (x)
Retained profit c/f	**x or (x)**

Balance Sheet as at dd/mm/yy

Fixed assets		
Tangible assets		
Premises	x	
Fixtures and fittings	x	
Plant and equipment	x	
Vehicles	x	x
Intangible assets		x
		x
Current assets		
Stock	x	
Debtors	x	
Bank	x	
Cash	x	
Prepayments	x	x
Current liabilities/creditors:		
Amounts falling due within one year		
Creditors	x	
Accruals	x	
Short-term loan	x	(x)
Net current assets (working capital)		x
Creditors:		
Amounts falling due after more than one year		
Long-term loan		(x)
		x
Capital and reserves		
Called-up share capital		x
Share premium pccount		x
Revaluation reserve		x
General reserve		x
Profit and loss account		x
		x

Cash Flow Statement for the Period Ended dd/mm/yy

Net cash inflows from operating activities		x
Returns on investments and servicing of finance		
Interest received	x	
Interest paid	(x)	
Interest element of finance lease rental payments	(x)	
Preference dividends paid	(x)	
Net cash outflow from returns on investments and servicing of finance		(x)
Taxation		
Corporation tax paid	(x)	
Net cash outflow for taxation		(x)
Capital expenditure and financial investment		
Payments for acquisition tangible fixed assets	(x)	
Payments for acquisition intangible fixed assets	(x)	
Receipts from sales of tangible fixed assets	x	
Net cash outflow from capital expenditure and financial investment		(x)
Equity dividends paid		
Dividend on ordinary shares	(x)	
Net cash outflow for equitty dividends		(x)
Financing		
Repayments of debenture stock	(x)	
Net cash outflow for financing		(x)
Increase/(decrease) in cash in the year		x or (x)

Income Statement for the Year Ended dd/mm/yy

Turnover	x
Cost of sales	(x)
Gross profit/loss	x
Other operating income	x
Distribution costs	(x)
Administration expenses	(x)
Other operating expenses	(x)
Profit from operations	x or (x)
Finance cost	(x)
Profit before tax	x or (x)
Income tax expense	(x)
Net profit from ordinary activities	**x or (x)**
Extraordinary items	x or (x)
Net profit for the period	**x or (x)**

Balance Sheet as at dd/mm/yy

ASSETS
Non-current assets

Property, plant and equipment	x	
Goodwill	x	
Royalties	x	
Investments in associations x		
Other financial assets	x	
		x
Current assets		
Inventories	x	
Trade accounts receivable	x	
Prepaymetns	x	
Cash and cash equivalents	x	
		x
TOTAL ASSETS		x

EQUITY AND LIABILITIES
Capital and reserves

Issued capital	x	
Reserves	x	
Accumulated profits/(losses)	x	
		x
Non-current liabilities		
Loan	x	
Current liabilities		
Bank overdraft	x	
Trade accounts payable	x	
Taxation payable	x	
Accrued costs	x	
		x
TOTAL CAPITAL AND LIABILITIES		

Publication

Publication by Plc prior to 1/1/2005 by Ltd prior to 1/1/2007	Publication by Plc post 1/1/2005 by Ltd post 1/1/2007
Profit and loss account	Income statement
Turnover	Revenue
Stock (opening and closing)	Inventory (opening and closing)
Operating profit	Profit from operations
Fixed assets	Non-current assets
Debtors	Receivables
Creditors: amounts falling due within one year	Current liabilities
Creditors: amounts falling due after more than one year	Non-current liabilities
Net current assets	Not shown

Appendix C Ratio Analysis Formulae

PROFITABILITY

Gross profit margin
$$\frac{\text{Gross profit} \times 100}{\text{Sales}}$$

Net profit margin
$$\frac{\text{Net profit (PBIT)} \times 100}{\text{Sales}}$$

Expenses to sales
$$\frac{\text{Expenses} \times 100}{\text{Sales}}$$

Return on capital employed (ROCE)
$$\frac{\text{Net profit (PBIT)} \times 100}{\text{Capital Employed}}$$

Return on owners' equity (ROE) before tax
$$\frac{\text{Net profit before tax} \times 100}{\text{Shareholders' funds}}$$

Return on owners' equity (ROE) after tax
$$\frac{\text{Net profit after interest \& tax} \times 100}{\text{Shareholders' funds}}$$

EFFICIENCY

Fixed asset turnover
$$\frac{\text{Sales}}{\text{Fixed assets}}$$

Total asset turnover
$$\frac{\text{Sales}}{\text{Net assets}}$$

Stock turnover
$$\frac{\text{Cost of sales}}{\text{Average stock}}$$

Stock days
$$\frac{\text{Average stock} \times 365}{\text{Cost of sales}}$$

Debtors days
$$\frac{\text{Trade debtors} \times 365}{\text{Credit sales}}$$

Creditors days
$$\text{Trade creditors} \times 365$$

LIQUIDITY

Current ratio
$$\frac{\text{Current assets}}{\text{Current Liabilities}}$$

Quick-acid test ratio
$$\frac{\text{Current assets - stock}}{\text{Current Liabilities}}$$

CAPITAL STRUCTURE

Gearing
$$\frac{\text{Fixed interest debt}}{\text{Shareholders funds}}$$

Interest cover
$$\frac{\text{Net profit (PBIT)}}{\text{Interest}}$$

INVESTMENT

Earnings per share
$$\frac{\text{Net profit after Interest, tax \& pref.dividend}}{\text{Number of shares}}$$

Price earnings ratio (P/E)
$$\frac{\text{Market price of share}}{\text{EPS}}$$

Dividend cover
$$\frac{\text{Profit available to pay dividend}}{\text{Dividends paid and proposed}}$$

Dividend yield
$$\frac{\text{Dividend per share} \times 100}{\text{Market price per share}}$$

Bibliography

Atrill P. and McLaney, E. (2001) *Accounting and Finance for Non-Specialists*, FT, Prentice Hall.

Black, Geoff (2002) *Accounting and Financial Reporting Standards*, FT, Prentice Hall.

Black, Geoff (2000*) Introduction to Accounting*, FT, Prentice Hall.

Business Eccountant, The, 'American Online "Confused" Balance Sheet with P&L', 21 May 2000.

Clarke, Peter J. (2002) *Accounting Information for Managers*, Oak Tree Press.

Dyson, J.R. (1997) *Accounting for Non-Accounting Students*, Pitman Publishing.

Failte Ireland Tourism Fact, 2003.

Glautier, M.W.E. and Underdown, B. (1997) *Accounting Theory and Practice*, Pitman Publishing.

Holmes, G. and Sugden, A. (1997) *Interpreting Company Report and Accounts*, Prentice Hall.

Kennedy, T.M., MacCormac, M.J. and Teeling, J.J. (1988) *Financial Management*, Gill and MacMillan.

Kotas, R. and Conlon, M. (1997) *Hospitality Accounting*, Thompson Learning.

Murphy, Eavan (2004) *Business and Company Law for Irish Students*, Gill and MacMillan.

Owen, Gareth (1998) *Accounting for Hospitality Tourism and Leisure*, Longman.

Revenue Commissioner's Guide to Value Added Tax: www.revenue.ie.

Schmidgall, R.S. (1998) 'The New Lodging Scoreboards: The Uniform System of Accounts for the Lodging Industry', *The Bottomline* (The Journal of Hospitality Financial and Technology Professionals), September 1998.

Schmidgall, R.S., Damitio, J.W., Duffy, P.A. and Singh, A.J. (1998) 'Capital vs Revenue Expenditure: A Survey of the Lodging Industry', *The Bottomline* (The Journal of Hospitality Financial and Technology Professionals), September 1998.

Smith, Terry (1992) *Accounting for Growth*, Century Business.

Wood, F. and Robinson, T. (1994) *Business Accounting: Irish Edition*, Pitman Publishing.

Wood, F. and Sangster, A. (2002) *Business Accounting 1*, Pitman Publishing.

Youell, R. (1998) *Tourism: An Introduction*, Addison Wesley Longman Harlow UK.

Annual Reports

Annual Reports Aerlingus.

Annual Reports Arnotts Plc.

Annual Reports Boots Plc.

Annual Reports Debenhams.

Annual Reports Gresham Hotels Plc.
Annual Reports ICG.
Annual Reports Jury'sDoyle Plc.
Annual Reports Marks and Spenser.
Annual Reports NEXT Group Plc.
Annual Reports Ryanair Plc.
Annual Reports Tottenham Hotspur Plc.

Other Sources

The Irish Times.
The Irish Times, Business Supplement.
The Phoenix, 20th Anniversary Issue.
Sunday Times, Business Supplement.

Websites

www.asb.org.uk
www.cro.ie
www.dosh.co.uk
www.forfas.ie
www.pegasus.co.uk
www.rai.ie
www.revenue.ie
www.sage.com
www.tassoftware.com